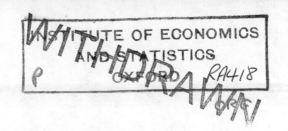
MACRO-ECONOMIC EVALUATION
OF ENVIRONMENTAL PROGRAMMES

ORGANISATION FOR ECONOMIC CO-OPERATION AND DEVELOPMENT

The Organisation for Economic Co-operation and Development (OECD) was set up under a Convention signed in Paris on 14th December 1960, which provides that the OECD
shall promote policies designed:
- — to achieve the highest sustainable economic growth and employment and a rising
standard of living in Member countries, while maintaining financial stability, and
thus to contribute to the development of the world economy;
- — to contribute to sound economic expansion in Member as well as non-member
countries in the process of economic development;
- — to contribute to the expansion of world trade on a multilateral, non-discriminatory
basis in accordance with international obligations.

The Members of OECD are Australia, Austria, Belgium, Canada, Denmark, Finland,
France, the Federal Republic of Germany, Greece, Iceland, Ireland, Italy, Japan, Lux-
embourg, the Netherlands, New Zealand, Norway, Portugal, Spain, Sweden, Switzerland,
Turkey, the United Kingdom and the United States.

.*.

CONTENTS

I

INTRODUCTION

In February 1974 the OECD published a macro-economic assessment of the cost of pollution control programmes and their general
economic policy implications in a number of OECD countries*. The
aim of that report was to place the additional pollution control expenditures over the next five to ten years within the context of other claims
on national resources so as to give a perspective to the debate on pollution control. That report offered a valuable insight on how pollution
control expenditures can be traced through the economy and gave mostly qualitative judgment on the impact of these expendirures on GNP
growth, prices, employment and balance of payments both in the
short and in the long run.

For the United States and to a limited extent for the Netherlands
the report was based on econometric studies and it was indicated in
the report that more complete econometric evaluation for a larger
number of countries was needed before a valid judgment on the measurement of the aggregate impacts of environmental expenditures and
their significance could be made. This present paper is a follow-up
to the 1974 report and brings together the more up-to-date econometric
studies on pollution control for a number of countries.

The present report discusses the usefulness of macro-economic
evaluation of environmental programmes both from the point of view
of the programmes and from the point of view of the economic development as a whole, including macro-economic policy formulations.
It contains the results and a comparative description of five macro-
economic models evaluating the environmental programmes for the
respective countries. The evaluation of the environmental programmes for Italy, Japan, the Netherlands and the United States is presented
in Appendices I - IV.

---

* Economic Implications of Pollution Control - A General Assessment, OECD,
Paris, February 1974.

II

THE GENERAL PURPOSE AND USEFULNESS
OF MACRO-ECONOMIC ENVIRONMENTAL STUDIES

The economic consequences of environmental programmes can be analysed from different points of view at different levels. From the point of view of the industry they are examined at the micro-level to establish their impact on the profitability of the individual firms or industries. Also at the micro-level the instruments employed in implementing environmental policies are examined for their efficiency both for achieving environmental standards and for being optimal from the economic point of view. Urban and regional evaluations are used for analysing, amongst other things, the equity aspects of environmental policies where the costs and benefits affect differently either geographic regions or consumer groups or various strata of the labour force.

At the macro-level both the scope and the purpose of the investigation is different. From the policy point of view the interest is twofold: a) what will be the demand on resources arising out of the particular environmental programme and the consequential effects of this additional demand on the other sectors, on the major economic variables and on economic goals; b) what environmental standards are achievable with a given environmental programme which is compatible with the overall economic aims.

The information developed in various OECD countries, and contained in this document provides a useful picture of the type of information macro-economic policy makers need to judge the impact of an environmental programme. From the broad policy point of view the interest is first and foremost in the reallocation of resources and in the consequential impact on output measured in conventional terms. While it is recognised that Gross National Product is not a perfect measure of output and a very imperfect measure of welfare, GNP is nevertheless an appropriate yardstick to judge the contribution of the various large scale programmes to national output. It is the only measure which gives an overall reflection in an aggregated form of the totality of environmental measures whether they arise from government expenditures directly or through regulation from private expenditures indirectly. It is the only way to measure the full economic impact of a set of environmental measures vis-à-vis an alternative set of environment measures or other policy proposals.

6

Along with a reasonable rapid growth of GNP a relatively high degree of price stability is also an explicit policy aim of OECD governments. It is therefore a valid question to ask how environmental programmes will effect the price level, both for internal consumption and for export prices. While micro-type analysis at the industry level could give a partial answer to some price changes, including some export prives, only macro-analysis could examine in a systematic way the impact on the general price level and on the much debated question of inflationary impact.

The unusually high level of unemployment, which is causing considerable concern for OECD government, focussed attention in recent years on the possible employment impact of environmental measure. Most econometric models can give a reasonable indication of the possible magnitudes involved of the employment. Quite apart from the effects of the total programmes there is an interest in the employment effects of specific measure as some countries are examining the possibility of using environmental policies as part of their anti-cyclical programme.

In the early 1970's a controversial issue, both from the national and the international point of view, was the international trade impacts of environment policies. While there is a concensus now that these are smaller than expected and that the compliance with the Polluter Pays Principle will further mitigate their impact, there is a need for a more thorough and wider evaluation. Again this needs a macro-type evaluation.

Most of the recent macro-economic studies examined include environmental subsectors specified by media. These subsectors can be used to calculate for the macro-model the investment requirements, etc. according to changes in environmental standards. Alternatively they could be used to calculate the standards achievable in line with the overall aims of macro-economic policies. It is a useful bridge which offers two-way communication between environmental and macro-economic policy makers.

The Case for Macro-Evaluation

The observations made in the preceeding paragraphs strongly suggest that there is a need for macro-type evaluation of programmes in countries which already operate or propose to put in operation major environmental programmes. This need is not always obvious because in most cases environmental programmes are expressed in emission or other similar standards and consequently the public and private expenditure implications and their consequential effects on growth, employment, prices and balance of payments are hidden. For this reason there is a need for presenting environmental programmes in emission and quality standards as well as in terms of expenditures which can then be translated in more meaningful macro-economic terms.

Secondly over the last three years the debate about environmental policies was conducted in terms of their impact on inflation and employment. The most comprehensive answer however imperfect this might be, can only be given through macro-economic evaluation. Other measurement by their nature would be too partial, such as given by the industry cost studies.

Thirdly by incorporating environmental programmes in the accepted framework of official macro-economic evaluation they would be automatically included in the institutional economic evaluation system and would be treated in the same way as health, law and order, education, etc. They would be accorded the same status of "public goods" which are normally provided through public expenditure programmes with the recognition that they have also wide ranging implications for the private sector.

Fourthly it would be possible to conduct not only a static but also a dynamic analysis through the macro-economic models. This is an important consideration taking into account that the introduction of environmental programmes is often followed by a rapid improvement in control technologies. The Polluter Pays Principle is intended to operate in such a way that the market mechanism would ensure rapid technological improvements. It is possible to incorporate in the macro models the changes in technical co-efficients reflecting improvements in control technology and perhaps also in productivity.

Fifthly if allowances for the different environmental standards can be made, and if the same type of models are used, the relative effects of programmes in the various countries can be compared. These international comparisons migh be difficult to pursue very far but there is a good case for adopting macro-economic approaches along similar lines.

III

A COMPARISON OF RESULTS OBTAINED

The results given by the four models examined* are expressed in Table 1 as percentage differences with reference to levels assumed when no expenditure on pollution control takes place. An attempt has been made to show the different results obtained by taking variants of proposed expenditure programmes (alternative phasings of programmes over time, alternative methods of programme financing, alternative cyclical situations), and whenever possible extreme values are given. For the Italian and Netherlands models, the percentages show differences from the levels predicted for the final year of Italy's Second Plan (1975) and as compared with a known reference year for the Netherlands (1973) ; for the American model the percentages given

---

*   The papers used are :

ITALY: "Anti-pollution policy: the effects on costs and prices in Italy", M. Lo
            Cascio (TECNECO Rome, 7/1973).
            "Pollution control measures to 1980. An economic and financial analysis
            for Italy" (OECD, 10/1975).

NETHER-   "The economic impact of pollution control policies" (2/1973, Central Plan-
LANDS: ning Bureau, The Hague)
            "Pollution, abatement and the economic structure" (H. den HARTOG,
            A. Houwelling, 1/1974. Vienne Conference on Input-Output Techniques).

UNITED   "Economic Consequences of Pollution Control" (Control Planning Bureau -
STATES: Monograph N° 20 - The Hague - September 1975).
            "A forecasting model applied to pollution control costs", by M.K. Evans.
            American Economic Review 5/1973.
            The Economic Impact of Pollution Control: Macro-economic and Industry
            Reports" (3/1975, Chase Econometrics.)
            "The Macro-economic Impacts of Federal Pollution Control Programs: 1976
            Assessment" - (Council of Environmental Quality and EPA).

JAPAN: "Macro-economic implications of environmental policies: the Japanese
            experience" (OECD, 12/1974).
            "Long-Term Environmental Conservation Program", Environment Agency,
            Tokyo, June,1977.

Table 1. RESULTS OBTAINED

	ITALY (1975)	NETHERLANDS (1973-1985)	USA (1976-1983)	JAPAN - I (1972-1977)	JAPAN - II (1975-1985)
I. Prices Consumer prices Export prices Total	+ 0.3 to + 0.5 % (Compared with level predicted for 1975)	+ 1 % + 1.7 % (change on 1985 after completion of the programme spread over 12 years	+ 4.7 % (1983) + 5.8 % (1983) (percentage differences with base-line projection)	+ 2.2 to + 3.8 % - 0.2 to + 3.1 % + 1.9 to + 3.1 % (percentage differences by 1977 with base projection)	+ 0.1 % ? + 0.2 % (differences between average yearly growth rates for model and base projection)
II. Level of private consumption	+ 0.3 to - 1 % (by volume)	- 6.4 %	- 4.5 % (durables - 1983) - 1.9 % (non durables - 1983)	Higher than forecasts until 1976 when the gap tends to close.	No forecast available for comparison
III. Level of private investment	- 2 to - 3 % (by volume, excluding anti-pollution	- 4.2 % (excluding housing)	+ 5 % (1977) - 0.3 % (1983)	Always higher than forecasts with largest gap in 1974	No forecast available for comparison
IV. Level of production	- 0.2 to 0.4 % (by volume)	- 5.1 % - 3.5 % (including anti-pollution	- 0.5 % (1977) - 2.2 % (1983)	+ 1.2 to + 2.6 % until 1974 + 0.1 to + 0.2 % over the period as a whole	- 0.01 % (difference between average yearly growth rate)
V. Employment		- 1.4 % - 1.2 % (including anti-pollution	+ 0.5 % (1977) - 0.2 % (1983)	Always higher than forecasts, with largest gaps from 1972 to 1974.	No figures available in the results
VI. Exports	+ 0 to - 0.2 % by value - 5 to - 8 % by volume	- 3.5 %	Trade balance commercial as with base-line projection: - 11.4 % (1977) - 7.7% (1983)	Decrease in 1972 and 1973 but forecast exceeded after 1975.	- 0.1 % (difference between average yearly growth rate)
VII. Imports	+ 7 to + 8 % by value + 0.7 to + 1.5% by volume	- 2.4 %		Higher than forecasts (largest gap in 1974)	No figures available in the results
VIII. Targets of environment sector 1. Targets of treatment.	Application of legal standards	Extent of elimination of back-logs: - collective water purification -: 69 % - first water purification and sanitation -: 81% - Adaptation of petrol run vehicles: 100% - Desulphurization of oil -: 86 % - Removal of solid waste matter -: 75 %	Application of legal standards up to 1982	Quantities eliminated, after completion of the programme, in 1977: - SO_2 : 3,900 10^6 tons (80 % od potential emissions in 1977 and 144% of effective emissions in 1971) - BOD : a) lower target 9,300 10^6 tons (62% of potential 1977 emissions and 107% effective 1971 emissions) b) higher target 13,750 10^6 tons (91% of potential 1977 emissions and 157% of effective 1971 emissions - Industrial wastes : a) Lower target 313 10^9 tons (75 % of potential 1977 emissions) b) Higher target : 418 10^9 tons (100% of potential 1977 emissions)	Quantities eliminated after completion of the programme, in 1985: - SO_2 : 72% of potential emissions in 1985 - NOx : 77% of potential emissions in 1985 - COD : 90% of potential generation in 1985 - Household waste; 98% of discharge quantity; - Industrial waste : no target ratio
2. Cumulated investments	(1971-1980) 5,519 10^9 tons at current prices	(1973-1985) 11.7 10^9 Gld at 1973 prices (annual cost of the environmental sector in 1985 is approximately 2% of GNP at market prices for that year including all running costs).	(1976-1983) 84.3 10^9 $ at 1974 prices (0.6% of GNP) and with all running costs: 249.3 x 10^9 at 1974 prices (1.7 % of GNP)	(1972-1977) a) Lower target 5.510 . 10^9 yen (1.5% of GNP - average annual rate) b) Higher target 9,850 10^9 yen 2.4% of GNP - average annual rate	(1975-1985) 20,000. 10^9 yen at 1975 price level.

10

correspond to differences with respect to levels forecast for certain years, the scenario used being a long term macro-economic outlook from 1976 to 1983 ; for the Japanese model I the results presented by the authors consist of absolute differences compared with the trend forecast under the Japanese Plan, which is why it was not possible to transform these into percentage differences, given the lack of statistical data regarding the trend. For the Japanese Model II the results presented were compared with a forecast for the growth rates without the investments for the control of pollution under examination.

A rapid glance at these findings shows that, if the results of the Japanese model I are temporarily excluded, the overall increase in prices brought about by passing on rises in production costs due to pollution control is not very large but is nevertheless sufficient to trigger some reduction in private consumption and in exports, one which is not fully offset by the multiplier effects of additional expenditure on the part of industries.

Price trends

The price trends obtained for all five models are fairly similar in that increases throughout the periods considered are small, but more marked for exports than for private consumption. The largest rates of increase obtained were for the American model and for the higher target variant of the Japanese model I in respect of the index of private consumption and of the overall index. If the trend findings provided by the American and Japanese models are examined, it will be seen that during an initial phase price rises tend to become more marked in comparison with the base projection owing to the cumulative effect of cost increases caused by staggering pollution control expenditure; during a subsequent period the gaps between the model and the base projection, tend to disappear, particularly in the case of export-price and capital-goods price indexes in the Japanese model I. This tendency may be ascribed to the effect of a progressively decreasing rate of production capacity utilisation, as stressed by the authors of this model.

Trends in private consumption

The effect of price increases and the play of demand elasticities are reflected by fairly considerable reductions in private consumption during the final year in the Italian and Netherlands models, and after an initial period during which expansionary effects prevailed in the American model. The situation is quite different in the Japanese model I, where the findings are consistently above the levels predicted by the base projection (even though the inflation index for private consumption is higher). The positive gap between these and the forecast figures however tends to narrow from 1976 onwards, and by the

11

beginning of the period the pattern of conumption shifts the emphasis from food to other items, without, however, involving the same income categories.

Investment trends

The figures given in some of the studies used do not clearly show whether the results stated for investment include amounts spent on anti-pollution equipment or not, yet the Italian and Netherlands models indicate a substantial decrease in productive investment by volume due to changes in induced investment. The findings of the American model show in the same way that, after a period of expansion culminating in 1976, productive investment declines and falls almost to the level predicted by the base projection. The situation again changes as regards results of the Japanese model I, in which private investment is always higher than that in the base projection, although the positive gap narrows somewhat from 1975 onwards. These results quite naturally reflect differences observed in respect of private consumption and exports.

Trends in the level of production and employment

The results obtained concerning these variables show the effect of trends just observed for the components of demand. The Italian model shows that the cyclical situation variants, by allowing the multiplier effects of anti-pollution investment to vary in extent, enable the level of production to be increased slightly or simply to be maintained. The results of the Netherlands model (according to the 1973 paper) show a fairly sharp decrease in the level of production (even when a calculation of the monetary value of pollution control activities is built in) and a decline in employment. Those of the American model begin by reflecting initially expansionary effects of pollution control expenditure (a seven percent fall in the volume of unemployment over that in the base projection), followed by an opposite movement.

In the same way, the result of the Japanese model I which are consistently higher than those of the base projection show more rapid growth in the first phase and considerably slower growth thereafter. In the Japanese Model II there is no significant difference between the growth rates of the model and of the base projection for the production. However, the level of the production in this model is greater than this of the base projection from 1976 to 1980.

Trends in foreign trade

As regards foreign trade, the results of the four models are characterised by a substantial increase in imports compared with the base projection, particularly during the initial phase owing to the acquisition of capital goods required for pollution control and to the impact of a rise in domestic demand. Exports in the Italian, Netherlands and American models are marked by fairly considerable loss of competitiveness by domestic products owing to higher production costs, whereas the Japanese model, although recording a similar phenomenon during an initial phase, yields surprising results for the second period, during which exports show extremely strong recovery after their competitiveness has improved owing to the lower rate of production capacity utilisation.

Conclusion on the Five Models

The results obtained by the Italian and Netherlands models appreciably differ from those of the Japanese model I, while the findings of the American model of the Japanese Model II fall somewhere in between. This may in part be due to the differences in period coverage, since the Italian and Netherlands models study the equilibrium reached for a given target year after an expenditure programme spread over several years, while the American and Japanese models primarily serve to describe the expansionary effects obtained over an initial period under the impact of this additional expenditure. The more pessimistic results obtained in the Netherlands model appear to be made even worse because they refer to an observed year, while in the other models contractionary effects are somewhat diluted because they are incorporated in the expansionary movement foreseen in their base projections. The possibility built into the Italian model, of modulating the responsiveness of multiplier effects according to the rate of production capacity utilisation or else comparisons with base projections using different forecast scenarios, as in the American model, make these two models fairly flexible and show how sensitive the conclusions drawn are to cyclical situations.

A comparison of the results derived in the American and Japanese model I may however well lead to quite different conclusions regarding the degree of dynamic response of these two economies. Thus the assumed cyclical trend shows no tendency to change direction in the case of the Japanese economy, where the volume of induced private investment is shown to be higher than the level forecast under the Plan for each of the years considered. The result is that production capacity increases far more rapidly than forecast throughout the period, although utilisation rate falls substantially each year during the second sub-period, while the cost of capital utilisation increases at a regular pace. In this model the declining rate of production capacity utilisation would hence appear to have a particularly powerful contractionary effect, thus serving to counteract the factors reducing private investment until the end of the period.

These differences as compared with results of the American model may also stem from the fact that the impact on the volume of investment

of increases in the expected rate of return on capital investment has
been formulated differently, or perhaps from the activating role attributed to the rate of production capacity utilisation in export functions,
an effect which would complement that which prices have on competitiveness. On a more general level, it will be noted that the models used
do not show all possible implications of adapting the machinery of production to pollution control measures. These effects appear to flow through
four separate channels:

1. Second round effects of increases in production costs due to the
   acquisition of pollution control equipment;
2. Multiplier effects of expenditure earmarked for the acquisition
   of this equipment and induced effects on investment, total
   demand, liquid assets and the cost of capital.
3. Effects of technological changes in the sectors involved.
4. Direct effects of reducing pollution levels and induced effects
   on production conditions, corrective measures (medical care,
   etc.) and consumer behaviour.

The effects flowing through the first two channels appear to the
best represented in the models used, while the effects flowing through
the fourth channel seem particularly difficult to build into a macro-
economic model. Conceivably, moreover, benefits for the community
preference function which accrue by reducing pollution are partially
cancelled by the resulting lower return in terms of GNP from various
industrial government activities after any substantial reduction in the
pollution level. Under these conditions, it is therefore, quite normal
that the models used should tend to show negative balances, except
when contractionary economic conditions are such that the expansionary
effects are felt with unusual force.

IV

FUTURE DEVELOPMENTS WITH
MACRO-ECONOMIC ENVIRONMENTAL STUDIES

The use of macro-economic environmental models is limited at present to a handful of OECD countries and even in those substantial improvements could be made in the application of the models.

a) At present the number of countries attempting to evaluate their programmes with macro-economic models is limited. Apart from the cases shown here there is work in some other OECD countries to develop an environmental sub-model which could be fitted into a more general macro-economic model of the country. As most OECD countries are now using macro-economic models, in some cases also in conjunction with extensive input-output tables, the framework into which environmental sub-models could be fitted is readily available. Given the rate at which environmental problems are multiplying, in both highly industrialized and other OECD countries, there is a strong case from the systematic evaluation of the overall environmental programme side-by-side with the partial analysis of the individual measures.

b) The main reason for the slow development of these environmental sub-models can be traced to the lack of environmental expenditure data and associated environmental changes:

    i) Private Capital Expenditure: in most countries there is no separate collection of private expenditure for environmental control purposes; as the majority of environmental expenditure, particularly in the early stage of the programme, is in this category there is an urgent need to collect this data separately as part of the annual and semi-annual investment survey; at this stage these data are included with other private capital expenditure largely in the enterprise sector; some expenditure might be undertaken also by the private household sector; in addition they are payments to the government sector for environmental services;

    ii) Private current expenditure: this is largely expenditure associated with the operation of capital equipment in the private enterprise sector; some information is becoming now available from industry surveys for certain industries in a limited number of OECD countries; in the current conventional treatment of environmental expenditures this information is needed to calculate the total cost in order to generate the impact of the environment programme on prices.

Government Expenditures: while some of the administrative costs are readily available from government accounts again only a few countries attempted to collate all the relevant data; they would consist of expenditure on administration and enforcement, expenditure on research, grants to the private sector, grants to lower levels of government, expenditure on abatement in government facilities and semi-government enterprises; this information could perhaps be obtained from a more detailed breakdown of the present functional classification of government expenditures.

In order of priorities given the possible cost of collection, expenditure by central government authorities might be obtainable at a relatively low cost; secondly sample surveys of large industrial plants in the major pollution industries would held to cover another substantial proportion of expenditures. These would be the minimum requirements for useful macro-economic studies.

c)   Whilst macro-economic models, incorporating an environmental, sector are capable of providing additional insights and information for policy formation and analysis purposes, two problem areas may be identified in the models currently available. Firstly, the model specification and formulation is exceedingly important. Failure to specify correctly or completely the relationships between environmental variables and other macro-economic variables may impose severe limitations and restrictions on the interpretation of, and confidence placed in, the results obtained, or may even give rise to misleading conclusions. Secondly, it is also necessary to examine the construction and definition of certain macro-economic concepts and measure to ascertain their validity. That is, do these constructs measure what they are supposed to measure or what is required that they measure? Both these problems are relevant to the discussion here.

i)   With regard to model specification the traditional view of the effects of an increase in the amount of resources allocated to environmental programmes is that real G.N.P. will fall (or rise more slowly) as less resources are then available for the production of the more traditional goods and services.

However, it is not clear that it will necessarily be true if certain other effects, not normally incorporated, are considered. There are a number of effects that may result in additions to G.N.P. as a consequence of the introduction of environmental programmes. For instance, there may be a productivity increase resulting from the increased efficiency of certain factors of production. Examples are improved health, or less corrosion of capital equipment. Alternatively the cost of inputs may fall as the quality of any natural resources used as inputs is improved. Increased productivity could also be achieved through technological innovation related to environmental control. Any of these effects may result in increased output, or in resources being released for use elsewhere, both cases generating an increase in G.N.P.

ii) With regard to measurement difficulties one encounters two problems. Firstly the well-known problem of G.N.P. and interpreting it as a measure of welfare, and the consequent need for an adjusted G.N.P. series, a welfare index, that can take account of environmental benefits due to any environmental programmes. Secondly there is the problem of incorporating environmental expenditure in G.N.P. Government expenditure on pollution control and pollution control services sold to households (e.g. waste disposal) would appear in G.N.P. as separate additional items. The problem arises with the pur- chases of pollution control facilities by industry, these being conventionally considered as intermediate goods. If the resultant additional intermediate costs are passed on fully in the way of price increases, then G.N.P. in current terms is unaffected, but real G.N.P. declines. If value added falls (e.g. profits fall) as a result of any price increases not fully reflecting increased costs then both current and real G.N.P. fall. Thus some method of including pollution control costs as intermediate products in real total product may be considered necessary in order to reflect more completely the impact of such environmental programmes.

ANNEXES

Annex I

The Models Used

The five studies examined in this paper are concerned with the implications of only those measures which fit into a traditional production framework*. These measures could

a) change the methods used in certain production operations to eliminate pollution at that stage;

b) or introduce additional operations to absorb emissions or reduce their effects;

c) or modify the characteristics of the products obtained.

Thus a common feature of the measures in question is to entail expenditure for the acquisition and installation of equipment and for its operation in the enterprises themselves or in specialised units. Such expenditure may therefore be classified in terms of programmes broken down by types of industry or trade; and may even be determined by specifying pollution treatment targets for individual sectors. Variants for carrying out these programmes may be defined either in terms of their phasing over time or in the light of financing policies as formulated by the public authorities. In the context of these different variants, the studies examined have tried to assess the overall implications of the measures taken by means of macro-economic models of their national economies. Certain aspects of these models will briefly be described before results are presented and compared.

The macro-economic models used by the authors of these studies have several, sometimes different characteristics; while an attempt has been made to show these in Table 1, in some cases this has not been possible, since the papers did not explicitly mention the mechanisms examined.

General characteristics of the models

The period covered by the five models is not identical. Thus the Italian and Netherlands models are simply annual equilibrium models, while the American and Japanese models cover several years. Each of the five models however deals with all implications of a programme

---

*   Except in the Dutch Study, in which additional pollution control branches are specified.

21

Table 1. CHARACTERISTICS OF THE MODELS USED

		ITALY	NETHER-LANDS	USA	JAPAN I	JAPAN II
I.	Type of Model					
	- Period covered	1975	1973–1985	1976–1983	1972–1977	1975–1985
	- Leontief model	+	+	+	+	+
	- Macro-economic relations	+	+	+	+	+
II.	Pollution aspects					
	- Coefficients of pollutants generated by industries	/	+	/	+	+
	- Coefficients of intermediate consumption deriving from pollution-control measures	/	+	/	/	/
	- Exogenously determined programme of pollution-control expenditure	+	/	+	/	/
	- Programme of pollution-control expenditure determined by establishing a percentage threshold for industrial emissions	/	+	/	+	+
	- Analysis of variants under programme of pollution-control expenditure	+	+	+	+	+
III.	Effects of spreading increases in production costs					
	- Mark-up factors applied to increases in production costs	+	/	+	+	/
	- Elasticities of private consumption with respect to product prices	+	+	+	+	/
	- Elasticities of exports with respect to relative prices	+	+	+	+	/

Table 1 (Cont'd)

	ITALY	NETHER-LANDS	USA	JAPAN I	JAPAN II
	1975	1973-1985	1976-1983	1972-1977	1975-1985
- Effect of the rate of production capacity utilisation on the desired level of selling prices or on the mark-up factor	/	/	+	+	/
- Effect on wage claims of a reduction in price increases caused by the pressure of unemployment	/	+	+	+	/
- Effects on wage claims of claims of increased inflationary pressures caused by a loss of purchasing power	/	/	+	?	/
IV. Multiplier effects and effects on the level of investment and production capacity					
- Classical multiplier effect (increase in the constant term in investment demand)	Effects restricted to the first round of expenditure	+	+	+	+
- Effect of total demand on private investment (induced investment)	+	+	+	+	
- Drain on liquid assets (higher interest rates and tigher credit conditions)	?	/	+	+	/
- effect of a higher desired rate of return on productive capital	/	/	+	?	/

of expenditure spread over a number of years, although effects are analysed only for the last year of the period in the Italian and Netherlands models, 1975 being the final year of an investment programme of twelve years duration for the Dutch economy. For the American model an analysis was carried out for the past period (1970-1975). There is a significant difference in the analysis between the US and the other macro-economic models and it was decided that the comparison should be only for the periods which are strictly comparable.

All five models used contain an interindustry input-output table enabling the impact on selling prices of increases in production costs attributable to pollution control measures for each industry, to be analysed; the effects of distributing these increases among industries are also taken into account. Each model also includes a number of macro-economic relationships in addition to the equilibrium relationships defined by the input-output model so as to modify the effects of distributing price rises at aggregate level and allow for the multiplier effects of committed expenditure. In the Japanese model II these macro-economic relationships are more aggregated than in the other models.

Aspects relating to discharges of pollutants and the determination of expenditure programmes by industry

The Italian and American models contain no relationships enabling the calculation of the volume of pollutants emitted by each industry; the expenditure programmes for each industry are thus determined exogeneously and are not explicitly referred to the amount of pollutants generated, unlike the method followed in the Netherlands and Japanese models. The Netherlands model appears to be the most complete in this respect since it brings in intermediate consumption and re-emissions of pollutants by pollution control industries. It therefore allows the efficiency of the industries to be measured and even the level of their activity to be quantified in money terms, evaluated at factor cost, assuming universal application of the Polluter-Pays Principle and treatment targets by type of pollutant.

Distribution of the impact of increases in production costs

In the Italian, American and Japanese I models changes in selling prices for each industry caused by the direct and indirect effects of pollution control expenditure are calculated by using cost-price elasticity coefficients. These coefficients, estimated from series in previous years, show how far each industry succeeds in transferring increases in its production costs to its selling prices. The values for the coefficients, which are normally less than unity, help to lessen the effects of cost increases inasmuch as certain enterprises are forced to accept lower profit margins. In the Japanese model II there is no cost-price elasticity coefficients like in the other models. Instead of this, it is supposed that price is decided by the industrial sector, with the marginal revenue being just equal to the marginal cost of production (including the whole unit cost of pollution control for the industry). Production cost increases give rise to another category of second round effects through the play of elasticities affecting the components of final demand (i. e. those of private consumption and exports in relation to prices for each category of product). In the Japanese second model the elasticities affecting the components of final demand are global and not disaggregated by product.

Out of the five models used two or three include more elaborate mechanisms into which feed-back effects are introduced:

- In the American and Japanese I models, the value of the mark-up elasticities is made dependent on the rate of production capacity utilisation and on the cost of labour, so that deflationary effects of a fall in total demand and of associated unemployment offset the inflationary effects on prices of the components of total demand. This mechanism has been omitted in the Japanese II model since there is no cost-price elasticity - consequently this second model offers no appropriate avenues for export and production changes over time.
- The American model also builds in a reverse mechanism, in which higher prices cause higher wage claims, which helps to increase the numerical value of cost-price elasticity and therefore hastens the pace of inflation. This mechanism, however, seems to have been left out in the Dutch model; it is assumed that any loss of purchasing power due to the effects of pollution control measures would be "ignored" by wage-earners and would result in lowered private consumption.
- The Italian model does not appear to include any explicit description of such causes and effects. Yet it should be noted that the authors of this model have defined a number of variants related to types of cyclical situations in which the degree of production capacity utilisation triggers demand multiplier effects. In this model the second round effects of cost increases will therefore be shown as identical for all the variants, whereas the multiplier effects will vary in size from one variant to another.

The mechanisms of spreading the impact of production cost increases should therefore in theory have a contractionary effect on the overall economy by bringing into play price elasticities of demand. Mechanisms curbing the spread of inflationary effects however seems to have been built into some of the models used, the level of production capacity utilisation being a central factor. It should be added that the policies followed by the public authorities as regards the financing of pollution control measures and the regulations governing the taxation of emissions may help to shift the impact of higher production costs among industries, as well as among enterprises and households, hence to alter their inflationary effects.

25

Multiplier effects of demand and induced effects of investment

In the five models used, an adjustment of the constant term in the investment function (or the introduction of an adequate variable, in the Netherlands and Japanese models) should give an increase in the volume of investment corresponding to the amount spend on pollution control, and in turn a larger increase in the volume of final demand via the traditional multiplier mechanism. In the Italian model, however, this effect is calculated directly from intermediate consumption in the input-output tables and the calculation does not go beyond the first round expenditure stage; it has moreover been noted that the size of multiplier effects in this model will depend on the different cyclical situations assumed.

Another category of effects is taken into account by deriving induced investment as a function of the level of total demand. While this emerges as a particularly important mechanism where the logic behind this type of model is concerned, it has not been explicitly described in the studies used. It should however, be noted that these effects will not necessarily be expansionary, given that the demand for capital goods resulting from the introduction of pollution control measures may be offset by a falling-off in induced investment due to a slow-down in private consumption and exports, and results would seem to indicate that this is exactly what takes place in the Italian and Netherlands models. Conversely, a rise in induced investment accentuates expansionary effects in the short term via the multiplier and also increases the production capacity of traditional industries in the medium term, thereby allowing utilisation rates to be relaxed in the years which follow.

A third kind of effect which must be taken into account in this type of model when introducing an additional demand for pollution control capital goods is the one caused by higher interest rates on the one hand and that of increases in the expected rate of return on invested capital (because of the non-productive nature of incremental investment) on the other. These two effects should tend to reduce the amount of private investment, a negative feed-back response which reduces the expansionary effect of pollution control expenditure. The effects of higher interest rates and tighter credit conditions seem to have been included in the American and Japanese I models, whilst certain variants of the Italian model provide for aid to enterprises from the public authorities designed to offset this effect in respect of anti-pollution equipment. The effect on the volume of investment of increases in the expected rate of return on invested capital appears only in the American model, although it is not formulated explicitly.

It can be seen, therefore, that the mechanisms postulated do not necessarily have expansionary effects, and that the impact of some of them are conditional (as on the rate of capacity utilisation), while others must certainly be regarded as helping to reduce overall demand.

26

Annex II

I. INTRODUCTION

The Issue and Scope of the Study*

While there has been growing concern about pollution control in industrialised countries, the number of empirical studies on its economic impacts have been rather limited. There are different views about whether or not the impacts are expansionary. The pessimists argue that the rise in cost due to pollution control tends to squeeze profit and investment, while consumption is also reduced because of increases in consumer prices. Thus, it is contended that economic growth is doomed to secular stagnation. The optimists, on the other hand, argue that there is a shift in growth rate from polluting to clean industries, merely resulting in better allocation of resources without significant slow-down in the rate of economic growth. Some even argue that the growth rate is likely to be accelerated during the transitional period due to a higher rate of investment and the introduction of new technology with lower pollution abatement cost. While price increases would be inevitable by internalising the external cost, it is argued that expansionary demand due to anti-pollution control is likely to exceed the contractionary forces affected by the cost increase.

The purpose of the present paper is to provide an econometric analysis of the impacts of anti-pollution measures for the short or medium-term period. The positive and negative impacts of economic growth, balance of payments and rate of inflation are discussed in as much detail as possible. Since longer-term econometric analysis has various difficulties in data availability and uncertainty of technological progress, the analysis is confined to the shorter perspective for which sufficient statistical data is available. Use has been made of an integrated analysis of a Leontief-type input-output model and a Keynesian-type macro-econometric model in order to assess both real as well as monetary impacts upon the Japanese economy.

The present analysis does not cover such items as damage costs, accumulated pollutants, technical progress, various administrative costs, public investment, etc. The damage costs were excluded mainly because of difficulties in definition and statistical measurement, although some of them, such as medical care, are not necessarily undefined. The

---

* See references 3), 4), 5), 6), 8), 9), 11) and 12) in the Bibliography.

problems would be better treated in the framework of social indicators or related indices in the context of a social welfare function.* Accumulated pollutants are left outside the study because of the lack of reliable information. Abatement costs for certain types of these pollutants are likely to become important, and they are usually dealt with by the government. Although the problem of technical progress is of vital importance for pollution control, it is explictly excluded because of the emphasis on shorter-term aspects. Government expenditures, including administrative costs for pollution control, are not taken up in the study because the emphasis is on the economic impacts in the private sectors.

The present study covers six types of pollutants: SO_x, NO_x, CO_x, particulates, BOD and industrial waste disposal. The other pollutants such as chemicals (mercury, PCB, etc.), house-hold waste, noise, smells, dust, submergence of ground, ocean pollution, etc. are excluded from our study for lack of reliable data.

For simplicity's sake it is assumed that all pollution abatement costs come from capital expenditures, thus disregarding all current expenses other than depreciation. In view of the insignificance of the latter items, this simplification would not distort the main results of the analysis.

In a separate paper the likely impacts of the oil price increase together with results of this study are analysed.

II.   ANALYTICAL FRAMEWORK

In assessing the overall impacts, three aspects have to be considered:

a)   expansionary impacts of anti-pollution investment ;
b)   rise in costs and prices on account of pollution control and the extent to which the increase in prices offsets the expansionary effect; and
c)   structural changes in sectoral demand and output.

The first type of impact, the expansionary effects, is analysed on the basis of certain assumed pollution control standards, projections for pollution generated on the basis of estimated output and the consequential abatement requirements. First the sectoral impacts are estimated in the Leontief-type input-output model of 60 x 60 sectors, modified for pollution control; these impacts are further analysed through Keynesian-type dynamic multipliers with a quarterly macro-model of about 140 equations. Induced private investment and consumption, together with wage, price and monetary impacts, are estimated with the latter model for the planning period, 1972-1977.

---

*   See reference 2) in the Bibliography.

The second aspect of the analysis on cost-price relations is also dealt with in the same framework of the Leontief model in order to obtain final results of sectoral price changes. These results are again converted to several final demand price deflators, after the adjustment of dynamic responses of cost-price relations. These effects of changes in deflators are then fed back into the macro-model so as to derive dynamic responses of final demand, output and money for the planning period.

Since the above two aspects of pollution control are closely inter-related, joint impacts are obtained by integrated use of the two models. Thus, the expansionary impacts of the first aspect, increased expend-itures, are likely to be counteracted to some extent by the contrac-tionary impacts of the second aspects, namely rising prices.

These joint effects are then further analysed on a sectoral basis with the Leontief model so as to assess sectoral changes in resource allocation. Generally, polluting industries tend to slow down, while less polluting or anti-polluting sectors tend to grow faster. Dynamic responses of these sectoral changes, however, vary according to in-dustry. Some respond immediately while others adjust themselves rather slowly. These relations can be analysed by dynamic price ad-justment functions and input-output interdependence.

The following procedures were used for analysing the above inter-relations.

a) estimation of direct pollution abatement costs at 60 - sector level;

b) estimation of direct and indirect price increases due to the rise in pollution costs at the 60 - sector level;

c) dynamic adjustment of prices and conversion to final demand deflators;

d) estimation of anti-pollution investment based on a) at 60 - sector level;

e) conversion of c) and d) to macro-model variables;

f) macro-model simulations;

g) reconversion of macro-model simulation to sectoral output and employment at 60 - sector level.

These steps are discussed in detail in Appendix A.

III.   THE RESULTS OF POLICY SIMULATION

A.   Goals of Pollution Control and Investment Requirements

1.   The Calculations

The desired goals for pollution control are indicated in Table 1. For 1977, two targets were considered; the lower target which is similar

29

to the present five-year plan* and the higher target which roughly corresponds to the one presently considered desirable by the authorities concerned.

Table 1.   GOALS FOR POLLUTION CONTROL

	1971	1977	
		LOWER TARGET	UPPER TARGET
AIR			
SO_x : amount of emission (million tons)	2.72	.97	.97
NO_x: amount of elimination (million tons)	–	0	5.49
Particulates, etc. (anti-pollution equipment, billion yen)	294	1915	1915
CO (additional cost per unit of automobile, 1 000 yen)	–	8.22	8.22
WATER			
BOD : amount of emission (million tons)	8.75	5.78 (120 ppm)	1.36 (20 ppm)
INDUSTRIAL WASTES			
Amount of emission (million tons)	2.23	104	0
Rate of elimination (%)	–	75	100

In the following, five cases of policy simulation are considered:

Case A   lower pollution control targets

Case B   higher pollution control targets

Case B1   higher pollution control targets for air pollution

Case B2   higher pollution control targets for water pollution

Case B3   higher pollution control targets for industrial wastes

---

*   See reference 8) in the Bibliography.

To achieve the stipulated pollution control target total output was first calculated for the 60 industries and then total pollution was obtained for SO_x, BOD and wastes with the use of coefficients of pollutants generated. These coefficients are given in Table 2. The difference between total pollution generated and the target specified gave the amount of pollution to be abated; both pollution generated and to be abated for the two targets are shown in Tables 3, 4 and 5 for SO_x, BOD and wastes respectively.

The next step was to calculate the investment requirements ; this was done by multiplying the quantity of pollutant to be abated by the "required investment per unit of pollution abatement" as shown in Table 6. The total capital stock required by 1977 for pollution control by industry (excluding CO) is given in Table 7. Three of the major pollutants; particulates, NO_x and CO_x were estimated directly because there were no satisfactory pollutant-generation coefficients available; the investment requirements for abating particulates and NO_x were also included in the industry breakdown in Table 8, which gives total anti-pollution investment requirements by type of pollutants for the individual years 1972-1977.

2. The Assumptions and the Results

As shown in Tables 3, 4 and 5, pollutants tend to be generated in selected industries, especially a) oil-consuming sectors such as chemicals, steel, electric power, transportation, and b) sectors with heavier water-pollution and industrial disposals such as pulp and paper, food manufacturing, non-ferrous metals, construction, etc.

Looking at the tables in more detail, air pollutants, SO_x, are generated mostly by electric power, other transport, iron and steel and chemicals which account for about 65 per cent of total SO_x. It is assumed here that these air pollutants, in all sectors, are to be reduced to one/fifth of those generated in 1972, with special emphasis on cleaner oil consumption.

As for water pollution of BOD, pulp and paper, food manufacturing and chemicals account for more than ninety per cent of the total. It is assumed here that total generated BOD is to be cut to one/third in the lower target and one/tenth in the higher target in 1977, with special reference to those three sectors.

Industrial disposals tend to be rather widely distributed as against other pollutants. Relatively higher shares are observed for basic metals and metal products, clothing, wood products, construction and electric power. It is assumed that those disposals are to be reduced gradually to one/fourth in the lower target and to zero in the higher target.

Table 2. CO-EFFICIENTS OF POLLUTANTS GENERATED (Pg)
(Ton per Million Yen of Output, 1965 prices)

SECTOR	SO_x	BOD	WASTES	SECTOR	SO_x	BOD	WASTES
1	0.0052			31	0.0004	0.0157	0.0658
2	0.0036			32	0.0955	0.0089	0.0658
3	0.0			33	0.0313	0.0195	0.1873
4	0.0018			34	0.0252	0.0194	0.5442
5	0.0028			35	0.0251	0.0373	0.5442
6	0.1242			36	0.0083	0.0010	0.6170
7	0.0020			37	0.0023	0.0006	0.6305
8	0.0359			38	0.0038	0.0008	0.0234
9	0.0101			39	0.0017	0.0013	0.0135
10	0.0053			40	0.0050	0.0013	0.0341
11	0.0551			41	0.0068	0.0007	0.0341
12	0.0130	0.3885		42	0.0071	0.0	0.0074
13	0.0011		0.1217	43	0.0010		0.0180
14	0.0184	0.3910	0.1217	44	0.0011		1.2854
15	0.0229	0.3921	0.1217	45	0.0045		1.2854
16	0.0118	0.3957	0.1217	46	0.0022		1.2854
17	0.0030		0.1217	47	0.4121		1.2854
18	0.0146	0.1731		48	0.0197		1.9180
19	0.0031	0.1715	0.0194	49	0.0001		
20	0.0123	0.1722	0.0194	50	0.0041		
21	0.0067	0.0002	0.0194	51	0.0001		0.0201
22	0.0070	0.0005	0.4421	52	0.0076		
23	0.0045	0.0004	0.2824	53	0.0006		0.0072
24	0.0233	1.2172	0.1952	54	0.1589		0.0072
25	0.0	0.0005	0.2321	55	0.0015		0.0072
26	0.0008	0.2999	0.0549	56	0.0005		0.0072
27	0.0214	0.0036	0.0790	57	0.0		0.0032
28	0.0392	0.4267	0.0167	58	0.0040		
29	0.0501	0.4280	0.1338	59	0.0054		0.0270
30	0.0432	0.0158	0.1338	60	0.0037		0.0186

NOTE: For sectoral classification, see Appendix C.

Table 3. AMOUNT OF SO$_x$ POLLUTANTS GENERATED AND ABATED (MILLION TONS) 1977

	G a)	A$_L$ a) A$_H$ c)		G a)	A$_L$ b) A$_H$ c)
1	14.1	2.9	31	0.3	0.1
2	0.6	0.1	32	357.0	74.6
3		0	33	207.0	43.3
4	3.2	0.7	34	276.8	57.8
5	2.0	0.4	35	75.6	15.8
6	105.0	21.9	36	57.1	11.9
7	0.2	0	37	34.0	7.1
8	0.1	0	38	70.9	14.8
9	0.9	0.2	39	18.7	3.9
10	0.1	0	40	17.4	3.6
11	63.0	13.2	41	13.4	2.8
12	25.8	5.4	42	38.9	8.1
13	1.5	0.3	43	9.3	1.9
14	15.8	3.3	44	7.5	1.6
15	96.1	20.1	45	23.6	4.9
16	32.4	6.8	46	12.4	2.6
17	3.3	0.7	47	1 494.5	312.2
18	10.1	2.1	48	8.6	1.8
19	2.6	0.5	49	0.1	0
20	46.4	9.7	50	85.2	17.8
21	16.3	3.4	51	0.5	0.1
22	19.2	4.0	52	12.5	2.6
23	8.1	1.7	53	3.6	0.7
24	95.7	20.0	54	700.5	146.3
25		0	55	3.3	0.7
26	0.2	0	56	3.2	0.7
27	27.0	5.6	57		
28	313.3	65.5	58	33.1	6.9
29	156.3	32.7	59	59.0	12.3
30	198.0	2 940.7	60	9.6	2.0
			Total	4 890.8	3 921.0

a) Pollutants Generated.

b) Abatement for Lower Target.

c) Abatement for Higher Target.

NOTE : For sectoral classification, see Appendix C.

Table 4. AMOUNT OF BOD POLLUTANTS GENERATED AND ABATED

(Million Tons) 1977

	$G^{a)}$	$A_L^{b)}$	$A_H^{c)}$		$G^{a)}$	$A_L^{b)}$	$A_H^{c)}$
1				31	12.3	1.5	5.1
2				32	33.8	0.7	11.7
3				33	129.7		
4				34	215.2		
5				35	115.1	15.6	95.2
6				36	7.1		
7				37	9.6		
8				38	14.6		
9				39	14.9		
10				40	4.7		
11				41	1.3		
12	766.3	679.9	751.9	42	0.2		
13				43			
14	331.8	294.3	325.5	44			
15	1,620.6	1,437.8	1,590.1	45			
16	1,060.4	940.8	1,040.5	46			
17				47			
18	118.3	70.9	110.4	48			
19	141.3	84.7	131.9	49			
20	645.4	386.9	602.4	50			
21	0.6			51			
22	1.4			52			
23	0.7			53			
24	4,984.5	3,373.1	4,715.9	54			
25	1.4			55			
26	56.9	53.3	56.3	56			
27	4.6			57			
28	3,414.7	1,423.6	3,082.9	58			
29	1,333.0	555.7	1,203.5	59			
30	71.9	9.0	30.0	60			
				Total	15,112.3	9,327.9	13,753.2

a) Pollutants Generated.

b) Abatement for Lower Target.

c) Abatement for Higher Target.

NOTE: For sectoral classification, see Appendix C.

Table 5. AMOUNT OF INDUSTRIAL WASTES GENERATED AND ABATED

(Million Tons) 1977

	G a)	A_L b)	A_H c)		G a)	A_L b)	A_H c)
1				31	322	241	322
2				32	4,377	3,282	4,377
3				33	22,522	16,891	22,522
4				34	37,356	28,017	37,356
5				35	11,611	8,708	11,611
6				36	27,112	20,334	27,112
7				37	2,159	1,620	2,159
8				38	1,574	1,181	1,574
9				39	2,343	1,757	2,343
10				40	743	557	743
11				41	91	68	91
12	1,510	1,132	1,510	42	616	462	616
13	1,064	798	1,064	43	74,668	56,001	74,668
14	654	490	654	44	54,465	40,848	54,465
15	3,193	2,395	3,193	45	42,062	31,547	42,062
16	2,090	1,567	2,090	46	45,253	33,940	45,253
17				47	43,472	32,604	43,472
18	84	63	84	48			
19	100	75	100	49			
20	458	343	458	50	2,610	1,958	2,610
21	6,736	5,051	6,736	51			
22	4,835	3,626	4,835	52	74	56	74
23	2,185	1,639	2,185	53	269	202	269
24	5,959	4,469	5,959	54	198	149	198
25	923	692	923	55	98	73	98
26	94	71	94	56	126	95	126
27	132	99	132	57			
28	6,684	5,013	6,684	58	1,398	1,049	1,398
29	2,609	1,957	2,609	59	1,271	953	1,271
30	1,885	1,413	1,885	60			
				Total	417,984	313,488	417,984

a) Pollutants Generated.

b) Abatement for Lower Target.

c) Abatement for Higher Target.

NOTE : For sectoral classification, see Appendix C.

Table 6. REQUIRED INVESTMENT PER UNIT OF POLUTION ABATEMENT (α)

(Thousand Yen Per Ton, 1965 Prices)

SEC-TOR	SOx	BOD	WASTES	SEC-TOR	SOx	BOD	WASTES
1	219			31	219	5,915	70
2	219			32	219	5,846	44
3				33	219	9,200	44
4	219			34	219		71
5	219		222	35	219		66
6	219		222	36	219	7,664	3
7			222	37	219		3
8			222	38	219		3
9	219		222	39	219		3
10				40	219		27
11	219		96	41	219		132
12	219	206	96	42	219		
13	219		96	43	219		176
14	219	208	192	44	219		
15	219	216	203	45	219		208
16	219	206	203	46	219		208
17	219		142	47	219		208
18	219	129	200	48	219		208
19	219	128	114	49			203
20	219		293	50	219		
21	219		52	51	219		203
22	219		52	52	219		203
23	219		166	53	219		
24	219	138	166	54	219		
25			73	55	219		
26		500	14	56	219		
27	219		14	57			
28	219	207	45	58	219		
29	219	209	3	59	219		
30	219		87	60	219		

NOTE : For sectoral classification, see Appendix C.

B. Sectoral Investment Requirements

Table 7 indicates the amount of capital required for anti-pollution by industry and provides the basis for calculating total incremental investment and cost required for pollution abatement. The table also implies that a relatively higher priority is placed on air pollution which accounts for about half the total capital required.

Replacement of anti-pollution capital stock has been disregarded in this exercise and the flow of fixed investment can be obtained directly as the increase in the capital stock by industry.

For both control targets, oil refineries and the electric power industry have the largest capital requirements; food, pulp and paper, chemicals and the basic metals industry will be the other major investors in pollution control investment.

Accumulated investment over six years in Table 8, is 5.5 trillion yen for the lower control target, while 9.8 trillion yen for the higher control target. In percentage of GNP, the average annual rate of this investment stands at about 1.5 to 2.4 per cent for 1970-1975. In terms of share by type of pollutants air pollution control accounts for the highest contribution. The lower share of the water pollution control is mostly due to the exclusion of public works for sewerage systems. As for the time pattern, the rates of increase of the anti-pollution investment are higher for the early three years, especially for SO_x, but it tends to decelerate for the later period. This changing time pattern is important in interpreting policy impacts as discussed later.

C. Sectoral Price Changes

Anti-pollution investment in the model used increases sectoral capital cost and prices accompanied by certain time lags and inter-industry repercussions. The total impacts of these changes on the price system including indirect as well as direct impacts of pollution control on sectoral prices over the planning period, are given in Table 9. Over the period to 1977, for both targets, relatively high price increases are observed for pulp and paper, leather products, petroleum refining, iron, electric power, automobiles, other transport. Smaller increases, but similar trends are indicated for dairy products, processed marine products and clothing.

As shown in Table 10, most of the larger changes are due to the cost for air pollution; but those for pulp and paper, leather products, dairy and marine products and non-ferrous metals are reflecting chiefly the cost for water pollution abatement. The price increase brought about by abatement of industrial wastes affected mostly clothing and wood products.

The total average price increase is rather insignificant, 1.9 and 3.1 per cent respectively for the two targets over the period. The figure is relatively low, partly because the total figure includes various machinery and equipment and services which are hardly affected by pollution controls.

Table 7. CAPITAL STOCK FOR POLLUTION CONTROL - 1977

(Billion Yen)

SECTOR	I a)	II b)	SECTOR	I a)	II b)
1	6.2	13.1	31	13.2	35.8
2	.3	.5	32	186.0	467.3
3	.0	.0	33	114.3	224.0
4	1.4	2.9	34	160.2	309.4
5	.9	1.9	35	192.4	855.0
6	45.9	97.5	36	31.1	61.2
7	.1	.1	37	28.9	50.3
8	.1	.1	38	39.3	76.9
9	.4	.8	39	15.9	27.7
10	.1	.1	40	10.1	19.4
11	27.5	58.5	41	6.4	13.1
12	177.0	213.0	42	0.0	40.2
13	18.4	25.1	43	20.9	31.0
14	73.7	96.5	44	15.5	23.3
15	392.5	489.0	45	19.8	34.5
16	243.5	291.7	46	15.6	25.1
17	1.5	3.1	47	741.5	1,505.6
18	14.2	24.5	48	3.8	8.0
19	12.8	20.4	49	.0	.1
20	73.7	125.5	50	71.7	125.1
21	104.1	144.5	51	.2	.5
22	82.0	116.0	52	6.6	13.2
23	36.8	51.8	53	5.8	8.9
24	570.3	823.7	54	309.4	654.8
25	13.8	18.5	55	3.0	5.1
26	26.9	28.7	56	3.3	5.5
27	14.7	28.9	57	.0	.0
28	457.5	963.3	58	35.8	59.2
29	193.5	407.7	59	45.2	80.6
30	798.2	1,027.0	60	4.2	8.9
			61	5,512.7	9,843.9

a) Lower Target
b) Higher Target.

NOTE: For industrial classification, see Appendix C.

Table 8. ANTI-POLLUTION INVESTMENT BY TYPE OF POLLUTANTS [a], [b]

	1972	1973	1974	1975	1976	1977	1972-1977
Case A:							
Lower Target							
1. SO_x	132	163	153	121	171	119	859
2. Particulates, etc.	294	363	341	271	382	264	1,915
3. NO_x							
4. CO [c]				(854)	(-10)	(45)	(889)
5. BOD	76	222	305	477	581	191	1,852
6. Wastes	73	91	107	204	315	97	887
Total [d]	574	840	906	1,073	1,448	672	5,513
Case B:							
Higher Target							
1. SO_x	132	163	153	121	171	119	859
2. Particulates, etc.	294	363	341	271	382	264	1,915
3. NO_x	369	456	429	340	479	331	2,404
4. CO [c]				(854)	(-10)	(45)	(889)
5. BOD	146	537	634	852	943	372	3,484
6. Wastes	73	173	205	309	293	129	1,182
Total [d]	1,013	1,693	1,762	1,893	2,267	1,216	9,844

a) Derived from I-0 model.
b) CO is not included in total.
c) Expenditures for anti-pollution.
d) Includes rounding errors.

Table 9.   THE IMPACT OF POLLUTION CONTROL ON PRICES SECTORAL PRICE CHANGES

(Percentage Increase by 1977)

SECTOR	I a)	II b)	SECTOR	I a)	II b)
1	.2	.3	31	.7	1.5
2	.1	.1	32	3.4	7.4
3	.0	.0	33	7.6	14.5
4	.7	1.0	34	2.5	4.7
5	.1	.1	35	1.4	5.3
6	3.2	6.1	36	1.1	2.1
7	.0	.0	37	.8	1.5
8	.0	.0	38	.4	.8
9	.3	.6	39	5.9	6.6
10	.0	.0	40	.5	.9
11	.0	.0	41	1.1	2.1
12	4.4	5.7	42	.3	.6
13	- .4	- .5	43	1.3	2.3
14	6.4	9.0	44	.8	1.4
15	2.9	3.8	45	1.4	2.5
16	3.1	4.2	46	1.3	2.4
17	.3	.6	47	6.2	11.8
18	.8	1.3	48	1.6	2.5
19	2.1	3.9	49	.0	.0
20	2.1	3.7	50	.9	1.3
21	3.2	4.8	51	.1	.1
22	2.3	3.5	52	1.5	2.7
23	1.6	2.6	53	.9	1.1
24	7.7	11.6	54	6.3	12.5
25	.4	.6	55	.2	.4
26	11.8	13.5	56	.1	.2
27	1.4	2.7	57	.0	.0
28	2.7	5.4	58	.5	.9
29	.4	.8	59	.6	1.0
30	6.6	8.5	60	2.1	4.1
			Average	1.9	3.1

a)   Lower Target.

b)   Higher Target.

NOTE: For industrial classification, see Appendix C.

Table 10. THE IMPACT OF POLLUTION CONTROL ON
PRICES SECTORAL PRICE CHANGES FOR THE HIGHER
TARGET BY TYPES OF POLLUTANTS

(Percentage Increase by 1977)

	AIR	WATER	WASTES		AIR	WATER	WASTES
1	.2	.1	.0	31	.7	.6	.2
2	.1	.0	.0	32	5.4	1.5	.5
3	.0	.0	.0	33	12.2	1.1	1.2
4	.4	.4	.1	34	4.0	.3	.4
5	.1	.0	.0	35	1.0	4.0	.3
6	5.6	.4	.1	36	1.7	.2	.2
7	.0	.0	.0	37	1.1	.2	.2
8	.0	.0	.0	38	.5	.3	.1
9	.5	.1	.0	39	6.1	.3	.2
10	.0	.0	.0	40	.7	.1	.1
11	.0	.0	.0	41	1.3	.6	.2
12	1.1	3.8	.8	42	.4	.2	.1
13	.2	.0	.7	43	1.4	.2	.7
14	3.8	4.2	1.0	44	1.0	.2	.3
15	1.0	2.2	.5	45	2.0	.2	.3
16	.9	2.7	.6	46	1.8	.2	.4
17	.4	.2	.0	47	10.5	.4	.9
18	.8	.5	.1	48	2.2	.2	.1
19	1.8	1.9	.2	49	.0	.0	.0
20	1.9	1.6	.2	50	1.0	.1	.2
21	1.4	1.0	2.4	51	.1	.0	.0
22	1.2	.3	2.0	52	2.4	.1	.2
23	1.0	.3	1.2	53	.9	.1	.1
24	2.5	7.9	1.2	54	12.1	.3	.2
25	.2	.2	.1	55	.3	.0	.1
26	1.4	11.3	.8	56	.2	.0	.0
27	1.9	.6	.2	57	.0	.0	.0
28	2.5	2.6	.2	58	.6	.1	.2
29	.3	.4	.0	59	.7	.1	.1
30	6.9	1.3	.3	60	3.5	.5	.2
				Average	2.2	.7	.3

NOTE: For classification see Appendix C.

As can be expected in the case of the higher target, the prices tend to rise further but there are substantial differences in the relative size of the increase between industries.

In Table 11, these sectoral prices are converted to final demand deflators which tend to affect the changes in demand components. The deflator for consumer prices is estimated to rise at a significantly lower rate, 1.4 and 2.1 per cent respectively, than the total of sectoral prices. Out of the 20 items listed, the deflators for light and fuels, fishing products, dairy products, eating out, etc. rise more than other items. It is rather striking that price effects of pollution control tend to affect items with relatively lower income elasticity. In other words, anti-pollution measures need to be accompanied by certain types of policies for income redistribution.*

With respect to exports, the price effect is relatively high for miscellaneous manufacturing products, metals, textiles and chemicals, while the lowest impacts are observed for machinery and equipment.

It is to be noted that the total export price deflator and the deflator for inventories is expected to rise faster than either the total sectoral price indicator or the consumer price deflator.

D. Macro-economic Impacts

As the next step, these results of the input-output model were then used for adjusting constant terms of private investment and price determination functions in the quarterly macro-model which includes financial as well as real transactions. The summary of the macro-economic simulation is given in Table 12 and the dynamic responses of the entire economy obtained from the model are shown in Appendix B.

1. GNP and Capacity

Although anti-pollution investment is here treated as non-productive and tends to raise the price deflators, especially capital cost, its expansionary impacts on real demand will stimulate real output and expenditures, especially for the earlier three years of the programme. It should also be noted that potential GNP, capacity of total economy, is also raised because of active induced investment. In both cases the rate of growth of real GNP is raised by 1.2 to 2.6 per cent for the earlier period, and by 0.1 to 0.2 per cent for the entire period respectively. Most of this expansion is accounted for by induced private investment including anti-pollution expenditures, a share of which is about half as much as the total investment. The private consumption also increases for the first three years and then levels off sharphy. Commodity exports in volume terms, indicate an

---

*   See references 3), 4), 5), 6), 8), 9), 11) and 12) in the Bibliography.

Table 11. THE IMPACT OF POLLUTION CONTROL ON PRICES OF FINAL DEMAND

(Percentage Increase by 1977)

CONSUMER PRICE DEFLATORS	I [a)	II [b)	PRICE [c) ELASTICITY
1. Cereals	1.3	1.7	
2. Vegetables	.4	.7	- .38
3. Fish	3.8	5.8	- .38
4. Dairy products	2.8	3.8	-1.06
5. Processed food	2.9	4.0	-1.33
6. Seasonings	2.5	3.3	- .97
7. Liquors	2.7	3.7	- .95
8. Cakes, etc.	1.7	2.3	- .69
9. Tobacco	.6	1.1	
10. Meals outside home etc. ..	4.8	7.0	
11. Apparels	1.5	2.4	-1.66
12. Light and fuels	5.2	8.8	-1.39
13. Water	–	.0	- .76
14. Rent	.2	.3	
15. Durables	.7	.9	
16. Health	.6	1.0	- .51
17. Transport and communication	2.1	3.8	- .73
18. Reading and recreation ...	.3	.6	- .85
19. Education	- .3	- .5	
20. Miscellaneous	.3	.4	
21. Average	1.4	2.1	
A. Foods	2.5	3.5	
B. Durables	.6	.9	
C. Others	1.0	1.7	

a) Lower Target.
b) Higher Target.
c) Taken from EPA report. (7)

Table 11 (Cont'd)

CONSUMER PRICE DEFLATORS	I [a)]	II [b)]	PRICE [c)] ELASTICITY
1. Foods	3.3	4.7	- .49
2. Textiles	2.7	4.9	- .90
3. Chemicals	1.8	3.6	- .87
4. Metals	3.6	7.1	-2.85
5. Machinery	1.5	2.1	-1.41
6. Others	4.9	8.2	-1.00
7. Average	2.5	4.1	-1.40

a) Lower Target
b) Higher Target.
c) Taken from EPA report.(7)

Table 12. SUMMARY OF MACRO-ECONOMIC SIMULATION
CASE FOR LOWER TARGET

	1972	1973	1974	1975	1976	1977
1. Output [a)]	731	2 134	2 638	1 876	1 702	580
a. price effect	-32	- 250	- 624	- 620	- 640	- 970
b. income effect	763	2,384	3,262	2,496	2,342	1,550
2. Capacity [a)]	150	919	2,105	3,065	3,721	4,218
a. price effect	- 6	-74	- 296	- 578	- 802	-1 081
b. income effect	156	993	2,401	3,643	4,523	5,299
3. Export Prices [b)]	.2	.2	-.2	-.5	-.2	-.3
a. price effect	0	.1	-.2	.4	.6	.9
b. income effect	.2	.1	0	-.9	-.8	-1.2
4. Inventory Prices [b)]	.1	.3	.2	.2	.5	.5
a. price effect	0	0	.1	.2	.2	.3
b. income effect	.1	.3	.1	0	.3	.2
5. Consumer Prices [b)]	0	.1	.7	1.5	2.1	2.2
a. price effect	0	.8	.2	.4	.7	1.0
b. income effect	0	-.7	.5	1.1	1.4	1.2

a) Billion yen in 1965 prices; additions to output and capacity.
b) Percentage changes.

opposite move; i.e. falling slightly in the first two years and then
starting to rise quickly thereafter because of price effects of earlier
pollution control and growing excess capacity for the latter period.

2. Prices

With respect to prices, it should be noted firstly that the inflationary pressures of the earlier period turn to be deflationary in the latter period due to growing excess capacity and level-off in the rate of growth of real output. This tendency is reflected more or less in the moves of various price deflators. Business investment prices, for example, start rising for the first half of the period and then tend to fall slightly for the second half. This implies that a) rising costs for pollution abatement, and b) expansionary pressures of business investment tend to raise the prices for earlier periods, but later they turn to be dominated by growing deflationary forces. Consumer price deflators, on the other hand, continue to rise until the last year, because of its rigidity against market conditions and larger increases in pollution abatement cost. Between these two extremes there are mixed types of price deflators. Deflators for private housing construction start rising fast, but in the last two years they turn to level off slightly. Export prices also follow a similar pattern to those of business investment but they turn to fall much earlier because of the increase in productivity and growing excess capacity in manufacturing.

3. Balance of Payments

There is an adverse trend in the balance of international payments. This is due mostly to the expansionary impact of the pollution abatement investment, but also to some extent, to the decline in exports and the rise in imports for earlier periods, brought about by a worsening in the terms of trade through the increase in the export and wholesale prices. The average annual value of these balance of payments deficits amount to about 1.5 billion dollars for the lower target and 2.6 billion dollars for the higher target. In the absence of government intervention in the foreign exchange market, such deficits could lead to a gradual devaluation of the yen. The significance of this balance of payments effect, however, would be certainly reduced, if similar pollution control costs were imposed in competing countries.

In regard to monetary transactions, there is a declining trend in money supply and a tightening of the money market; this is reflected in the increase in government surplus and continuous deficits in the balance of payments. Thus the interest rate on call money and bank loans tends to rise so that they produce a negative impact on business investment. This kind of automatic stabilising effect of the money market would be somewhat reduced if the exchange rate of the yen were left to float and to be devalued somehow. In other words, inflationary pressures of pollution control would be greater under the floating exchange rate system than in the case of fixed rate systems. This also implies that counter-cyclical policy tends to have stronger impacts under the floating exchange rate system.

In Table 12, the price effects are derived from the input output model, while the income effects are obtained as residuals between the total effect and the price effect. Thus the income effects are regarded as direct and indirect impacts of anti-pollution investment through the Keynesian-type multiplier. The price effects on output are significantly smaller than the income effects but tend to gradually increase. For capacity of output a continuous increase is indicated again with the price effects being significantly smaller than the income effects.

Though the overall impacts on price deflators tend to vary, the sensitive deflators such as export prices, indicate rather negative signs in the later period, while the price effect tends to increase gradually. For the other deflators, the positive income effects are slightly higher than the price effects.

These patterns imply that the empirical results favour the optimists' view which emphasises the expansionary impacts of the pollution control ; however, the contractionary effects are not necessarily insignificant and they tend to grow, though only slightly, in the longer-term.

E. Sectoral Output and Employment

With the input-output model the aggregate levels of final demand are converted to final bill of goods and then to sectoral levels of output and employment through the same technical coefficients and import coefficients as those used for the price analysis.

A similar changing pattern can also be observed with respect to income and price effects of pollution control. In accordance with macro variables, most of the sector output expands greatly, centering around machinery industries for earlier periods and later they turn to level off gradually due to relatively increasing price effects of pollution control.

The main features in sectoral changes of output are: a) increases in general and electric machinery and transport equipment, primary and fabricated metals, b) decline in food and primary products, textiles and electricity and gas, and c) relatively stable or slight decline in chemicals and paper, as shown in Table 13. At 60 - sector level a declining tendency of oil refining can also be noted.

The first group in the above is naturally affected by the expansion of anti-pollution investment. The second group is adversely affected by the price effects of private consumption and exports. The decline of the share of agricultural output is mostly attributed to the decline of food consumption due to the increase in water and air pollution cost. This tendency implies that the price effects of anti-pollution are likely to adversely affect the lower income classes as they depend more on these essential goods with low income elasticity. (See, for instance, W. Baumol (3), in the Bibliography.)

46

Table 13. SECTORAL OUTPUT
PERCENTAGE INCREASE

	STANDARD CASE	LOWER TARGET	HIGHER TARGET
1	3.92	3.90	3.83
2	8.72	8.73	8.68
3	7.72	7.73	7.45
4	6.07	6.00	5.98
5	10.15	10.32	10.15
6	10.12	10.13	10.15
7	9.93	10.17	10.27
8	11.38	11.55	11.65
9	10.73	11.57	12.20
10	14.43	15.00	15.38
11	10.58	10.87	10.98
12	11.10	11.17	11.67
13	11.97	12.12	12.15
14	10.57	10.43	10.35
15	10.57	10.65	10.65
16	8.22	8.30	8.33
17	11.38	11.58	11.63
18	10.18	10.27	10.28
19	10.22	10.22	10.18
20	10.07	10.13	10.15
Average	10.43	10.60	10.67

NOTE: For industrial classification see Appendix C.

The third group is relatively stable, contrary to expectations, as they are regarded as highly polluting industries. Although their price effects are significant as shown in Table 9, indirect income effects of final demand have compensated the negative impacts of prices. This is also the case with basic steel in which negative price effects on exports are cancelled by the positive income effect of anti-pollution investment.

As for employment, a very similar pattern is observed at 20 - sector level. Total employment increases for the first three years and, though it tends to level off later, the employment level is still higher in 1977 for both lower and higher targets. As indicated in Table 15, the increase in employment centers around machinery, metals and construction industries for the early period, while there is a slight decline for primary sectors, food, pulp and paper and other manufactured goods. In terms of structural changes, there is a noticeable

47

Table 14.　COMPONENTS OF SECTORAL OUTPUT

	1974			1977		
	S a)	I b)	II c)	S a)	I b)	II c)
1	3.01	2.92	2.82	2.52	2.50	2.49
2	.55	.55	.55	.54	.54	.54
3	4.76	4.45	4.53	4.55	4.48	4.45
4	2.40	2.36	2.30	2.15	2.13	2.12
5	1.70	1.69	1.68	1.67	1.66	1.65
6	4.49	4.44	4.36	4.52	4.50	4.49
7	8.80	8.95	9.09	8.59	8.41	8.41
8	2.71	2.73	2.76	2.80	2.80	2.80
9	6.37	6.76	7.13	6.01	6.20	6.32
10	7.26	7.48	7.66	7.60	7.73	7.82
11	6.13	6.18	6.23	5.89	5.91	5.92
12	11.50	11.44	11.32	11.71	11.65	11.61
13	10.21	10.31	10.40	10.97	10.97	10.95
14	1.88	1.86	1.82	1.91	1.88	1.87
15	8.37	8.29	8.21	8.46	8.42	8.41
16	2.12	2.08	2 00	2.08	2.08	2.08
17	5.58	5.55	5.49	5.78	5.77	5.76
18	2.55	2.52	2.48	2.57	2.56	2.56
19	8.55	8.39	8.13	8.81	8.75	8.72
20	1.06	1.05	.10	1.05	1.05	1.05
Total	100.00	100.00	100.00	100.00	100.00	100.00

a) Standard Case.
b) Lower Target.
c) Higher Target.

NOTE : For industrial classification see Appendix D.

shift of employment from the primary and tertiary sectors to the secondary sector, especially in machinery industries.　The declining shares of employment in the tertiary sector are noted for trade and service sectors, though there is a slight increase in their absolute levels.

This finding also supports the earlier observed trend in output that pollution control does not tend to reduce but to increase the share of industrial activity as against primary or tertiary activities.

Table 15.   COMPONENTS OF SECTORAL EMPLOYMENT

	1974			1977		
	S a)	I b)	II c)	S a)	I b)	II c)
1	13.0	12.9	12.7	9.3	9.3	9.0
2	0.3	0.3	0.3	0.3	0.3	0.3
3	2.0	2.0	2.1	2.1	2.1	2.1
4	4.1	4.1	4.1	4.1	4.1	4.2
5	0.6	0.6	0.6	0.6	0.6	0.6
6	1.2	1.2	1.2	1.2	1.2	1.8
7	1.5	1.6	1.6	1.6	1.6	1.6
8	3.0	3.0	3.1	3.3	3.3	3.4
9	2.4	2.4	2.5	2.3	2.4	2.4
10	3.4	3.5	3.6	3.8	3.9	4.1
11	2.1	2.1	2.2	2.2	2.2	2.3
12	7.3	7.4	7.5	7.7	7.7	7.7
13	8.9	9.0	9.2	10.0	10.0	10.1
14	0.5	0.5	0.6	0.6	0.6	0.6
15	20.8	20.7	20.4	21.0	21.0	20.9
16	0.6	0.6	0.6	0.7	0.7	0.7
17	7.1	7.2	7.3	7.9	8.0	8.1
18	2.4	2.4	2.4	2.6	2.6	2.6
19	18.6	18.4	18.0	18.5	18.4	17.9
20	0	0	0	0	0	0
Total	100.0	100.0	100.0	100.0	100.0	100.0

a)   Standard Case.
b)   Lower Target.
c)   Higher Target.

NOTE :   For industrial classification see Appendix D.

IV.   CONCLUSIONS

Although the analysis does not cover all types of pollutants and the models used are not originally designed for environmental studies, the results of the study provide useful macro-economic guidelines and can be summarised in the following way.

Firstly, in regard to the effects on economic growth, the expansionary impacts of anti-pollution investment and related demand are greater than contractionary effects of costs and prices for the earlier three years: in the latter part of the period the expansionary impacts are gradually reduced. As compared with the U.S. case, the demand effects seem to be greater because of an active response of induced business investment.* On a sectoral basis, the expansionary impacts are largely accounted for by various engineering industries except in the automobile sector, while slightly decelerating tendencies are noted for food, pulp and paper, sundry goods and energy sectors. In this context, the policies towards energy-saving technology and structural adjustment are quite compatible with those for anti-pollution. The growth rates of basic steel and chemical industries are not significantly affected. This implies that from a macro-economic point of view the internalisation of the external costs gives rise to accelerating effects on output and employment at least for short-term and favourable impacts on welfare in the long-run. It should also be noted that the aggregate capacity in terms of potential GNP will expand and this can be utilised through ordinary demand management policy. The pessimistic view on economic growth appears to be exaggerated as it is chiefly based on a micro-economic view-point.

Secondly, some qualifications are needed in the evaluation of the above tentative conclusion. For instance, the price effects on exports are likely to be offset somewhat by similar tendencies abroad. The assumption of constant technology for anti-pollution is likely to overestimate the required pollution abatement investment. On the other hand, a) replacement investment accompanied by cleaner technology and efficiency, and b) public investment for sewerage systems, which are excluded from the present study, rather tend to underestimate the effects of expansion. Another important international aspect is direct investment abroad. Investment decisions between domestic or foreign sites are often dependent on the relative cost for anti-pollution; this problem had not been evaluated and remains to be solved in the paper.

The third issue discussed was the relationship with other economic policies. Demand management, as noted above, needs to be restrictive for the earlier three years, and to be expansionary for the later period in order to keep a stable economic growth. Mixed use of floating exchange rate systems will make for the efficiency of the stabilisation policy. As for income distribution, tax and social security policies need to be more strengthened in favour of lower income classes because of relative increases in the prices of living necessities as a result of pollution control.

---

* See reference (4) in the Bibliography.

Appendix A

A. Estimation of Pollution Abatement Costs and Investment

First, we estimated three types of pollution matrix as below :

1) Pg, ij - Pa, ij = Pe, ij

   Where Pg is coefficients of pollution generated per unit of
   output, Pa is coefficients of pollution abatement cost per unit
   of output, and Pe is coefficients of pollution emitted per unit
   of output.   The size of each matrix ij is 6 x 60 which contains
   six pollutants and sixty sectoral divisions.   These pollutants
   are, as noted before, SOx, NOx, COx, particulates and other
   air pollutants, BOD, and industrial wastes.   The environmental goals of the government are usually stated as:

2) $\sum\limits_{j}$ Pe, ij.Xj $= \sum\limits_{j}$ (Pg, ij - Pa, ij) Xj

   Where Xj is sectoral output.   Required anti-pollution investment and increase in capital cost are derived from Pa, ij
   which are directly or indirectly regulated by the government,
   once the sectoral output levels are roughly assumed.   The
   relationship between pollution abatement and investment is:

3) I_π, ij $= \Delta K_\pi$, ij

4) K_π, ij $= \alpha$ ij Pa, ij Xj

5) C_π, ij $= \alpha_\pi$ i. K_π, ij.

   Where I_π is pollution abatement investment, K_π is pollution
   abatement equipment, α is coefficients of investment required per unit of pollutant, C_π is pollution abatement cost
   and π is rate of depreciation of K_π.   The results of our
   estimation of Pgij and α ij are shown in Table 1 and Table 2.

B. Estimation of Direct and Indirect Price Increase and Conversion to Final Demand Deflators

Our sectoral price study is based on an expanded input-output
model which includes a newly constructed price block.   The latter

consists of two sub-systems: a) static and b) dynamic, defined as below.

(static system)

6) $\quad P_d^* = pA = (\quad + K + \tau\ )\ \hat{v}$

7) $\quad p^* = p_d^*\ (I - \mu\ ) + p_m \cdot \mu$

Where p_d^* is imputed price of domestic producers, p^* is imputed price of supply, p_m is import price, A is technical coefficient matrix, $\omega\ =\ \dfrac{\omega \cdot Lw}{\cdot V}$ (unit labour cost in terms of value added), is wage rate, $K = \dfrac{(r + d\ )K}{V}$ capital cost including tax, d = depreciation cost), $\tau\ =\ T/V$ $\mu\ =\ M/\ (X + M)$, i.e. diagonal matrix of import dependency $\hat{v}\ =\ V/X$, i.e. diagonal matrix of value-added ratio. p_d^*, p^*, p_m, ω , χ and τ are row vectors.

The above price block is further transformed into the following dynamic one by introducing external market conditions and the rate of capacity utilisation.

(dynamic system)

8) $\quad P_d - P_{d-1}\ =\ \lambda\ (p_d^e - p_{d-1})$

9) $\quad p_d^e\ =\ f\ (p_d^*,\ p_m,\ \omega\ )$

10) $\quad p = p_d\ (I - \mu\ ) + p_m \cdot \mu$

11) $\quad p_c^*\ =\ p \cdot Bc$

12) $\quad p_e^*\ =\ p \cdot Be$

13) $\quad p_c\ =\ f(p_c^*,\ t)$

14) $\quad p_e\ =\ f(p_e^*,\ t)$

Where p_c^* is consumer price deflator by 20 major groups, p_e^* is export price deflator by 6 major groups, Bc is convertor-matrix of 60 x 20, Be is convertor-matrix of of 60 x 6, p_d^e is expected value of domestic output price

δ is rate of capacity utilisation, λ is adjustment coefficients. p_d, p, p_c, p_e are actual values.

As easily noted, the increase in anti-pollution costs C affects K and then p_d^* and p^*, and finally the entire price system through interindustry dependence and dynamic adjustments. A similar price adjustment was made for other final demand deflators such as those for various investment, government consumption and change in inventories.

C. Conversion to Macro-Model Variables

The results of the above analysis on sectoral investment and prices need to be further adjusted to quarterly macro-variables, as our macro-model is based on quarterly data and the impacts of anti-pollution investment are not explicitly included in the specification of the model. Since the model has about 17 functions of price deflators for different final demand items and three private business investment functions, constant terms of those functions have been adjusted by using the aggregate amounts derived from the input-output model. A similar adjustment was also made for private capital stock, as the anti-pollution investment has no productive impacts on capacity and rate of utilisation. This implies that while being expansionary in macro-economic terms, the anti-pollution investment is unproductive and inflationary in micro-economic terms.

Several qualifications, however, are needed to the above approach. Firstly, a favourable impact of replacement investment is not explicitly considered which tends to increase environmental efficiency through its vintage effect. Secondly, regional aspects in relocation of industrial plants which also affect pollution standards of the government are neglected. Thirdly, coefficients of pollution generated are assumed to be constant over time but there is an increasing tendency of technical progress in this area. Lastly, government investment, especially that for sewerage systems which tends to have a substantial impact on environment and the economy is not included in the present study.

In view of these qualifications, it should be pointed out that the aggregate required anti-pollution investment and price increase tend to be over-estimated in some sectors, while under-biased in the public investment.

D. Macro-Model Simulation

Based on the adjustments derived from the input-output model, dynamic impacts on aggregate variables have been obtained by the EPA Quarterly Macro-Model with about 140 equations for 1972 to 1977. [13]. Since this model consists of three sectors: primary secondary and tertiary, the policy impacts can be analysed for sectoral output, employment, investment, as well as various price deflators. Monetary impacts are also obtained in terms of money supply, financial transactions and various interest rates.

In order to distinguish the effects between those of aggregate demand and of prices, an attempt is made to run the model separately for these two different impacts. This lends itself to the analysis of the policy impacts in view of the complex nature of the present study.

E. Estimation of Sectoral Output and Employment

The results of the macro-model simulation are again converted to sectoral demand, trade, output and employment by the input-output model. The final demand structure is also affected by the change in relative prices, especially for exports and private consumption. Thus, polluting sectors tend to be adversely affected while other sectors tend to respond rather expansionary. As discussed later, their response patterns are different according to the dependency on anti-pollution activities, price sensitivity, etc.

Appendix B

MACRO-ECONOMIC VARIABLES

A. Real and Price Variables

(1965 prices, billion yen)

CY		1972	1973	1974	1975	1976	1977
V	I	731	2,134	2,638	1,876	1,702	580
	II	1,301	4,192	5,596	3,611	2,501	746
V^c	I	150	919	2,105	3,065	3,721	4,218
	II	267	1,714	4,173	6,128	7,124	7,684
C	I	19	87	152	138	72	-50
	II	34	165	317	301	158	-54
C_f	I	1	1	-14	-50	-97	-147
	II	3	3	-20	-87	-175	-262
C_d	I	3	14	21	9	- 8	-13
	II	5	26	44	21	-19	-30
C_o	I	15	72	144	179	176	111
	II	26	136	293	367	352	238
C_g	I	0	-2	-4	-6	-11	-15
	II	0	-2	-6	-11	-15	-23
I_g	I	-9	-33	-41	-63	-120	-147
	II	-17	-61	-79	-110	-207	-276
I_h	I	18	59	77	13	-32	-87
	II	32	114	163	26	-92	-170
I_p	I	585	1,906	2,557	2,045	1,929	1,230
	II	1,040	3,702	5,363	3,982	2,993	1,795

I   Lower Target.
II   Higher Target.

55

	CY	1972	1973	1974	1975	1976	1977
$I_p 1$	I	8	7	1	-2	2	11
	II	17	17	5	-1	9	30
$I_p 2$	I	444	1,397	1,827	1,366	1,310	633
	II	754	2,715	3,838	2,562	1,867	798
$I_p 3$	I	133	502	729	682	617	585
	II	269	971	1,520	1,422	1,116	967
J_p	I	224	501	406	89	127	-202
	II	398	1,009	908	89	-1	-386
E	I	-11	-32	9	89	119	120
	II	-20	-61	4	181	275	252
E_c	I	-13	-37	3	85	116	124
	II	-22	-69	-10	174	272	260
M	I	94	351	516	430	382	269
	II	165	673	1,074	847	608	392
O	I	4.1	12.7	16.4	12.4	11.5	5.8
	II	7.3	24.9	34.7	24.0	17.3	8.2
K_p	I	76	818	2,362	3,698	4,380	4,831
	II	138	1,532	4,769	7,654	8,838	9,302
V/V_c	I	.8	1.6	.7	-1.1	-2.0	-3.6
	II	1.5	3.2	1.8	-2.3	-4.4	-6.7
p^c	I	0	.1	.7	1.5	2.1	2.2
	II	0	.2	1.1	2.8	3.9	3.8
P_{cf}	I	.2	1.0	2.7	4.2	5.1	5.2
	II	.3	1.8	4.9	7.8	9.2	8.8
P_{cd}	I	.1	.3	.4	.2	.3	.6
	II	.2	.6	.7	.4	.3	.6
P_{co}	I	-.1	-.4	-.3	.5	1.1	1.2
	II	-.2	-.8	-.8	.8	2.1	2.2
P_{cg}	I	0	.1	.1	.3	.5	.6
	II	0	.1	.5	.5	.6	1.0

CY		1972	1973	1974	1975	1976	1977
P_{ig}	I	.2	.6	.8	1.1	1.7	1.8
	II	.3	1.2	1.6	1.9	3.0	3.5
P_i	I	.3	1.0	1.0	.4	-.3	-1.3
	II	.5	1.8	2.1	.7	-1.1	-3.1
P_h	I	.2	.6	.9	1.3	1.7	1.6
	II	.3	1.1	1.8	2.3	2.9	2.8
P_j	I	.1	.3	.2	.2	.5	.5
	II	.3	.5	.4	.3	.8	1.1
P_e	I	.2	.2	-.1	-.4	-.1	-.2
	II	.4	.5	-.2	-.9	-.5	-.4
P_{ec}	I	.2	.2	-.2	-.5	-.2	-.3
	II	.4	.4	-.4	-1.2	-.8	-.7
P_m	I	-.1	-.4	-.6	-.6	-.6	-.5
	II	-.1	-.7	-1.1	-1.2	-.9	-.7
P	I	-.1	-.2	-.2	.2	.5	.8
	II	-.2	-.5	-.5	.2	.9	1.3
P_w	I	.3	.5	.3	.2	.5	.4
	II	.5	.9	.5	-.0	.6	.6
P_{wi}	I	.3	.5	.3	.1	.5	.3
	II	.6	1.0	.5	-.1	.4	.2
P_{wf}	I	.0	.1	.2	.2	.2	.3
	II	.0	.2	.3	.4	.4	.5
P_{wo}	I	.0	.2	.3	.6	.8	1.1
	II	.1	.2	.6	1.2	2.0	3.1
P_k	I	.2	.8	1.1	1.2	1.5	1.7
	II	.4	1.4	2.1	2.3	2.4	2.6
W	I	4.2	21.7	50.5	71.7	76.1	55.7
	II	7.4	40.3	100.2	144.5	145.0	97.2

NOTE :

V	$=$	real GNP
V^c	$=$	potential GNP
C	$=$	real private consumption
C_f	$=$	do., for food
C_d	$=$	do., for durables
C_o	$=$	do., for others
C_g	$=$	real government consumption
I_g	$=$	real government investment
I_h	$=$	real private housing investment
I_p	$=$	real private business investment
I_p^1	$=$	do., primary sector
I_p^2	$=$	do., for secondary sector
I_p^3	$=$	do., for tertiary sector
J_p	$=$	change in private inventories
E	$=$	exports
E_c	$=$	commodity exports
M	$=$	imports
O	$=$	industrial production (1940 = 100)
K_p	$=$	business capital stock
P	$=$	consumer price deflator
P_c	$=$	do., food
P_{cf}	$=$	do., durables
P_{cd}	$=$	do., for others
P_{co}	$=$	government investment deflator
P_{cg}	$=$	business investment deflator
P_i	$=$	private housing deflator
P_h	$=$	inventory deflator
P_j	$=$	export price deflator
P_e	$=$	commodity export deflator
P_{ec}	$=$	import price deflator
P_m	$=$	wholesale price deflator, industrial products

NOTE (suite) : P_{wi} = do., other

P_{wo} = user cost of capital

W^k = wage rate (1000 yen)

P_{wf} = do., farm products

B. MONETARY VARIABLES

(billion yen)

1. Money supply (= 2 + 3 + 4.)	I	−196	−948	−1,304	−626	−289	−1,967
	II	−347	−1,812	−2,849	−1,232	97	974
2. Credit to private sectors	I	−26	−25	239	623	608	449
	II	−45	−64	361	1,297	1,389	841
3. Credit to public sectors	I	−83	−498	−823	−675	−441	−343
	II	−148	−935	−1,705	−1,379	−616	−303
4. Credit to abroad	I	−87	−424	−719	−573	−456	−302
	II	−154	−935	−1,705	−1,379	−616	−303
5. Call money rate(%)	I	.01	.01	.24	.26	.18	.15
	II	.02	.16	.48	.54	.31	.19
6. Interest rate on bank loan (%)	I	0	.02	.04	.05	.03	.03
	II	0	.03	.09	.10	.06	.05

I. Lower Target
II. Higher Target

Appendix C

INDUSTRIAL CLASSIFICATION

60-SECTOR	7-SECTOR
1. General crop	
2. Industrial crop	
3. Livestock for textiles	1. Agriculture, Forestry
4. Livestock	Fishing
5. Forestry	
6. Fisheries	.
7. Coal mining	
8. Iron ores	
9. Nonferrous metallic ores	2. Mining
10. Crude petroleum and natural gas	
11. Other mining	
12. Meat and Dairy products	
13. Grain products	
14. Manufactured sea foods	
15. Other food	
16. Beverages	
17. Tobacco	
18. Natural textiles	
19. Chemical textiles	3-1. Light Manufacturing
20. Other textiles	Industries
21. Wearing apparel	
22. Wood products	
23. Furniture	
24. Pulp and paper	
25. Printing and Publishing	
26. Leather products	
27. Rubber products	
28. Basic Chemicals	3-2. Heavy Manufacturing
29. Other chemicals	Industries

60-SECTOR	7-SECTOR
30. Petroleum products	
31. Coal products	3-1. Light Manufacturing
32. Ceramics	Industries
33. Primary iron	
34. Steel products	
35. Primary Non-ferrous Metals	
36. Fabricated Metals	3-2. Heavy Manufacturing
37. Machinery	Industries
38. Electrical machinery	
39. Automobile	
40. Other transport equipment	
41. Instrument and related products	3-1. Light Manufacturing Industries
42. Miscellaneous manufacturing	
43. Residence	
44. Non-residence	4. Construction
45. Public engineering work	
46. Other engineering work	
47. Electricity	
48. Gas	5. Public Utilities
49. Water and sanitary service	
50. Wholesale and retail trade	6. Commerce and Services
51. Real estate	
52. Railway transport	
53. Road transport	5. Public Utilities
54. Other transport	
55. Communications	
56. Bank and other financial institutions	
57. Government services	6. Commerce and Services
58. Public services	
59. Other personal services	
60. Unallocated	7. Unallocated
61. Total	8. Total

Appendix D

INDUSTRIAL CLASSIFICATION

20-SECTOR

---

1. Agriculture
2. Mining
3. Food
4. Textiles
5. Pulp and Paper
6. Chemicals
7. Primary Metals
8. Metal Production
9. Machinery
10. Electrical Machinery
11. Transport Equipment
12. Other Manufacturing
13. Construction
14. Public Utilities
15. Trade
16. Real Estate
17. Transport and Communication
18. Banking and Insurance
19. Services
20. Unallocated

BIBLIOGRAPHY

1. BAUMOL, W. :   Environmental Protection and the Distribution
                        of Incomes, in Problems of Environmental
                        Economics (Paris, 1972)

2. CAZES, B.   :   Environmental Quality Indicators and Social
                        Indicators, in Problems of Environmental
                        Economics (Paris, 1972)

3. DORFMAN, R and DORFMAN, N.S., ed. : Economics of
                        the Environment (New York, 1972)

4. ENVIRONMENTAL PROTECTION AGENCY : The Economic
                        Impact of Pollution Control - A Summary
                        of Recent Studies (Washington, 1972)

5. FAZIO, A.G. and LO CASCIO, M. : Evaluation of the Economic
                        Effects of Anti-Pollution Public Policy:
                        Proposal for an Econometric Analysis Model,
                        in Problems of Environmental Economics
                        (Paris, 1972)

6. FØRSUND, F.R. and STRØM, S : Outline of a Macro-Economic
                        Analysis of Environmental Pollution: A
                        Multi-sectoral Approach, in Problems of
                        Environmental Economics (Paris, 1972)

7. ECONOMIC COUNCIL : The 4th Report of Committee on Econo-
                        metric Methods, 1973 (in Japanese)

8. ECONOMIC PLANNING AGENCY: Annual Economic Report,
                        1973 (in Japanese)

9. MEADOWS, D.L., et. al. : Limit to growth 1972

10. ECONOMIC PLANNING AGENCY : Economic and Social Plan,
                        1977 (1972)

11. OECD   :   Problems of Environmental Economics
                        (Paris, 1972)

12. SHISHIDO, S. :   Quality of Life and Economic Growth -
                        Accelaration vs Decceleration (JERI, 1972)

13. SHISHIDO, S. et.al. : Supply and Demand Management with the
                        EPA Quarterly Macro-Model, 1972

Annexe III

PROGRAMME OF POLLUTION-CONTROL MEASURES TO 1980 - AN ECONOMIC AND FINANCIAL ANALYSIS FOR ITALY

1. Introduction

The main problems to be considered in defining a pollution control programme are the cost of instituting the various technological measures and the effect of this expenditure on the national economy.

A first estimate of the expenditure necessary for equipment to deal with the main forms of pollution was made in Italy in 1969 as part of an ISVET research project commissioned to assess the economic costs and benefits of government pollution control measures. * Using the appropriate methodology, the study gives a general estimate of the scale of investment and operating costs that would be required between 1970 and 1985 in order to reach more or less optimum clean air and water standards.

This paper updates the figures given in that study and goes into greater depth, correcting the clean air and water standards to be reached and setting them out in more detail. This is based on a finer analysis of the costs and takes into account certain targets that legislation has since defined, e.g. as regards air pollution caused by industrial emissions. **

The pollution control costs that have been worked out relate to the following general targets for the various types of pollution:

a) air pollution caused by household heating: full conversion of all old and new apparatus ;

b) air pollution caused by vehicle emissions: gradual introduction between now and 1980 of tighter standards for permitted emission levels, under which, firstly, "clean-air-package" and, secondly, "main-air-ox" type devices would become compulsory ;

---

* A report on this study has been brought out by G. SCAIOLA, "L'intervento pubblico contro gli inquinamenti" (Public pollution-control action), ISVET series 16, published by F. Angeli, Milan, 1971.

** The estimates are still very general and approximate because it is not yet possible, on the national scale, to work out a functional correlation between the quantity of pollutants discharged to atmosphere, control costs and environment quality. These estimates are, however, the quantitive structure that the pollution control programme has to fit and, as such, they should have a definite operational significance.

c)   industrial air pollution: complete conversion of plants already existing in 1971 and all new plants;

d)   domestic sewage: completion of 50 per cent of the sewer system and installation of 50 per cent of the necessary treatment plants planned for 1985;

e)   industrial water pollution: conversion of 90 per cent of plants existing in 1971 and all new plants;

f)   sea pollution caused by oil tankers: provision of facilities for treating tanker cleaning and ballast water in 21 oil ports;

g)   ground pollution by solid urban waste: installation of incinerating equipment and other disposal systems capable of handling 50 per cent of solid urban wastes produced by 1980.

The estimates for the finance required for pollution control equipment up to 1980 take into account the increase in pollution implicit in the production and population growth forecasts for the above-mentioned date.   The total figure for the finance required is L. 5,518,000 million at current prices.

This general pattern of targets and pollution control costs was then looked at in terms of three possible schemes based on two primary variables:

a)   the sequence of investment over time (i.e. the phasing of the environmental quality targets) ; and

b)   the extent of state participation in pollution control costs borne directly by the private sector and local authorities. *

Each of the three schemes is based on a particular combination of values for these two variables.   As far as investment phasing is concerned, in all three schemes there would be immediate introduction of compulsory pollution control systems for new industrial plant and the stepped conversion of household heating appliances would be completed by 1975; but as far as old plants are concerned two possibilities have been considered: low-gear and high-gear rates of conversion to comply with the regulations.

In the ten-year period between 1971 and 1980, low-gear conversion would mean a total investment bill of L.3,631,000 million (of which L. 1,166,000 million would be spent (by 1975) whereas high-gear conversion would cost L. 5,503,000 million (of which L.2,178,000 would be spent during the first five years).

---

*   This would last for the ten years start-up period, without prejudice to the "Polluter Pays" principle recently adopted by the EEC, apart from the necessary exceptions (which, precisely, relate mainly to the transitional phase during which the pollution control regulations would be instituted).

As regards the sharing of the cost between economic agents (those responsible for pollution control), three possibilities are considered. Whilst all three include government assistance for local communities but none for domestic pollution-control measures (heating and motor vehicles) - they differ in the help to be given to business firms. The three alternatives are as follows:

A. no assistance

B. low-interest loans for capital expenditure on control equipment for all forms of industrial pollution (excluding solid wastes) ;

C. as for B, plus tax reliefs for equipment used to control industrial water pollution.

Any combination of one of the two phasing alternatives and one of the three possible patterns of government assistance constitutes a potential pollution-control scheme.

As indicated above, only three of these possible schemes (A, B and C) have been studied since it was thought that they gave a wide enough range:

Scheme	Pattern of assistance	Investment phasing
A	= A	low-gear
B	= B	higher-gear
C	= C	low-gear

In scheme A, the process of converting production plant already existing at the time that the regulations entered into force would be slow.

Even though all new production plant would have to be equipped with pollution-control systems, the total amount of investment for cleaning industrial effluent would not be high during the first years. Running expenses would be wholly paid by the firms and include amortization of the capital invested (at 8 per cent per annum) plus plant operating and maintenance costs.

In scheme B, old plant has to be converted to comply with the regulations at a quicker pace. The total investment for pollution control systems and the related running expense would therefore be higher in the early years than for scheme B.

On the other hand, the firms concerned would be relieved of some of the burden because the government would bear part of the amortization cost (loans at 4 per cent instead of 8 per cent for certain parts of the investment depending on the year in which the money was spent) and because there would be tax reliefs - certain percentages of the capital invested in pollution-control equipment would be deductible for tax purposes.

In scheme C the phasing would be the same as in scheme A and loans would be available to firms on favourable terms as in scheme B, but there would be no tax reliefs.

In all three schemes the water rate for both industrial and domestic use, would be raised (increasing revenue by about L. 80,000 million).

By establishing the extra costs that firms in the various industries would have to meet under the three schemes (1975) it was possible to arrive at the increase in production costs and selling prices in the various sectors for each scheme, with the help of an econometric model for 1975, for which year forecasts are available for the national economy broken down by sectors of production (then figures were used as a basis for the forecasts in the draft of Italy's second five-year plan).

The industries hardest hit by the increase in production costs (in all three schemes) are as follows :

a)   the paper industry, which is particularly affected both by the cost of the equipment and by the increase in the industrial water rate (an increase in cost ranging from 21 to 33 per cent for the three schemes);

b)   chemical and related industries (16 to 23 per cent) ;

c)   power generation and distribution (about 15 per cent) ;

d)   non-metallic ore conversion (11 to 20 per cent) ;

e)   oil and coal products (9 to 15 per cent) ;

f)   metal industries (9 to 15 per cent);

g)   rubber (7 to 13 per cent).

Overall, the increase in industrial production costs for 1975 is fairly slight.

A comparison between the figures for the three schemes shows that the increase in running expenses is highest for scheme B in all industries, in spite of the tax concessions and low-interest rates, because of the faster rate at which the industrial system has to be converted to the pollution control standards laid down by the applicable regulations. The increase is lower in scheme A (low-gear conversion) and lower still in scheme C - low-gear conversion plus low-interest loans.

The industries that suffer most if the rate of investment in pollution-control equipment is quickened are those involved in the conversion of non-metallic ores (11 per cent increase in cost for scheme C, but 20 per cent for scheme B), rubber (7 versus 13 per cent), oil and coal

products (9 versus 15 per cent), chemical and related industries
(16 versus 23 per cent), and paper and board (21 versus 33 per
cent).

A comparison between the figures for scheme C and those for
scheme A shows which industries are particularly helped by soft
loans: paper and board (25 per cent higher cost in scheme A but only
21 per cent higher in scheme C), rubber (10 versus 7 per cent) and,
to a lesser extent, the chemical and related industries (18 versus 16
per cent), and metal industries (10 versus 9 per cent).

The effect on prices directly attributable to the cost of having
and running pollution-control equipment in use in 1975 can be calculated
by multiplying the direct effect on costs by sectoral coefficients of
price/cost elasticity.

The total effect on production costs includes not only those increases
caused directly by pollution-control expenditure itself but also the indirect increases, that is to say those generated as the primary increase
in the cost of intermediate goods percolates through the general system
of industrial costs and prices as a result of the economic interdependence
between the various industries.

Industries suffering the biggest increases in production costs due
to these indirect effects are as follows

a)   oil and coal products, where the total effect in the three
schemes varies from 18 to 29 per cent. Deducting the direct effect
of about 9 to 15 per cent, the indirect effect on costs is approximately
9 to 14 per cent.

b)   power generation and distribution: indirect effect on costs
estimated at about 1 to 16 per cent.

c)   rubber: about 4 to 6 per cent;

d)   conversion of non-metallic ores: about 4 to 5 per cent;

e)   textiles: about 3 to 5 per cent;

f)   chemicals and related products: 3 to 5 per cent;

g)   clothing and soft furnishings: about 3 to 4 per cent;

h)   construction: about 3 to 5 per cent.

The biggest total effect on selling prices arises in the following
industries:

a)   oil and coal products, where the increase in prices would
range from about 18 to about 30 per cent, in the three schemes;

b)   chemical and related industries: about 19 to 28 per cent;

c)   conversion of non-metallic ores: about 9 to 16 per cent;

d)   foodstuffs and beverages: about 4 to 7 per cent;

e)   textiles: 4 to 7 per cent.

A comparison between the increase in costs and the increase in selling prices shows that, in the industries most affected by the pollution-control measures, those where average profit margins would shrink the most are:

a)   the metal industries, where, in the three schemes, the increase in selling price varies from 5 to 8 per cent and that in production costs from 11 to 19 per cent;

b)   the rubber industries, where the increase in selling prices varies from 4 to 7 per cent compared with an increase in production costs ranging from 11 to 19 per cent;

c)   the non-metallic ore conversion industries, where the increase in selling prices varies from 10 to 17 per cent compared with an increase in production costs varying from 15 to 26 per cent.

These sectoral differences in the cost of pollution control measures suggests that the relevant legislation should perhaps be applied with sufficient discretionary margins to allow for the differing extents to which these industries influence the general system of prices and for the cyclical and structural situation of the market they specifically supply.

Estimated effects on the system of industrial costs and selling prices for 1975 are therefore relatively limited in extent, one reason being the fact that only 30 per cent of existing production plant would, according to the schemes being considered, be converted in that year to comply with the pollution-control legislation.

If the legislation were to be applied in full then the effect on prices would be far greater.

To sum up: econometric analysis shows that it would be feasible to implement a pollution-control programme during the next five years because the economy could cope with its effects without serious difficulty. At the same time it shows the usefulness, in the process of converting industry to the new standards, of economic support from the public sector on a flexible basis, taking its anti-cyclical effect into account, and with some sectoral differentiation in order to prevent unwanted disequilibria.

2.   Estimated cost of technical pollution-control measures

Establishing what financial resources would be required to implement an effective pollution-control policy and the ways in which finding them could be shared by the state, industry and consumers, is one of the basic steps in framing a co-ordinated programme of action.

As mentioned at the beginning of this report, a first estimate of the cost of a programme for controlling the main forms of pollution in Italy, was prepared in 1969-70 as part of an ISVET cost/benefit study on a government pollution-control plan.

In the present study we felt it would be useful to go into further depth, to correct and describe more fully the pollution control standards to be achieved and to use a finer breakdown of sectoral costs in order to take account, among other things, of certain specific objectives that have since been defined by the Government, e.g. regarding industrial air pollution.

The cost analysis relates to the following main forms of pollution:

a)   air pollution caused by domestic heating;

b)   air pollution caused by motor vehicle emissions;

c)   air pollution caused by industry;

d)   water pollution caused by urban effluents' domestic sewage;

e)   water pollution caused by industry;

f)   seawater pollution caused by oil tankers;

g)   ground pollution caused by solid urban wastes.

This latter item (ground pollution caused by solid wastes) has thus been added to the classification adopted for the 1969-70 study. On the other hand, certain other possible forms of pollution have not been considered (those caused by the use of chemical products in agriculture, radio-active waste, noise, etc.).

The estimates are still only very approximate indications, because it is not yet possible to define a functional correlation at national level between the quantities of pollutants discharged to the environment, the cost of pollution-control equipment and the quality of the environment. Because of all the theoretical, operational and technical difficulties involved in establishing such a relationship the only valid method would be to take a geographical approach and to study well-defined homogeneous areas. Failing such an approach, an assessment of financial requirements at national level cannot be based on any precise definition of the environment quality targets to be reached; the best that could be done was to establish approximate pollution abatement thresholds achieved with modern treatment techniques that are already in use (mainly in other countries).

Finance requirements have been assessed to 1980 for technical measures designed to cope with the present level of pollution and that of the potential future pollution implicit in production and population growth between now and that date. The figures make no allowance for the cost fo the administrative structures that would be necessary in order to set up the investigatory and monitoring systems for enforcing pollution control legislation.

With regard to points c) and e) (industrial pollution), an assessment has been made for each industry that creates pollution; the purpose was to evaluate the effect of pollution control costs on the system of sectoral prices, on the trade balance, and on the formation and use of resources, by constructing an econometric model using the matrix of the sectoral interdependencies of the Italian economy (see paragraph 4).

Table 1 summarises the capital expenditure estimates. It is pointed out, again, that these estimates relate to very high, more or less optimal, pollution control levels. There may be lower, and yet acceptable, levels of pollution control for which the capital cost would not be so high.

3. Proposals for public financial assistance in relation to various possible investment phasing possibilities

Once the financial criteria for public investment are defined, the various possibilities have to be quantified.

These possibilities need to include forecasts with regard to the phasing of the investment programmes since public support for the pollution control process is the variable instrument that can be used to reconcile environmental objectives (spaced out over time) with the need to avoid big price increases and production cuts in individual sectors.

Table 1.   ESTIMATED INVESTMENT REQUIREMENTS TO 1980

(for high standard of pollution control)

ENVIRONMENT	SOURCE	CAPITAL EXPENDITURE IN LIRE '000 MILLION AT CURRENT PRICES 1971-1980
Air	Domestic heating	50
	Motor vehicles	459
	Industry[1]	765
Water	Urban areas[2]	2,160
	Industry[3]	1,864
	Oil tankers	21
Ground	Urban areas	200
	TOTAL	5,519

1. Of which L.379,000 million relate to 1970 production in the industrial sectors concerned and L.385,000 million is the estimated investment to cover the forecast increase in production over the period 1971-1980.
2. Of which L.1,700 million would be spent on the sewer system and L.460,000 million on treatment plants scaled to the Italian population forecasts for 1985.
3. L. 1,354,000 million relate to production by the industries considered in 1970 and L. 511,000 million for the forecast increase in production between 1971 and 1980.

Three possible alternative schemes will therefore be outlined, quantified as to the pattern of expenditure between now and 1980 and defined by the forms and levels of the State's financial commitment.

They have been chosen from among the possible combinations between three levels of public financial commitment and two rates of phasing the pollution control measures. There are thus two extreme and one intermediate programme.

On this basis, in spite of the small number of combinations, it is felt that the range of solutions put forward is sufficiently broad.

Each scheme is broken down under the following headings for each form of pollution*:

a)   financing;

b)   volume and phasing of investment by industrial sector;**

c)   volume and phasing of running expenses, broken down by economic agents (firms, households, local authorities, central government).

This breakdown seemed necessary in order at a later stage to be able to provide an estimate of the economic effects of alternative pollution-control schemes as set out in section 4.

Table 2 summarises the characteristics of the three possible schemes, particular attention being paid to the level of government financial assistance. Details as regards the phasing of the pollution control programme, however, are given in the section in which each of the three possible schemes is discussed.

3.1.   Scheme A: low-gear, with low level of public support

This scheme is based on the following assumptions:

a)   strict application of the "polluter-pays" principle in industry, i.e. no government help to polluting industries;

b)   slow application of pollution control measures (because of the absence of any state encouragement) even though they might be specifically laid down in the legislation;

c)   gradual provision, as local finance allows, of public facilities (sewage system, sewage plant, disposal of solid urban wastes).

This scheme should therefore involve minimum economic cost to the community.

---

*   The forms of pollution considered are: domestic heating, motor vehicle emissions, air pollution caused by industrial emissions, industrial waste water effluents, domestic sewage, solid urban waste and oil tankers.

**   Details for industrial sectors are given in section 4 with reference to the econometric calculation of the effect of pollution control legislation.

Table 2.   ALTERNATIVE POLLUTION CONTROL SCHEMES

		State financial assistance*
		Phasing of investment
	low-gear	
low SCHEME A	medium SCHEME C	
- industrial pollution control costs wholly borne by firms themselves.	- government support and incentives for industry (credit facilities).	
- government assistance at a slow rate for public waste treatment plant (credit facilities and grants).	- governement assistance at a slow rate for public waste treatment plant (credit facilities and grants).	high
		High-gear SCHEME B
		- extensive public support and incentives for industry (credit facilities and tax reliefs)
		- government support at a faster rate for public waste treatment plant (credit facilities and grants).

(*)   Uniform level for local authorities; at varying rates for industry.

Overall, however, it would not appear to be the most realistic of the three because it would be difficult - particularly in the present economic situation - to refuse all state assistance to industry for pollution control.

Public financial support

In this first scheme, state support for each of the sectors concerned would be as follows:

a) Household heating

Under present legislation, this problem ought to have been solved but this is not confirmed by estimates of the extent to which the rules concerned have been implemented. These are only estimates, and not checked facts, since the provisions of the implementing regulation for Act 615, requiring that a census of heating installations be taken in zones A and B by the fire service, has not been complied with.

It is fairly certain that, alongside the installation of plant in conformity with the law in new buildings, the conversion of old plant will continue during the next few years.

Government action is likely to incline towards a system of more effective controls and severer penalties although there would not appear to be any case for the use of public finance except in the event that the control zones (zones A and B defined in Act 615 of 13th July, 1966) were extended. An effective air pollution control policy might instead be achieved by suitably pricing certain "clean" fuels (e.g. methane) in order to provide an incentive for their use in future heating installations.

b) Motor vehicle emissions

Here there would be no financial assistance from the state except, possibly, to help finance applied research in this area. Government action could take the form of tax reliefs to help absorb the extra cost of producing low-lead petrol, should such a measure be included in future legislation on the subject. This possibility, however, would appear to be remote and uncertain, one reason being that the specialists are far from unanimous in their conclusions regarding the dangers of lead.

c) Industrial air pollution

Recent regulations on this subject require that pollution control equipment be installed in new industrial plant and that old establishments be converted.

In this first scheme there is no provision for financial support from the government except for the grant of guaranteed loans for the necessary investment. Thus all pollution control expenditure would be borne by the production units causing the pollution.

d)   Industrial liquid effluents

Here, too, there is no provision for any government support.
This would apply whether government action were purely a matter of
laying down effluent standards or whether the "penalty-bonus" system
were used since this would put no financial burden on the State.

e)   Domestic sewage

As regards the local authorities it is not a question of providing
incentives in order to accelerate the rate at which pollution control
measures are taken.   The problem here is the difficult financial situation they are in and their need of considerable state support.   The
phasing of pollution control investment and the completion of the
drainage system* should be jointly planned by the central and local
governments; priority should no doubt be given to the large towns and
tourist areas but otherwise, as has been said, this is a matter of
central and local planning.

In this connection there is even a case for creating a national fund
for use by the government to help local authorities in the manner and to
the extent that may be judged the most appropriate in each individual
case.   But if a general yardstick is wanted, it would seem that the
state ought to provide local authorities with:

- guaranteed loans on favourable terms (4 per cent interest) for
  an amount equal to 30 per cent of the investment involved;
- outright grants for 70 per cent of the investment.**

On this basis, local authorities would be left to meet direct running
expenses and to pay back 30 per cent of the investment.

One way of meeting these costs, to which reference has already
been made, is for the local authorities to increase the water rate,
scaling the tariff in relation to category of user and quantity used over
and above "normal family consumption".

f)   Solid urban wastes

The same problems arise as in the previous case.   The point is
that the building of plants for the disposal of solid waste (whatever
technique is used, whether it be incineration, combustion, or controlled
tipping) is the responsibility of the local authorities (communes, groups

---

*   It should be noted that even though the completion of the sewage system does
not come specifically under the heading of pollution control, being part of normal urban
infrastructure, it has been included in this proposal for state assistance because it is the
necessary preliminary to all specific pollution control measures.

**   This, in fact, repeats what was provided under Decree No. 1090 of 13th March,
1968, which is regarded as adequate from the financial standpoint.   The fact that the sewage
system has not been built in spite of these incentives is considered to be mainly attributable
to organisational shortcomings.

75

of communes and, in the extreme case, regions, depending on the cost of the plant and the need for it to be fully utilised). Like sewage systems, these installations are therefore public facilities.

In this area, the proposal is that the State should provide the local authorities with :

- guaranteed loans on favourable terms covering 30 per cent of the investment;
- outright grants for the remaining 70 per cent.

To find the resources they would need, local authorities could consider raising the urban refuse collection rate and, where the rate is already high, to divide it into two parts, the first related to the assumed quantity of waste (calculated and adjusted indirectly, e.g. on the basis of the number of people in the household and/or surface area occupied) and the other related to the assumed income (based, for example, on surface area per head and the quality of the dwelling itself).

g) Seaborne oil transport

The control of oil pollution at sea will certainly be covered by legislation in the very near future. The main principles of the measures to be taken against this type of pollution have already been laid down at the London Convention and in the international agreements that followed.

An important point here is that any measure in favour of the Mediterranean basin (increasingly affected by oil pollution and dumping) is obviously of particular interest to Italy.

It is therefore to be expected that legislation will soon be introduced and that one of the first measures will relate to the installation of equipment in oil ports for the collection and teeatment of any oil tanker ballast water that is discharged. Systematic pollution by hydrocarbons is attributable to many causes but the discharging of oil tanker ballast and cleaning water is one of the worst sources of deep sea pollution and one of the most expensive, in terms of investment, to eradicate.

It is also likely that the government will take financial steps to encourage the construction of such facilities by port groups. But in this first scheme, as for industrial pollution, it is envisaged that the cost of installing facilities in ports for treating tanker ballast and cleaning water will be wholly borne by the refining industry.

Volume and phasing of investment

As already indicated, investment in this low-gear pollution control scheme would be thinly spread out over time.

The factors on which this assumption are based, singly or in combination, are as follows:

- slow introduction of pollution-control legislation;
- enactment of legislation which is not complied with or else is ineffective;
- extended periods for the conversion necessary to comply with the legislation;
- low-level of government financial assistance.

The general pattern of expenditure, broken down by the sectors concerned and by source of finance (industry, households or government) is shown in Table 3.

Running expenses

In addition to investment requirements, we need to consider the running expenses for the pollution-control equipment used in each sector and the distribution of these running expenses among the various economic agents (industry, households and central and local government).

The overall picture of running expenses, and the basic assumptions on which the calculations have been made, can be seen in the following terms:

a) Domestic heating

Operating costs here primarily arise out of the additional cost of gas-oil compared to fuel oil, after allowing for any other advantages deriving from the use of this fuel.

A point to note is that the higher cost of gas-oil compared with fuel oil is partly a matter of difference in tax treatment (this is expected to continue in the future).

Secondly, there is the cost of paying back the investment in building work. This has been calculated on the basis of equal annual payments equivalent to 9.4 per cent of the investment, which corresponds to a 25-year repayment plan at eight per cent interest.

The pattern of running expenses (extra cost of gas-oil and repayment of building work) would work out as follows, (with, of course, a one-year timelag). (see page 78).

b) Motor vehicle emissions

For this sector, in the scheme we are considering, no action is foreseen - prior to 1975 - that would involve extra cost for the use of special devices or for any resultant extra petrol consumption.

Between 1975 and 1980 it is expected that measures will be introduced requiring devices of the "clean air package" type to be used. The higher vehicle production costs and prices that this would mean (treated as investment costs) are written-off under this heading over a period equivalent to the average life of a vehicle.

The payments have been worked out on a basis of equal annual instalments equivalent to 14.9 per cent of the investment, representing a 10-year repayment plan at eight per cent interest.

('000 million 1970)

YEAR	1971	1972	1973	1974	1975	1976	1977	1978	1979	1980
Repayments	54	58	65	70	75	82	89	96	104	112
Gas-oil	–	0.94	1.88	2.82	3.76	4.70	4.70	4.70	4.70	4.70
Total	54	58.95	66.88	72.82	79.76	86.70	93.70	100.70	108.70	116.70

Table 3. SCHEME A: INVESTMENT BREAKDOWN

('000 million, 1970)

YEAR	INDUSTRIAL LIQUID EFFLUENTS		INDUSTRIAL AIR POLLUTION		OIL PORTS	TOTAL INDUSTRY	DOMESTIC HEATING	MOTOR VEHICLE EMISSIONS	TOTAL HOUSE-HOLDS	SEWAGE SYSTEM	WATER TREATMENT PLANT	SOLID URBAN WASTES	TOTAL PUBLIC FINANCE	GRAND TOTAL
	OLD PLANT	NEW PLANT	OLD PLANT	NEW PLANT										
1971	-	-	-	-	-	-	10	-	10	-	-	-	-	10
1972	-	-	20	31	2	53	10	-	10	20	5	10	35	98
1973	72	48	40	34	2	196	10	-	10	40	10	10	60	266
1974	145	50	40	36	2	273	10	-	10	60	15	10	85	368
1975	145	52	60	40	2	299	10	-	10	80	25	10	115	424
Total '71-'75	362	150	160	141	8	821	50	-	50	200	55	40	295	1,166
1976	145	51	80	37	2	315	-	21	21	100	35	10	145	481
1977	145	52	84	38	2	321	-	22	22	100	35	12	147	490
1978	145	54	84	43	3	339	-	24	24	100	35	12	147	500
1979	216	56	-	46	3	321	-	25	25	100	35	12	147	493
1980	216	58	-	50	3	327	-	27	27	100	35	12	147	501
Total '76-'80	867	271	248	214	13	1,613	-	119	119	500	175	58	733	2,465
Total '71-'80	1,229	421	408	355	21	2,434	50	119	169	700	230	98	1,028	3,631
Outstanding balance	216	-	-	-	-	-	-	-	-	1,000	230	100	-	1,566

79

The amounts involved (with a one-year timelag, of course, in each case) would be as follows:

(Lire '000 million 1970)

YEAR	1971	1972	1973	1974	1975	1976	1977	1978	1979	1980
Repay-ments	–	–	–	–	–	–	3.13	6.40	8.00	12.00

c)   Industrial air pollution

According to information provided by industry the cost of operating and maintaining the various types and systems of dust trapping and gas scrubbing equipment varies considerably from one industry to another and depends on the type of equipment, efficiency required and cost of electric power.   On average it comes to about 23 per cent of annual investment.

Amortization costs have been calculated as equal annual instalments of 14.9 per cent, equivalent to a ten-year repayment plan at eight per cent interest.

Overall, with the phasing of investment allowed for in this scheme, running expenses would break down as shown in the table on page 82 with, of course, a twelve-month timelag.

d)   Liquid industrial effluents

The cost of operating and maintaining industrial waste water treatment plant is very much the same for all industries and has been estimated to average 15 per cent of investment costs.

Amortization has been calculated on the basis of equal annual instalments equivalent to a 20-year repayment plan at eight per cent interest.

Overall, with the phasing of investment allowed in this scheme, running expenses would break down as shown in Table A on page 81 with, of course, a twelve-month timelag.

e)   Domestic sewage

The cost of running and maintaining drainage systems and sewage works for urban waste has been put at two per cent and nine per cent respectively.

Amortization has been allowed for at equal annual instalments of 8.3 per cent of the capital cost for sewage systems (40 years at eight per cent interest).   For the treatment plant itself, the annual instalment is equivalent to ten per cent, i.e. 20 years at eight per cent interest.

The general picture for running expenses in this scheme with, of course, a twelve-month timelag is shown in Table B on page 81.

Industrial air pollution: running expenses

(Lire '000 million, 1970)

YEAR	1974	1971	1972	1973	1975	1976	1977	1978	1980	1980
Item										
Operating and maintenance costs	–	–	11.73	28.75	46.23	69.23	96.14	124.20	153.41	164.00
Amortization	–	–	7.59	18.62	29.95	44.85	62.28	80.46	99.38	106.23
Total	–	–	19.32	47.37	76.18	114.08	158.42	204.66	252.80	207.23

Table A. LIQUID INDUSTRIAL EFFLUENT, RUNNING EXPENSES

(Lire '000 million, 1970)

YEAR	1971	1972	1973	1974	1975	1976	1977	1978	1979	1980
Item										
Operating and maintenance costs	-	-	-	18.00	47.25	76.80	106.20	135.75	165.66	206.40
Repayments	-	-	-	12.00	31.50	51.20	70.80	90.50	110.40	137.60
Total	-	-	-	30.00	78.75	128.00	177.00	226.20	276.06	344.00

Table B. MUNICIPAL SEWAGE - RUNNING EXPENSES

(Lire '000 million, 1970)

YEAR	1971	1972	1973	1974	1975	1976	1977	1978	1979	1980
Item										
Operating and maintenance costs for :										
- sewage system	-	-	0.40	1.20	2.40	4.00	6.00	8.00	10.00	12.00
- treatment plant	-	-	0.45	1.35	2.70	4.95	8.10	11.25	14.40	17.55
Total	-	-	0.85	2.55	5.10	8.95	14.10	19.25	24.44	29.55
Repayments for :										
- sewage system	-	-	1.66	4.98	9.96	16.60	24.90	33.20	41.50	49.80
- treatment plant	-	-	0.50	1.50	3.00	5.50	9.00	12.50	16.00	19.50
Total	-	-	2.16	6.48	12.96	22.10	33.90	45.70	57.50	69.30
TOTAL	-	-	3.11	9.03	18.06	31.05	48.00	64.95	81.94	96.85

f) Solid urban waste

Here, operating costs depend upon the disposal system that is used. Operating and maintenance costs for incineration plant come to about L. 3,000 per year per tonne treated; the equivalent figure for controlled tipping is L. 500. A period of 15 years, at eight per cent, for controlled tipping.

In the scheme we are considering (low-gear phasing of the L. 98 million investment) running expenses would be as follows:

Solid urban waste - running expenses
Lire '000 million, 1970

YEAR	1971	1972	1973	1974	1975	1976	1977	1978	1979	1980
Item										
Operating and maintenance costs	–	–	2.2	4.4	6.6	8.8	11.0	13.8	16.6	19.4
Repayments	–	–	1.2	2.4	3.6	4.8	6.1	7.5	9.1	10.5
Total	–	–	3.4	6.8	10.2	13.6	17.1	21.3	25.7	29.9

g) Seaborne oil transport

The basis on which operating and maintenance costs have been worked out in this case is L. 20-35 per m^3 of treated water, depending on the size of the plant.

The volume of water to be handled in the next few years has been based on the quantities of crude oil handled in the ports concerned. Amortization has been calculated on the basis of annual instalments equal to ten per cent of the investment figure, i.e. 20 years at eight per cent.

The overall picture of running expenses in this case (with a twelve month timelag) is as follows:

(Lire '000 million, 1970)

YEAR	1971	1972	1973	1974	1975	1976	1977	1978	1979	1980
Item										
Operating and maintenance costs	–	–	0.08	0.16	0.24	0.32	0.40	0.48	0.60	0.72
Repayments	–	–	0.20	0.40	0.60	0.80	1.00	1.20	1.50	1.80
Total	–	–	0.28	0.56	0.84	1.12	1.40	1.68	2.10	2.52

Distribution of financial burden among economic agents

Though the direct cost of pollution control falls on industry, households, local authorities and the state, indirectly it is borne by the whole of the community. This latter effect, mainly caused by the extent to which pollution control costs met by industry percolate through to the system of prices, is analysed in section 4.

For this scheme, the distribution of running expenses among the various economic agents is set out in Table 4 under the following headings:
- industry - for liquid effluents, air pollution and seaborne oil transport ;
- households - for heating and motor vehicle emissions*;
- local communities - domestic sewage and solid urban wastes;
- the state - financial support for local communities.

The direct cost to the Treasury arising out of the above arrangements (totalling L. 245 million for the period 1971-1980) covers the capital input and the interest rate relief for loans made to local authorities to enable them to have the necessary pollution control facilities installed.

The cost to be met by the local authorities would total L.237,000 million for the period 1971-1980. The enable them to find the money the drinking water rate and the rates for domestic refuse collection might possibly be increased.

Were the drinking water tariff to be increased [this would be variable over the country and in inverse proportion to the present tariffs (L. 0-30) and average, say L. 10] the extra yield would be about L. 40,000 million. **

3.2. Scheme B: High-gear introduction of pollution control with major financial help from the state

This second pollution control scheme is based on the following principles:
a) Rapid and effective introduction of the relevant regulations ;
b) General financial assistance to industry and local authorities***;

---

* In annual fact, pollution control costs for "household" heating and motor vehicle emissions also have to be met by industry and the local authorities, though to a lesser extent. In these fields, however, the latter economic agents may be considered to behave "as though they were" households.

** Under Bill No. 695 this revenue would go to the Treasury which would then redistribute it to the local authorities as called for by the investment schemes planned by the Ministry for Public Works, which would allow Communes in the south of the country - that already charge high water rates and for which no increase is foreseen.

*** It should be noted that this policy of support for polluting industries departs from the "polluter pays" principle (which is strongly advocated in international circles too, e.g. the OECD, for the express purpose of avoiding distortions and undesirable effects on international trade). In actual fact, although the principle is theoretically desirable (since it would take into account the real cost of resources and their better distribution), many countries already operate a policy of support and encouragement to firms having to install pollution control equipment particularly in the initial phases of pollution control programmes.

Table 4.   DISTRIBUTION OF RUNNING COSTS AMONG ECONOMIC AGENTS

(Lire ' 000 million, 1970)

YEAR	INDUSTRY				HOUSEHOLDS			LOCAL AUTHORITIES			STATE		
	LIQUID EFFLUENTS	AIR POLLUTION	OIL PORTS	TOTAL	DOMESTIC HEATING	MOTOR VEHICLE EMISSIONS	TOTAL	DOMESTIC SEWAGE	SOLID URBAN WASTES	TOTAL	DOMESTIC SEWAGE	SOLID URBAN WASTES	TOTAL
1971	-	-	-	-	54	-	54	-	-	-	-	-	-
1972	-	-	-	-	50	-	59	-	-	-	-	-	-
1973	-	19	0.3	19.3	67	-	67	1.26	2.24	3.50	1.75	1.16	2.91
1974	30	47	0.6	77.6	73	-	73	3.78	4.42	8.20	5.35	2.38	7.73
1975	79	76	0.8	155.8	80	-	80	7.55	6.63	14.18	10.51	3.57	14.08
Total 70-75	109	142	1.7	252.7	333	-	333	12.59	13.29	25.88	17.61	7.11	24.72
1976	128	114	1.1	243.1	87	-	87	13.45	8.84	22.29	17.60	4.76	22.36
1977	177	158	1.4	336.4	94	3	97	20.87	11.28	32.19	27.13	5.82	32.95
1978	226	205	1.7	432.7	101	6	107	28.28	13.84	42.12	36.67	7.46	44.13
1979	276	253	2.1	531.1	109	8	117	35.74	16.70	52.44	46.20	9.00	55.20
1980	344	270	2.5	616.5	117	12	129	43.12	19.73	62.85	55.73	10.17	65.90
Total 75-80	1,151	1,000	8.8	2,159.8	508	29	537	141.46	70.39	211.85	183.33	37.21	220.54
TOTAL 70-80	1,260	1,142	10.5	2,412.5	841	29	870	154.05	83.68	237.73	200.94	44.32	245.26

c)   flows of investment, overall, concentrated over a short period of time.

Out of various schemes considered this one presents the community with the biggest bill, particularly during the period 1971-1975. It therefore constitutes the opposite extreme to scheme A in which investment would be more spread over time.

The financing arrangements and the phasing over time that has been assumed for this scheme are described in the following paragraphs in which consideration is also given to their effects on the economic system and on public finance.

Public financial support

In this scheme, state support for each of the sectors concerned would be as follows:

a)   Domestic heating
      As for scheme A - i.e. no assistance.

b)   Motor vehicle emissions
      As for scheme A - i.e. no assistance.

c)   Industrial air pollution.

If the rate of investment is to be speeded up, i.e. to be made more rapid than envisaged in current regulations, public financial assistance would have to be planned so as to achieve the following objectives:

- to enable the necessary loans to be raised for non-productive investment;
- to lighten the burden on industry and particularly on firms passing through a difficult period;
- to speed up the conversion of existing plant.

The following measures are thereofre proposed:

- guaranteed loans, equivalent on average, to 60 per cent of the investment, and varying according to the industry concerned and the location and size of the firm (e.g. 100 per cent. for firms and slack industries and 50 per cent for large firms in growth sectors) ;
- low-interest loans (four per cent) to firms as an incentive to carry out the necessary conversion work quickly. For this purpose the facilities offered would be scaled as follows :
  100 per cent of the loan would be guaranteed for equipment installed in 1972;
  80 per cent of the loan would be guaranteed for equipment installed in 1973;
  60 per cent of the loan would be guaranteed for equipment installed in 1974;

40 per cent of the loan would be guaranteed for equipment installed in 1975;

20 per cent of the loan would be guaranteed for equipment installed in 1976.

d) Liquid industrial effluents

Considerable state support is envisaged in this case because of the heavy cost of waste water treatment in practically all sectors of production. The facilities provided would fall under the following headings:

- guaranteed loans averaging about 60 per cent of investment, scaled in relation to the industry concerned, and the location and size of the firm ;
- loans at four per cent in order to quicken the pace of conversion. This facility would be on reducing scale over time as in the case of industrial air pollution (from 100 per cent guaranteed in 1972 to 20 per cent guaranteed in 1976) ;
- tax relief in the form of a "deduction for investment" i.e. deduction of part of the investment from taxable income, over and above normal depreciation. *

Firms would be free to avail themselves of these facilities provided that:

- the total amount of the deduction does not exceed 100 per cent of the investment;
- the maximum period during which the deduction is allowed does not exceed 10 years;
- the annual amount of the deduction does not exceed a certain percentage of the investment (20-30 per cent) as laid down by the responsible authorities in the light of the cyclical situation.

Arrangements would be made for each of the above concessionary measures to be varied in relation to the industry concerned, and to size and location of firm.

e) Domestic sewage

As for scheme A, there would be a capital contribution convering 70 per cent of local authorities' expenditure. The remaining 30 per cent could be raised by loans at four per cent from the Cassa Depositi

---

* The purpose of this measure would be to quicken the pace at which pollution control is brought into effect but at the same time, it can be used as an anti-cyclical variable. It would appear reasonable to provide that firms installing pollution control equipment should be entitled to an investment deduction as from the year in which the equipment is brought into service - within the limits of the percentages laid down by the government year by year.

e Prestiti. Again, as in scheme A, the water rate would be increased in order to provide the necessary funds to finance the work of completing the drainage system and the installation of water treatment plant.

f) Solid urban wastes

As in scheme A, the financing pattern would be the same as for domestic sewage, with an increase in the local rates for the collection and disposal of refuse to enable municipalities to raise some part of the finance required themselves.

g) Seaborne oil transport

It is envisaged that public help for the oil refining industries having to install ballast and cleaning water treatment plants in oil ports would be of the same kind and on the same scale as that foreseen for liquid industrial effluents, i.e. guaranteed loans, loan facilities and deductions of certain percentages of investment from taxable income in accordance with the same scales as those set out under (d).

Volume and phasing of investment

In scheme B, the financing plan, implying a considerable state commitment to help industry to implement the pollution control programme, is coupled with a faster timetable.

This would seem reasonable because the rate at which investment would be phased depends upon the type and scale of financial incentives offered. A further advantage with this scheme, is that it provides an indication of the maximum level of expenditure for the community and for the state in a national co-ordinated pollution control programme.

The general pattern of expenditure, broken down by sector concerned and by source of finance (industry, households or government) is shown in Table 5.

Running expenses and their distribution among economic agents

The high-gear phasing of investment in scheme B alters the scale of annual running expenses in comparison with scheme A. Similarly the change in the arrangements for government assistance - which now includes public support for industry, also alter the distribution of the financial burden among the economic agents.

The basis of calculation for running expenses (amortization, and operating and maintenance costs) does not of course change as compared with scheme A. * The resultant running expenses for each year broken

---

* The only exception relates to motor vehicle emissions because, apart from the amortization of the main-air-ox device (included in scheme B), running expenses also cover the increase in petrol consumption (estimated at 7 per cent)implied by the use of this device. Running expenses are therefore relatively heavy, rising from L. 25, 000 million in 1976 to L. 132, 000 million in 1980

Table 5. SCHEME B: INVESTMENT PROGRAMME

Lire ' 000 million, 1970

YEAR	LIQUID INDUSTRIAL EFFLUENTS		INDUSTRIAL AIR POLLUTION		OIL PORTS	TOTAL INDUSTRY	HOUSEHOLD HEATING	MOTOR VEHICLE EMISSIONS	HOUSEHOLD TOTAL	DRAINAGE SYSTEM	WATER TREATMENT PLANT	SOLID URBAN WASTE	TOTAL GOVERNMENT EXPENDITURE	GRAND TOTAL
	OLD PLANT	NEW PLANT	OLD PLANT	NEW PLANT										
1971	-	-	-	-	-	-	10	-	10	-	-	-	-	10
1971	89	46	48	31	5	219	10	-	10	60	15	18	93	322
1973	140	48	80	34	5	307	10	-	10	90	25	18	133	450
1974	250	50	120	36	5	461	10	19	29	100	35	18	153	643
1975	250	52	160	40	6	508	10	20	30	150	45	20	215	753
Total '71-'75 ..	729	196	408	141	21	1,495	50	39	89	400	120	74	594	2,178
1976	250	51	-	37	-	338	-	75	75	200	60	24	284	697
1977	250	52	-	38	-	340	-	80	80	200	60	24	284	704
1978	-	54	-	43	-	97	-	84	84	200	60	24	284	465
1979	-	56	-	46	-	102	-	88	88	200	60	24	284	474
1980	-	58	-	50	-	108	-	93	93	200	60	24	284	485
Total '71-'80 ..	500	271	-	214	-	985	-	420	420	1,000	300	120	1,420	2,825
TOTAL '71-'80	1,229	467	408	355	21	2,480	50	459	509	1,400	420	194	2,014	5,003
Outstanding balance..........	-	-	-	-	-	-	-	-	-	300	40	-	-	-

89

down by economic agent involved and source of pollution are given in Table 6.

3.3. Scheme C: Low-gear introduction of pollution control, moderate financial help from the state

Between the two schemes considered (scheme A with long completion times and no state assistance for polluters in the private sector; scheme B with maximum state aid, a somewhat faster rate of implementation and substantial public support for firms taking steps to control pollution) there are, of course, several intermediate possibilities that might be envisaged by combining and modulating the pattern of government assistance with the phasing of investment.

The intermediate scheme (scheme C) considered here is based on the following criteria:

a) public support for firms through guaranteed loan facilities as for scheme B, but no generalised tax reliefs for firms having to treat liquid effluents;

b) low-gear investment phasing in the private sector and for the building of sewage treatment plant (as in scheme A). This would seem a realistic criterion in the difficult economic situation through which the production system is now passing; the introduction of an accelerated public works programme over the next few years as an anti-cyclical measure would certainly be desirable but seems hardly feasible in the absence of legislative and operational machinery enabling the necessary finance to be raised.

In order that the local authorities may find the necessary resources to cover part of the public expenditure, there would be increases in the refuse collection rate, and the domestic and industrial water rates, on the same basis as for the schemes already described.

Pattern of public finance

The following table summarises the government assistance applicable in scheme C for the various sources of pollution:

DOMESTIC HEATING	MOTOR VEHICLE EMISSION	INDUS-TRIAL AIR POLLU-TION	LIQUID INDUS-TRIAL EFFLU-ENTS	SEA-BORNE OIL TRANS-PORT	DOMESTIC SEWAGE	SOLID URBAN WASTE
No assistance		Guaranteed loans (60 per cent) Loans at 4 per cent interest on percentages decreasing over time			70 per cent grants to local authorities Loans at 4 per cent for the remaining 30 per cent.	

90

Table 6. DISTRIBUTION OF RUNNING COSTS AMONG ECONOMIC AGENTS

Lire '000 million, 1970

YEAR	INDUSTRY							LOCAL AUTHORITIES										STATE*
	LIQUID EFFLUENTS	AIR POLLUTION	OIL PORTS	TOTAL	DOMESTIC HEATING	MOTOR VEHICLE EMISSIONS	TOTAL	DOMESTIC SEWAGE	SOLID URBAN WASTE	TOTAL	DOMESTIC SEWAGE	SOLID URBAN WASTE	TOTAL LOCAL AUTHORITIES	LIQUID INDUSTRIAL EFFLUENTS	INDUSTRIAL AIR POLLUTION	OIL PORTS	TOTAL INDUSTRY	TOTAL STATE
1971	—	—	—	—	54	—	54	—	—	—	—	—	—	—	—	—	—	—
1972	—	—	—	—	59	—	59	—	—	—	—	—	—	—	—	—	—	—
1973	31.55	28.72	0.62	60.89	67	—	67	3.78	5.48	9.26	11.21	0.72	11.93	2.19	1.22	0.08	3.53	15.46
1974	76.08	70.51	1.25	147.84	73	—	73	9.92	8.18	18.10	28.29	4.12	32.41	4.66	2.63	0.15	7.50	39.91
1975	148.15	128.18	7.31	283.64	80	2.8	82.8	17.15	12.21	29.36	47.81	6.29	54.10	7.60	4.08	0.19	11.94	66.04
Total '71-'75	255.78	227.41	9.18	492.37	333	2.8	335.8	30.85	25.87	56.72	87.31	11.13	98.44	14.45	7.93	0.42	22.97	121.41
1976	221.66	202.74	2.71	427.11	87	30.8	117.8	27.43	16.24	43.67	76.53	8.36	84.89	9.58	5.32	0.23	15.19	100.08
1977	295.93	216.65	2.71	515.29	94	68.0	162.0	41.14	20.32	61.46	114.82	10.48	125.30	10.56	5.43	0.23	16.28	141.58
1978	371.43	231.05	2.71	605.19	101	106.9	207.9	54.84	25.41	80.25	153.11	13.09	166.20	10.56	5.43	0.23	16.28	182.48
1979	384.95	247.34	2.71	635.00	109	145.4	254.4	68.57	30.49	99.06	191.39	15.71	207.10	10.55	5.43	0.23	16.28	223.38
1980	398.95	264.88	2.71	666.54	117	186.5	303.5	82.29	35.50	117.79	229.68	18.30	247.98	10.55	5.43	0.23	16.28	264.26
Total '76-'80	1,672.92	1,162.66	13.55	2,849.13	508	537.6	1,045.6	274.27	127.96	402.23	765.53	65.94	831.47	51.80	27.04	1.15	80.31	911.78
Total '71-'80	1,928.70	1,390.07	22.73	3,341.50	841	540.4	1,381.4	305.12	153.83	458.95	852.84	77.07	929.91	66.25	34.97	1.57	103.28	1,033.19

*   The indirect annual cost in tax revenue foregone by allowing investment on treatment plant for liquid effluent and oil tanker cleaning and ballast water to be deductible has not been calculated. It has however been worked out for the period 1971-1980 as a whole.

A variant of this scheme could consist in confining these facilities to firms having to convert old plant; new plant would bear the full burden of pollution control measures. It should perhaps be reiterated that in every case the principle of different treatment according to sector, location and size of firm should be applied. Under this heading would also come tax reliefs for sectors or firms finding themselves in specially difficult cyclical situations.

Nevertheless, for cost calculation purposes in scheme C, it has been assumed that the pattern of public support would be as set out in the previous scheme and that all firms required to institute pollution control equipment would benefit.

Phasing of investment

This would be the same as for scheme A, as shown in Table 3 where total expenditure is broken down by the various economic agents involved (industry, households, government).

Running expenses and their distribution among economic agents

Table 7 shows annual running expenses (based on the same assumptions as for schemes A and B) broken down by economic agent involved.

Public spending and forms of financing

In this third scheme, public expenditure would total L.550,700 million, of which L.237,700 would have to be met directly by the local authorities and L.313,000 million by the central government.*

As in the other schemes a part of the public expenditure would be met by increasing the refuse collection rate, and the domestic and industrial water rates (not including that for water used, in electricity generation).

The yield from these increases, which would total about L.100,000 a year, would go into a national fund set up by the government with a credit institution.

4. Economic effects of government measures

The introduction of an overall plan to control the main sources of pollution could have serious effects on the national economy and in particular on the system of industrial costs and prices, the levels and pattern of final demand and foreign trade, income and employment in the various production sectors and, more generally, on the whole

---

*   For the period 1971-1980.

Table 7. DISTRIBUTION OF RUNNING EXPENSES AMONG ECONOMIC AGENTS

(Lire '000 million, 1970)

YEAR	INDUSTRY				HOUSEHOLDS			LOCAL AUTHORITIES			STATE							
	LIQUID EFFLUENTS	AIR POLLUTION	OIL PORTS	TOTAL	DOMESTIC HEATING	MOTOR VEHICLE EMISSIONS	TOTAL	DOMESTIC SEWAGE	SOLID URBAN WASTE	TOTAL	DOMESTIC SEWAGE	SOLID URBAN WASTE	TOTAL	INDUSTRIAL LIQUID EFFLUENTS	INDUSTRIAL AIR POLLUTION	OIL PORTS	TOTAL INDUSTRY	GRAND TOTAL
1971	-	-	-	-	54	-	54	-	-	-	-	-	-	-	-	-	-	-
1972	-	-	-	-	59	-	59	-	-	-	-	-	-	-	-	-	-	-
1973	-	18.21	0.068	18.278	67	-	67	1.26	2.24	3.50	1.75	1.16	2.91	-	0.79	0,032	0,822	3,732
1974	28.04	45.30	0.542	73.882	73	-	73	3.78	4.42	8.20	5.25	2.48	7.73	1.96	1.70	0,058	3,718	11,448
1975	74.50	73.59	0.722	148.812	80	-	80	7.55	6.63	14.18	10.51	3.57	14.08	4.50	2.41	0,078	6,988	21,068
Total '71-'75	102.54	137.10	1.332	240.972	333	-	333	12.59	13.29	25.88	17.51	7.21	24.72	6.46	4.90	0,168	11,528	36,248
1976	121.57	110.97	1.009	232.549	87	-	87	13.45	8.84	22.29	17.60	4.76	22.36	6.43	3.03	0,091	9,551	31,911
1977	169.28	154.60	1.303	325.183	94	3	97	20.87	11.28	32.15	27.13	5.82	32.95	7.72	3.40	0,097	11,217	44,167
1978	217.65	201.60	1.603	420.853	101	6	107	28.28	13.84	42.12	36.67	7.46	44.13	8.35	3.40	0,097	11,847	55,977
1979	267.65	249.60	2.003	519.253	109	8	117	35.74	16.70	52.44	46.20	9.00	55.20	8.35	3.40	0,097	11,847	67,047
1980	335.65	266.60	2.403	604.653	117	12	129	43.12	19.73	62.85	55.73	10.17	65.90	8.35	3.40	0,097	11,847	77,747
Total '76-'80	1,111.80	983.27	8.321	2,103.491	508	29	537	141.46	70.39	211.85	183.33	37.21	220.54	39.20	16.63	0,479	56,309	276,849
TOTAL 71-80	1,214.34	1,120.47	9.653	2,344.463	841	29	870	154.05	83.68	237.73	200.84	44.42	245.26	45.66	21.53	0,647	67,837	313,097

process of resource formation and utilisation. An analysis of the typology of the various kinds of effects and the problems they raise is attached. *

In order to quantify these phenomena and to make it possible to assess the economic implications of the various options that have been examined above, an econometric model was constructed, the results of which are set out in later paragraphs.

4.1.   Methodological aspects

The model that was used, based on systems-analysis principles, breaks down logically into the following three phases:

a)   Analysis of the effects of pollution control regulations on production costs and selling prices in the industries affected, and of the subsequent indirect effects on the whole of the national system of industrial costs and prices.

The increase in production costs in polluting industries is based on a costing system covering amortization and the cost of operating and maintaining pollution-control equipment in use in 1975, after deducting tax reliefs and loan facilities described in schemes A, B and C above.

The direct influence on selling prices of the increase in production costs in these sectors was measured by means of a system of parameters based on statistics using regression analysis and specially prepared chronological series of industrial process and costs.

The calculation of these coefficients (in terms of the elasticity of the total cost variable, i.e. less profit, amortization and overheads) follows the "mark-up" logic in a largely oligopolistic market and is designed to define the trend in gross proportional margin as a function of the variation of one of the cost components.

The sum of the secondary effects of the increases in price in those sectors directly affected by pollution control regulations on national industrial cost and price levels and structures was measured by means of a system of parameters combining price/cost elasticity coefficients with the technical coefficients taken from the matrix of sectoral inter-dependence in 1975, drawn up in order to quantify the second Italian 5-year plan.

b)   Analysis of changes in sectoral level and structure of the various components of final demand attributable to:

- changes in price, whose effect may be seen in terms of increases in the cost of living and changes in relative prices;

---

* See A. G. Fazio and M. Lo Cascio: "Evaluation of the Economic Effects of Anti-Pollution Public Policy: Proposal for an Econometric Analysis Model" in Problems of Environmental Economics, OECD, Paris, 1972.

- any increases that may be made in the tax burden to meet pollution control expenditure borne directly by the state and other public bodies;
- the emergence of public and private demand for capital goods required for pollution control and the consequent effect of the multiplier on income.

The falling households' real purchasing power as a result of the increase in price levels and possibly the heavier tax burden, was considered solely in relation to the overall level of consumer expenditure and not in relation to the various sectoral components. This estimation was made in terms of the marginal propensity to consume (statistically easier to establish) by using chronological series of private consumption and national income expressed at constant prices.

Changes in the pattern of consumption due to changes in prices, in the various schemes, were defined with the help of functional relationships between the sectoral shares of consumption and the corresponding prices. The parameters for these equations were estimated on the basis of regression analysis using historical series for consumption and prices by production sector specially prepared for this purpose.

The additional demand in respect of pollution control equipment was based on the investment phasing criteria that have been referred to. In the process, an attempt was made to identify the industries to which this demand would be likely to go in relation to each form of pollution (liquid effluents, air pollution, refuse, etc.).

The effects on income arising out of this expansion in final demand for capital goods were estimated by inverting the 1975 matrix of technical coefficients. This technique was used for measuring the first-round effect of the multiplier on the home market.

c) Analysis of the effects on international trade and on the process of resource formation and utilisation.

The effects of the increase in prices in the various sectors of production on the scale and pattern of imports and exports (it could happen that national firms might become less competitive on domestic and foreign markets) were analysed in the same terms as similar approaches used for quantitative assessment:

- for imports, by identifying the functional relationships between sectoral levels of imports and those between prices obtained on the home market by Italian firms and those obtained by foreign firms;
- for exports, by identifying existing functional relationships and those between prices obtained by Italian firms on international markets and those obtained by competing countries. *

---

* World demand was also introduced as an explanatory variable since this synthesises other causes for changes in exports and provides an estimate in which changes in the terms of trade are allowed for.

In order to measure the levels of production, added value and sectoral employment resulting from the changes in the system of prices and the new values assumed by the various sectoral components of final demand brought about by the introduction of pollution control measures, use was made of a widely employed methodology, namely Leontieff's "open model" for analysing sectoral interdependence. With such a model it is possible to define the sectoral levels of production, added value, and therefore employment, corresponding to predetermined levels of final sectoral demand, given a certain production technology expressed by means of a system of technical coefficients.

By changing the coefficients of the 1975 matrix to allow for price changes in the various sectors of production, and by solving the model in terms of the new components of final demand, it was possible to obtain the vectors of production, added value and employment for the second Italian five-year plan.

In relation to these components, therefore, the solutions of the proposed model brought to light the net effects on the process of national resource formation attributable to the introduction of pollution control measures in accordance with the various institutional arrangements envisaged. The net effects on the utilisation of resources, on the other hand, were derived from a similar approach relating to the sectoral components of final demand.

4.2. Effects on production costs and selling prices in the various sectors of production

In all three pollution control schemes discussed (cf. section 3 above) the firms concerned would have increased production costs because of the cost of operating the pollution control equipment. In addition there would be the increase in the domestic and industrial water rates.

It may be helpful, for a better understanding of what follows, to sum up the main aspects of the three schemes that are being considered.

In scheme A there would be a low-gear process of conversion for production plants in existence when the regulations entered into force. Even allowing for the fact that all new production units would have to be equipped with pollution-control systems, investment for the treatment of industrial effluents and waste would amount to only a small total in the early years. Running expenses are wholly borne by the firms themselves and include the annual amortization of the invested capital (at eight per cent) plus the cost of operating and maintaining the equipment.

In scheme B, existing plant would be adapted to comply with the regulations at a more rapid rate. The annual investment figures and running expenses for pollution control equipment would therefore be higher in the early years than for scheme A.

Firms would, however, be partly relieved of the burden beacause some of the amortization cost is borne by the Government (in the form of loans at 4 per cent instead of 8 per cent for certain percentages of the investment varying with the year in which the equipment is bought) and because of the proposed tax relief resulting from the deduction from the annual tax base of certain percentages of the capital invested in pollution control equipment.

Scheme C provides for the same investment phasing as Scheme A, and the same loan facilities for firms as in scheme B. There would, however, be no tax relief.

As already pointed out, the water rate (industrial or domestic) would go up in all three schemes; this would produce an increase in revenue of about L. 80 000 million.

Increases in production costs attributable directly to pollution control measures in the three schemes, and in relation to the various sectors of production,* are shown in Table 8(a).

The hardest hit sectors in all three schemes are the following:

a) paper industry, badly hit both by the high cost of operating the pollution control equipment and by the increase in the industrial water rate (the increases ranges from 21 to 33 per cent over the three schemes);

b) chemical and related industries (16 - 23 per cent);

c) power generation and distribution (around 15 per cent);

d) conversion of non-metallic ores (11 - 20 per cent);

e) oil and coal products (9 - 15 per cent);

f) metal industries (9 - 15 per cent);

g) rubber industries (7 - 13 per cent).

Overall increases in industrial production costs in 1975 are relatively slight.

Comparing the results obtained for the three schemes it can be seen that the increase in running expenses is highest in scheme B, for all sectors of production, because of the faster rate at which firms would have to convert to comply with the pollution control standards set by the regulations - in spite of the tax reliefs and loan facilities. The increase is not so large in scheme A (low-gear conversion) and smaller still in scheme C (low-gear conversion and loan facilities).

The industries that suffer most if the process of investment in pollution control equipment is speeded up are: conversion of non-metallic ores (11 per cent increase in cost for scheme C but 20 per cent in scheme B), the rubber industries (7 versus 13 per cent), oil and coal products (9 versus 15 per cent), chemical and related industries (16 versus 23 per cent), and paper and board (21 versus 33 per cent).

---

* The burden borne by each of the sectors of production was established in the light of the various control techniques used and therefore of the different investment and operating costs in the various industries for the three different referred to (cf. 2).

Industries that are particularly helped by the grant of loans on favourable terms may be identified by comparing the results obtained for scheme C and those obtained for scheme A. They are the paper and board industry (25 per cent increase in costs in scheme A but only 21 per cent in scheme A), rubber (10 versus 7 per cent), and to a lesser extent, the chemical and related industries (18 versus 16 per cent), and the metal industries (10 versus 9 per cent).

Effects on prices directly attributable to the cost of operating the pollution control equipment in use in 1975 can be calculated by multiplying the direct effects on costs by the sectoral coefficients of price/cost elasticity [given in Table 8(b)]. The total effect on production costs given in the second column of Table 8(c) includes not only the increases that are directly attributable to pollution control costs but the indirect increases, i.e. those attributable to the percolation of the initial increase in the price of intermediates through the system of industrial costs and prices because of the economic interdependence of the various sectors of production.

The industries suffering the highest increases in production costs through these indirect effects are as follows:

a)   oil and coal products (total effects, in the three schemes, ranging from 18 to 29 per cent;) direct effect ranging from about 9 to 15 per cent; and therefore indirect effect on costs ranging from about 9 to 14 per cent;

b)   power generation and distribution - indirect effect on costs estimated at about 10 to 16 per cent;

c)   rubber industries - about 4 to 6 per cent;

d)   conversion of non-metallic ores - about 4 to 5 per cent;

e)   textiles - about 3 to 5 per cent;

f)   chemical and related industries - about 3 to 5 per cent;

g)   clothing and soft furnishings - about 3 to 4 per cent;

h)   construction, about 3 to 5 per cent.

Industries suffering most in terms of total effect on selling prices* are as follows:

a)   oil and coal products, where selling prices would go up by about 18 to 30 per cent for the three schemes;

b)   engineering and related industries (about 19 to 28 per cent);

c)   conversion of non-metallic ores (about 9 to 16 per cent);

d)   food and beverages (about 4 to 7 per cent);

f)   textiles (4 to 7 per cent).

A comparison between increases in cost and increases in selling prices suggests that those sectors where average profit margins would shrink to the greatest extent because of pollution control measures are:

_____

*   See Table 8(d).

a) the metal industries - selling prices up by 5 to 8 per cent compared with an increase in production costs of from 11 to 19 per cent, in the three schemes;

b) the rubber industries - selling prices up by 4 to 7 per cent, production costs up by 11 to 19 per cent;

c) conversion of non-metallic ores - an increase in selling price of 10 to 17 per cent compared with an increase in production costs of 15 to 26 per cent.

In view of the fact that the financial burden of pollution control varies from industry to industry it would be right for the relevant regulations to make sufficient allowance for the specific situation of each industry both as regards its influence on the general system of prices and the cyclical and structural situation of the market it serves.

The effect on the system of industrial costs and prices, as estimated for 1975, are limited in scale, the reason being that in that year only 30 per cent of existing production units would, according to the assumptions on which the schemes are based, be converted to comply with the pollution control regulations.

4.3. Effects on levels and sectoral structure of final demand

All the results obtained by using the model show only slight changes in the levels and pattern of final demand for all three schemes, the main reason being the limited extent to which prices in most sectors of production would appear to be affected by the relevant regulations.

The most important changes would relate to the expansion of demand for pollution control capital goods, particularly in the construction and chemical engineering industries. The scale of this additional demand varies with the rate at which conversion to comply with the regulations would proceed in the various schemes.

For scheme B it is evaluated at about L. 780,000 million and for schemes A and C at about L. 440,000 million. As regards capital goods demand in other sectors, no major changes have been made in this first solution of the model, compared with the I.S.P.E. forecasts, which were simply adjusted to allow for the increase in prices.

As will be seen, this assumes that other components of final demand do not change in such a way as to require firms to alter their forecasts regarding their stock of capital equipment.

In addition, effects on international trade and therefore on the balance of payments, should not seriously influence the degree of liquidity of the system in all three schemes, nor require the monetary authorities to provide special loan facilities (in addition to those already envisaged for financing pollution control equipment). Similarly, the financial requirements for pollution-control investment (in both the public and private sectors) should not have any major effect on the degree of monetary liquidity and on interest rates.

The values assumed by the investment vector in schemes A, B and C, established on the above basis, are shown in Table 9 (a).

The demand for consumer goods is dealt with under two headings; public sector consumption and private sector consumption.

It was assumed that public consumption would not alter subsequent to the introduction of pollution control regulations.

This would appear to be the only feasible assumption, because:

a) the annual cost to the State and other public bodies is not, even in schemes B, on such a scale as to call for any major changes to the various items in the state budget;

b) the largest part of the amount entered in the national accounts under the heading of public consumption (as in "input-output" accounting systems and therefore in the I.S.P.E. forecasts), relates to services provided by the Government, whose monetary value is expressed on the basis of the expenditure met by the state, about 90 per cent of which is made up of wages and salaries which ought to remain as they are given an increase in consumer prices ranging, on average, from 0.3 to 0.6 per cent ;

c) lastly, because any change in the level and pattern of public spending, and in particular that under the heading of "public consumption", that were to follow the introduction of the regulations would simply not be foreseeable.

As regards private consumption, four separate possible answers have been calculated for each of the schemes discussed in order to provide a range of solutions that would cover a variety of situations that cannot be forecast with any precision four years in advance and thus provide a framework within which the situation that does eventually materialise may be expected to be found.

It is important that the terms of the problem of evaluating the effect of pollution control measures on private consumption should be clearly understood. This evaluation is decisive because on it hinges the calculation of the changes in the process of resource formation and utilization.

If there is any increase in selling prices in the various sectors of production there will be a decrease in the real purchasing power of households - on the assumption that earnings per physical unit of product remain unchanged. The decrease in purchasing power could be greater if taxes were increased in order to cover part or all of state of local authority spending on pollution control. The effect of this would be to reduce, in real terms, the total level of consumption; in monetary terms this amount would have to be revalued to the extent of the increase in selling prices in the various sectors of production. Allowance, however, would have to be made for the effect on earnings of expansion generated by the additional demand for pollution control capital goods - estimated, as already stated, at between L.450 and

800 million.   If this demand resulted in increased production – in the construction and mechanical engineering industries and in all sectors in general – without bottlenecks (by making greater use of existing capacities) there should be an increase in real income available to households as a result of the investment multiplier. *

There is no way of establishing, in advance, the scale or limits of a situation which by its very nature depends on cyclical factors. It is, however, reasonable to conclude that, should that situation materialise, the aggregate of consumption would not suffer any major weakening in real terms.   In monetary terms, however, it would need to be revalued in accordance with the changes in the prices of its various sectoral components. **

In this case too, the effects may of course vary in relation to the extent of the financial coverage of pollution control costs assumed by the state and other public bodies.

It is for all these reasons that a range of possible solutions has been calculated for the consumption sector, instead of one single solution, in relation to the financing arrangements proposed for each of schemes A, B and C.   This range covers four types of possible situation:

a)   presence of real effects of the multiplier on income, no increase in taxation;

b)   presence of real effects of the multiplier on income plus heavier taxation on the household sector to meet the cost to the State and local authorities of pollution control expenditure in the various schemes A, B and C, after deducting the yield from the industrial water rate;

c)   no effects on income and heavier taxation on households, as under b);

d)   no real effects on income and no heavier taxation on households.

Tables 9 (b), 9 (c), 9 (d), and 9 (e) show the values assumed by the consumption vector for the four above alternatives in relation to the three schemes.

---

*   As already pointed out, these effects have been calculated for the first-round effect of the multiplier, using the inverted 1975 matrix of technical coefficients.   The monetary values of these effects on income lies between L.500 and 800 million, depending on the rate at which conversion to comply with the standards proceeds.

**   In this connection it may be noted that, as against the positive effects of the multiplier on real income as a result of the additional capital goods demand, there would be the negative "multiplier" effects of the fall in demand for export goods and in the demand for national production goods as a result of their replacement by imports because of the change in the terms of trade with other countries.   These negative effects, however, could well in certain circumstances be far less marked than the positive effects.   The problem will, in any case, be considered again at a later stage.

In calculating the vectors, account was taken of changes in price not only in regard to the monetary revaluation of the components and the reduction of real consumer purchasing power, but also, as noted, with regard to relative prices, so as to allow for the effect of substitution between the various categories of products included in the aggregate under consideration.*

It would seem unnecessary to make a point-by-point analysis of the results given in the tables since this would be tantamount to a comprehensive study of the changes in the process of resource formation and utilisation in the various sectors of production in relation to the various cyclical possibilities that might be forecast for the reference year and the various alternatives as regards the financing and phasing of pollution control measures.

4.4.   Effects on international trade and on the process of resource formation and utilisation

On the basis of variations in the terms of trade as between national and foreign products caused by the increases in price introduced by the various industries in Italy, an estimate was made of the differential effects on the I.S.P.E. total and sectoral forecasts for imports in 1975. The assumption was made that prices in countries competing with Italy on the home market would not be subject to similar changes in trend values.

The Table 10 (a) shows levels of imports by sector for 1975 for schemes A, B and C and the resultant changes in each case in relation to the I.S.P.E. values.

In general the biggest increases occur with scheme B (overall average increase: 1.5 per cent). The increases with schemes A and C are smaller (0.8 per cent and 0.7 per cent respectively).

The situation varies with sector of production. The industries which appear to be most affected are:

- rubber (varying from 4.97 per cent for scheme B to 3.25 per cent for scheme C);
- oil and coal products (4.69 to 3.49 per cent);
- chemicals (2.62 to 1.87 per cent);
- metal industries (1.42 to 0.93 per cent);
- textiles (1.23 to 0.82 per cent).

---

*   The results obtained for each of the three schemes do not suggest that changes in price will have any major effect on the product structure of aggregate consumption. Nevertheless some changes of some importance in absolute terms are found in the chemicals and oil and coal products sectors (increases of about L.20,000 and 10,000 million respectively), and in agriculture, food, and clothing and apparel (increases of about L. 35,000, 10,000 and 5,000 million, respectively).

The process of substitution between Italian and imported goods and services would operate on only a very minor scale in the other sectors.

Estimates were also made of the extent to which Italian exports (overall and sectoral figures) would suffer in 1975 as a result of changes in the terms of trade with foreign countries in relation to the relevant I.S.P.E. forecasts.

This fall in exports, however, would be accompanied by an increase in their value (in monetary terms) because of the higher prices demanded by the various national industries. The relevant results are shown in Table 10 (b).

In purely monetary terms, the changes would appear to be slight as can be seen from Table 10 (b). In quantity, however, total exports would fall by 4.5 per cent in the case of scheme A, by 7.92 per cent in scheme B, and by 4.96 per cent in scheme C.

The industries where the contraction is most significant are:

- chemical and related industries (scheme B: 2.7 per cent; scheme C: 1.9 per cent);
- conversion of non-metallic ores (varying from 2 per cent to 1.3 per cent);
- metal industries (from 3 to 1.4 per cent);
- textile industries (from 0.5 to 0.7 per cent).

One significant fact emerging from the analysis of the effects of pollution control measures on foreign trade is a distinct worsening of our trade balance.

Estimates for the three schemes show the following net movement in the balance of payments current account (for Italy):

- scheme A: 180
- scheme B: 229   (Lire '000 million at 1970 prices, adjusted to allow for the increase in export prices).
- scheme C: 160

The effect of the pollution control measures on the various components of final demand, foreign trade and the system of industrial costs and prices, brings about a change in the process of national resource formation and utilisation.

As has already been noted, it is not possible to quantify this phenomenon in isolation from the cyclical and structural situation of the Italian economy and the way in which the financial burden borne by the state and other public bodies is met.

In this case too, four possible alternatives have therefore been identified for each of the three schemes (A, B and C) and relating to extremes in cyclical situations and coverage of the financial burden borne by the state as already described in section 4.3.

The results obtained in terms of gross national product, and shown in Table 10 (c), indicate that, if the economic situation is such that the factors of production are not being fully utilised, particularly in the key industries (construction and mechanical engineering), leaving an unused margin of production capacity, it is better to opt for the faster rate of conversion to the new pollution control standards and at the same time to provide the tax reliefs and loan facilities which, at least partly, would reduce the extra burden on costs and therefore on the competitiveness of Italian industry. Though non-productive, the additional spending on capital goods would help towards the typically Keynesian objective of expansion in monetary demand for anti-cyclical purposes, possibly corrected by measures of encouragement to the production process (first and second eventuality). There would also be a further increase in prices, more marked in scheme B, on top of their spontaneous and non-disquieting increase.

If, on the other hand, there were to be any tightness on the factors of production market and on the system or prices (third and fourth eventuality) during the period under consideration, and if at the same time existing production capacities were being used to a greater extent, it would be better to plan for a slower rate of conversion to comply with the pollution control standards and to provide tax reliefs and loan facilities. The point is that, in real terms, resources for the provision and installation of pollution control equipment would have to be used to the detriment of other components of final demand (because of the lower purchasing power of money and the higher taxation) with adverse effects on the formation of income.

The problem may be summed up in the following terms: whilst there would be an increase in income arising out of the expansion in demand for capital goods (for pollution control) there would also be a decrease because part of the demand for national production equipment would be replaced by imports (and exports might possibly fall).

In scheme B (maximum state assistance) the positive effects on income might be estimated at about L. 800,000 million and the negative effects at L. 200,000 million.*

Insofar as the net effect (the difference between the two) were real, the approach to take could be of the type out-lined in scheme B. But if the net effect were to be purely monetary in nature, this would present problems as regards the propensity of households to consume and therefore as regards the formation of savings and the possible sacrifice of certain other components of public expenditure. The increase in prices arising out of the steeper increase in costs in scheme B would come on top of the existing tight situation with regard to prices and probably inflationary demand.**

Table 10 (d) gives the range of effects in terms of real consumption in the case of the four alternative cyclical eventualities and the three

---

    *   As already pointed out, the calculation has been carried out at sectoral level and taking into account the first round effects of the multiplier only.

    **   This latter type of effect on prices has not been evaluated.

schemes. If real consumption, or rather the real propensity to consume, is regarded as a constraint with regard to the introduction of pollution control measures, there are two conclusions to be drawn:

a) a slow process of conversion is always to be preferred;
b) where there are real income effects (first and second eventuality) it is better to lighten the load borne by firms through loan facilities and/or tax reliefs, and where there are none it is better to make firms bear the whole cost of industrial pollution control.

A more detailed definition of these results is given by reference to the sectoral effects of developments in the process of resource formation.

Tables 10(e) and 10(f) give the percentage changes in gross product of the various sectors of production in 1975, as compared with the I.S.P.E. forecasts for the same year, in the case of scheme A and scheme B and for the first and third cyclical eventuality.*

The sectors suffering significant reductions in gross product, in all cases, are:

- paper and board: reduction in gross product, of 6 to 8 %;
- mining, 3 to 5 per cent;
- power generation and distribution: 3 to 4 per cent;**
- metal industries: 2.8 to 3.5 per cent;
- mechanical engineering, 0.35 (scheme B and third cyclical eventuality) to 3.7 per cent (scheme A, first cyclical eventuality);
- conversion of non-metallic ores: 0.8 to 2 per cent.

Sectors which, because of the increase in the final and intermediate demand affecting them, or because of changes in prices, find their gross product increasing, are:

- printing and publishing: gross product up by 2.8 to 3.6 per cent;
- oil products: +1.4-3.4 per cent;
- rental of housing: +0.5+1.8 per cent.

It may, incidentally, be noted that there is no close correlation between those sectors in which selling prices go up and those where added values take the deepest plunge. In the rubber industry for example, where production costs go up steeply but selling prices increase to a lesser extent, the gross product remains the same. Then there are certain sectors which, although prices do not go up very

---

* The sectoral calculations were confined to the most significant schemes and eventualities in the detailed analysis.

** This decrease is largely due to the contraction in profit margins as a result of expected government control on prices in this sector. At a later stage this could be adjusted in relation to the high level of the direct and indirect increase in production costs.

much, find their gross product falling (e.g. mechanical engineering). It would therefore be important that the measures designed to assist the hardest-hit industries should be varied in accordance with the cyclical or structural nature of the negative effects which the pollution control regulations might have on the various sectors of production.

Table 8a.   INCREASES IN PRODUCTION COSTS* IN THE VARIOUS SECTORS DUE TO DIRECT AND INDIRECT EFFECTS

	SECTOR OF PRODUCTION	SCHEME A		SCHEME B		SCHEME C	
		DIRECT EFFECT IN %*	TOTAL EFFECT IN %*	DIRECT EFFECT IN %*	TOTAL EFFECT IN %*	DIRECT EFFECT IN %*	TOTAL EFFECT IN %*
1.	Animal and crop farming, forestry, trapping	6.187	n.a.	6.187	n.a.	6.187	n.a.
2.	Fishing	-	1.689	-	2.370	-	1.555
3.	Mining	4.159	5.471	5.939	7.777	3.351	4.534
4.	Food and beverages	0.004	n.a.	0.004	n.a.	0.004	n.a.
5.	Tobacco	3.685	6.501	4.858	9.192	3.068	6.032
6.	Textiles	0.025	3.659	0.025	4.887	0.025	3.241
7.	Clothing and apparel, soft furnishings	1.451	4.559	1.941	6.140	1.203	4.036
8.	Leather, hides and footwear	0.026	2.213	0.026	3.007	0.026	2.039
9.	Woodworking industries	10.098	12.353	15.571	18.848	9.461	11.536
10.	Metal industries	0.503	2.851	0.503	3.911	0.503	2.680
11.	Mechanical engineering (not including repair work)	0.584	n.a.	0.672	n.a.	0.467	n.a.
12.	Manufacture of transport vehicles	-	2.013	-	2.827	-	1.860
13.	Car, motorcycle, cycle and sundry mechanical repairs	12.693	16.298	20.391	25.625	11.735	15.048
14.	Conversion of non-metallic ores	18.017	21.378	23.756	28.522	16.692	19.767
15.	Chemical and related industries	10.465	20.061	15.571	29.796	9.533	18.277
16.	Oil and coal products	10.020	14.214	13.420	19.109	7.583	11.417
17.	Rubber	25.461	n.a.	33.967	n.a.	21.813	n.a.
18.	Paper and board	0.032	2.098	0.032	2.838	0.032	1.937
19.	Printing and publishing	0.036	2.845	0.036	3.997	0.036	2.616
20.	Other manufacturing industries	0.192	3.604	0.192	5.337	0.192	3.343
21.	Construction	15.162	n.a.	15.652	n.a.	15.062	n.a.
22.	Power generation and distribution	0.491	n.a.	0.491	n.a.	0.491	n.a.
23.	Gas production and distribution, methane distribution		-		-		-
24.	Water supplies	1.201	4.251	1.201	5.660	1.201	3.971
25.	Distributive and related industries, hotels, shops, etc.	0.161	2.057	0.161	2.963	0.161	1.884
26.	Transport, ancilliary transport and communications activities						
27.	Credit institutions, insurance companies, finance management	0.041	0.445	0.041	0.581	0.041	0.418
28.	Various services	0.142	2.133	0.142	2.978	0.142	1.965
29.	Rental of housing	0.624	3.367	0.624	4.479	0.624	3.178
30.	Government services	-	-	-	-	-	-

* By physical unit.

n.a. : not available at the moment.

107

Table 8b.   SECTORAL PRICE-COST ELASTICITIES

Sector of Production

1.	Animal and crop farming, forestry, trapping	0
2.	Fishing	0
3.	Mining	1.00
4.	Food and beverages	0.90
5.	Tobacco	0
6.	Textiles	0.75
7.	Clothing and apparel, soft furnishings.	0.75
8.	Leather, hides and footwear	1.00
9.	Woodworking industries	0.70
10.	Metal industries	0.45
11.	Mechanical engineering (not including repair work)	0.35
12.	Manufacture of transport vehicles	0
13.	Car, motorcycle, cycle and sundry mechanical repairs	1.00
14.	Conversion of non-metallic ores	0.65
15.	Chemical and related industries	1.00
16.	Oil and coal products	1.00
17.	Rubber	0.35
18.	Paper and board	0
19.	Printing and publishing	1.00
20.	Other manufacturing industries	0.75
21.	Construction	1.00
22.	Power generation and distribution	0
23.	Gas production and distribution, methane distribution	0
24.	Water supplies	0
25.	Distributive and related industries, hotels, shops, etc.	1.00
26.	Transport, ancilliary transport and communications activities	1.00
27.	Credit institutions, insurance companies, finance management	1.00
28.	Various services	1.00
29.	Rental of housing	1.00
30.	Government services	0

Table 8c. INCREASES IN SELLING PRICES IN THE VARIOUS SECTORS DUE TO DIRECT AND INDIRECT EFFECTS IN 1975

SECTOR OF PRODUCTION	SCHEME A		SCHEME B		SCHEME C	
	DIRECT EFFECT IN %*	TOTAL EFFECT IN %*	DIRECT EFFECT IN %*	TOTAL EFFECT IN %*	DIRECT EFFECT IN %*	TOTAL EFFECT IN %*
1. Animal and crop farming, forestry, trapping	–	–	–	–	–	–
2. Fishing	–	–	–	–	–	–
3. Mining	3.743	1.689	5.345	2.370	3.016	1.555
4. Food and beverages	–	4.924	–	6.999	–	4.081
5. Tobacco	–	–	–	–	–	–
6. Textiles	2.764	5.176	3.644	6.894	2.301	4.524
7. Clothing and apparel, soft furnishings	0.019	2.744	0.019	3.665	0.019	2.431
8. Leather, hides and footwear	1.451	4.559	1.941	6.140	1.203	4.036
9. Woodworking industries	0.018	1.549	0.018	2.105	0.018	1.427
10. Metal industries	4.544	5.559	7.001	8.481	4.257	5.191
11. Mechanical engineering (not including repair work)	0.176	0.998	0.176	1.369	0.176	0.938
12. Manufacture of transport vehicles	–	–	–	–	–	–
13. Car, motorcycle, cycle and sundry mechanical repairs	–	2.013	–	2.827	–	1.860
14. Conversion of non-metallic ores	8.250	10.554	13.254	16.656	7.628	9.781
15. Chemical and related industries	18.017	21.378	23.756	28.522	16.692	19.767
16. Oil and coal products	10.465	20.061	15.571	29.796	9.533	18.277
17. Rubber	3.507	4.975	4.697	6.688	2.564	3.996
18. Paper and board	–	–	–	–	–	–
19. Printing and publishing	0.032	2.098	0.032	2.838	0.032	1.997
20. Other manufacturing industries	0.027	2.134	0.027	2.953	0.027	1.962
21. Construction	0.192	3.604	0.192	5.337	0.192	3.343
22. Power generation and distribution	–	–	–	–	–	–
23. Gas production and distribution, methane distribution	–	–	–	–	–	–
24. Water supplies	–	–	–	–	–	–
25. Distributive and related industries, hotels, shops, etc.	–	–	–	–	–	–
26. Transport, ancilliary transport and communications activities	–	–	–	–	–	–
27. Credit institutions, insurance companies, finance management	1.201	4.251	1.201	5.660	1.201	3.971
28. Various services	0.161	2.057	0.161	2.963	0.161	1.884
29. Rental of housing	–	–	–	–	–	–
30. Government services	–	–	–	–	–	–

* By physical unit.

109

Table 8d. PERCENTAGE INCREASES IN SELLING PRICES
IN THE VARIOUS SECTORS OF PRODUCTION BETWEEN
NOW AND 1980 DUE TO TOTAL NET EFFECTS
OF POLLUTION CONTROL MEASURES

SECTOR OF PRODUCTION	SCHEME A	SCHEME B	SCHEME C
1. Animal and crop farming, forestry, trapping	-	-	-
2. Fishing	-	-	-
3. Mining	4.43	3.68	3.46
4. Food and beverages	15.65	14.85	11.20
5. Tobacco	-	-	-
6. Textiles	14.09	13.22	10.40
7. Clothing and apparel, soft furnishings	7.26	6.72	5.47
8. Leather, hides and footwear	12.37	11.57	9.25
9. Woodworking industries	4.00	3.68	3.11
10. Metal industries	13.64	13.12	11.83
11. Mechanical engineering (not including repair work	2.23	2.06	1.88
12. Manufacture of transport vehicles	-	-	-
13. Car, motorcycle, cycle and sundry mechanical repair	4.97	4.41	4.09
14. Conversion of non-metallic ores	29.29	27.61	25.19
15. Chemical and related industries	55.83	52.14	42.41
16. Oil and coal products	50.22	38.94	43.63
17. Rubber	15.02	13.95	10.53
18. Paper and board	-	-	-
19. Printing and publishing	5.32	4.83	4.16
20. Other manufacturing industries	5.46	5.01	4.33
21. Construction	9.22	8.51	7.83
22. Power generation and distribution	-	-	-
23. Gas production and distribution methane distribution	-	-	-
24. Water supplies	-	-	-
25. Distributive and related industries, hotels, shops, etc.	9.48	8.06	8.15
26. Transport, ancilliary transport and communications activities	4.63	3.71	3.98
27. Credit institutions, insurance companies, finance management	0.93	0.81	0.79
28. Various services	7.24	6.63	6.17
29. Rental of housing	-	-	-
30. Government services	-	-	-

Table 9a. LEVELS OF ITALIAN INVESTMENT (AND RELEVANT CHANGES) BY SECTOR OF PRODUCTION

SECTOR OF PRODUCTION	ISPE ESTIMATES (NO POLLUTION CONTROL PROGRAMME) LIRE '000 MILLION. 1970	ESTIMATED FIGURES FOR SCHEME A		ESTIMATED FIGURES FOR SCHEME B		ESTIMATED FIGURES FOR SCHEME C	
		ABSOLUTE VALUE	PERCENTAGE CHANGE	ABSOLUTE VALUE	PERCENTAGE CHANGE	ABSOLUTE VALUE	PERCENTAGE CHANGE
1. Animal and crop farming, forestry, trapping	24	24	–	24	–	24	–
2. Fishing	–	–	–	–	–	–	–
3. Mining	–	–	–	–	–	–	–
4. Food and beverages	–	–	–	–	–	–	–
5. Tobacco	–	–	–	–	–	–	–
6. Textiles	–	–	–	–	–	–	–
7. Clothing and apparel, soft furnishings	12	12	–	12	–	12	–
8. Leather, hides and footwear	12	12	–	12	–	12	–
9. Woodworking industries	375	376	2.67	376	2.67	376	2.67
10. Metal industries	34	41	205.88	44	294.11	40	176.47
11. Mechanical engineering (not including repair work)	4,275	4,093	-42.57	3,736	-126.08	4,093	-42.57
12. Manufacture of transport vehicles	1,422	1,422	–	1,422	–	1,422	–
13. Car, motorcycle, cycle and sundry mechanical repairs	324	324	–	325	3.09	324	–
14. Conversion of non-metallic ores	131	129	-15.27	129	-15.27	130	- 7.63
15. Chemical and related industries	85	79	-70.59	78	-82.35	80	-58.82
16. Oil and coal products	–	–	–	–	–	–	–
17. Rubber	8	8	–	8	–	8	–
18. Paper and board	–	–	–	–	–	–	–
19. Printing and publishing	–	–	–	–	–	–	–
20. Other manufacturing industries	4	4	–	4	–	4	–
21. Construction	10,875	10,757	-10.85	10,933	5.33	10,754	-11.13
22. Power generation and distribution	–	–	–	–	–	–	–
23. Gas production and distribution, methane distribution	–	–	–	–	–	–	–
24. Water supplies	–	–	–	–	–	–	–
25. Distributive and related industries, hotels, shops, etc.	–	–	–	–	–	–	–
26. Transport, ancillary transport and communications activities	–	–	–	–	–	–	–
27. Credit institutions, insurance companies, finance management	–	–	–	–	–	–	–
28. Various services	–	–	–	–	–	–	–
29. Rental of housing	–	–	–	–	–	–	–
30. Government services	–	–	–	–	–	–	–
TOTAL	17,581	17,281	17.06	17,103	-27.19	17,279	-17.18

N.B. The absolute values are given at 1970 prices, revalued to allow for the increase in the three schemes, A, B and C.

Table 9b. LEVELS OF CONSUMPTION, AND RELEVANT CHANGES BY SECTOR OF PRODUCTION - FIRST ALTERNATIVE

SECTOR OF PRODUCTION	ISPE ESTIMATES (NO POLLUTION CONTROL PROGRAMME) LIRE '000 MILLION, 1970	ESTIMATED FIGURES FOR SCHEME A		ESTIMATED FIGURES FOR SCHEME B		ESTIMATED FIGURES FOR SCHEME C	
		ABSOLUTE VALUE	PERCENTAGE CHANGE	ABSOLUTE VALUE	PERCENTAGE CHANGE	ABSOLUTE VALUE	PERCENTAGE CHANGE
1. Animal and crop farming forestry, trapping	7,305	7,337	4.38	7,345	5.48	7,334	3.97
2. Fishing	433	434	2.31	433	–	434	2.31
3. Mining	30	30	–	30	–	30	–
4. Food and beverages	12,410	12,482	5.80	12,506	7.74	12,474	5.16
5. Tobacco	1,168	1,167	– 0.86	1,167	– 0.86	1,168	–
6. Textiles	937	942	5.34	942	5.34	941	4.27
7. Clothing and apparel, soft furnishings	3,199	3,212	4.06	3,214	4.60	3,211	3.75
8. Leather, hides and footwear	957	960	3.13	962	5.22	961	4.18
9. Woodworking industries	770	772	2.60	774	5.19	773	3.90
10. Metal industries	–	–		–		–	
11. Mechanical engineering (not including repair work)	1,149	1,154	4.35	1,156	6.09	1,153	3.48
12. Manufacture of transport vehicles	1,577	1,581	2.54	1,582	3.17	1,581	2.54
13. Car, motorcycle, cycle and sundry mechanical repair	1,012	1,013	0.99	1,013	0.99	1,013	0.99
14. Conversion of non-metallic ores	136	140	29.41	140	19.41	138	14.71
15. Chemical and related industries	1,672	1,693	12.56	1,699	16.15	1,692	11.96
16. Oil and coal products	2,348	2,388	17.04	2,406	24.70	2,385	15.76
17. Rubber	252	253	3.97	254	7.94	253	3.97
18. Paper and board	60	59	-16.67	59	-16.67	59	-16.67
19. Printing and publishing	776	776	–	776	–	777	1.29
20. Other manufacturing industries	287	289	6.97	290	10.45	289	6.97
21. Construction	45	45	–	45	–	45	–
22. Power generation and distribution	771	775	5.19	777	7.78	775	5.19
23. Gas production and distribution, methane distribution	202	202	–	202	–	202	–
24. Water supplies	86	84	-23.26	84	-23.26	84	-23.26
25. Distributive and related industries, hotels, shops, etc.	1,708	1,702	– 3.51	1,704	– 2.34	1,692	– 9.37
26. Transport, ancilliary transport and communications activities	1,697	1,708	6.48	1,710	7.66	1,706	5.30
27. Credit institutions, insurance companies, finance management	806	802	– 4.97	800	– 7.44	803	– 3.72
28. Various services	4,452	4,468	3.59	4,471	4.27	4,467	3.37
29. Rent of housing	4,131	4,150	4.60	4,156	6.05	4,146	3.63
30. Government services by physical unit	9,400	9,400	–	9,400	–	9,400	–
TOTAL	59,776	60,018	4.05	60,097	5.37	59,986	3.51

N. B. The absolute values are given at 1970 prices, revalued to allow for the increase in prices in the three schemes, A, B and C.

Table 9c. LEVELS OF CONSUMPTION AND RELEVANT CHANGES, BY SECTOR OF PRODUCTION - SECOND ALTERNATIVE

SECTOR OF PRODUCTION	ISPE ESTIMATES (NO POLLUTION CONTROL PROGRAMME) LIRE '000 MILLION, 1970	ESTIMATED FIGURES FOR SCHEME A		ESTIMATED FIGURES FOR SCHEME B		ESTIMATED FIGURES FOR SCHEME C	
		ABSOLUTE VALUE	PERCENTAGE CHANGE	ABSOLUTE VALUE	PERCENTAGE CHANGE	ABSOLUTE VALUE	PERCENTAGE CHANGE
1. Animal and crop farming, forestry, trapping	7,305	7,322	2.33	7,305	-	7,313	1.10
2. Fishing	433	433	-	431	- 4.62	433	-
3. Mining	30	30	-	30	-	30	-
4. Food and Beverages	12,410	12,456	3.71	12,438	2.26	12,438	2.26
5. Tobacco	1,168	1,164	- 3.42	1,161	- 5.99	1,165	- 2.57
6. Textiles	937	940	3.20	937	-	938	1.07
7. Clothing and apparel, soft furnishings	3,199	3,206	2.19	3,197	- 0.63	3,202	0.94
8. Leather, hides and footwear	957	958	1.04	957	-	958	1.04
9. Woodworking industries	770	770	-	770	-	771	1.30
10. Metal industries	-	-	1	-	-	-	-
11. Mechanical engineering (not including repair work)	1,149	1,151	1.74	1,150	0.87	1,150	0.87
12. Manufacture of transport vehicles	1,577	1,578	0.63	1,573	- 2.54	1,577	-
13. Car, motorcycle, cycle and sundry mechanical repairs	1,012	1,011	- 0.99	1,007	- 4.94	1,010	- 1.98
14. Conversion of non-metallic ores	136	140	29.41	139	22.06	138	14.71
15. Chemical and related industries	1,672	1,689	10.17	1,690	10.77	1,687	8.97
16. Oil and coal products	2,348	2,383	14.91	2,393	19.17	2,378	12.78
17. Rubber	252	252	-	253	3.97	252	-
18. Paper and board	60	59	-16.67	59	-16.67	59	-16.67
19. Printing and publishing	776	774	- 2.58	772	- 5.15	775	- 1.29
20. Other manufacturing industries	287	288	3.48	288	3.48	288	3.48
21. Construction	45	45	-	45	-	45	-
22. Power generation and distribution	771	773	2.59	773	2.59	773	2.59
23. Gas production and distribution, methane distribution	202	202	-	201	- 4.95	201	- 4.95
24. Water supplies	86	84	-23.26	83	-34.88	84	-23.26
25. Distributive and related industries, hotels, shops, etc.	1,708	1,698	- 5.85	1,695	- 7.61	1,687	-12.30
26. Transport, ancilliary transport and communications activities	1,697	1,704	4.12	1,701	2.36	1,701	2.36
27. Credit institutions, insurance companies, finance management	806	800	- 7.44	796	-12.41	801	- 6.20
28. Various services	4,452	4,458	1.35	4,447	- 1.12	4,454	0.45
29. Rental of housing	4,131	4,141	2.42	4,133	0.48	4,134	0.73
30. Government services.	9,400	9,379	- 2.23	9,349	- 5.43	9,373	- 2.87
TOTAL	59,776	59,888	1.87	59,773	0.05	59,815	0.65

N.B. The absolute values are given at 1970 prices, revalued to allow for the increase in prices in the three schemes A, B and C.

113

Table 9d. LEVELS OF CONSUMPTION, AND RELEVANT CHANGES BY SECTOR OF PRODUCTION - THIRD ALTERNATIVE

SECTOR OF PRODUCTION	ISPE ESTIMATES (NO POLLUTION CONTROL PROGRAMME) LRE '000 MILLION, 1970	ESTIMATED FIGURES FOR SCHEME A		ESTIMATED FIGURES FOR SCHEME B		ESTIMATED FIGURES FOR SCHEME C	
		ABSOLUTE VALUE	PERCENTAGE CHANGE	ABSOLUTE VALUE	PERCENTAGE CHANGE	ABSOLUTE VALUE	PERCENTAGE CHANGE
1. Animal and crop farming forestry, trapping	7,305	7,294	- 1.51	7,268	- 5.07	7,291	- 1.92
2. Fishing	433	431	- 4.62	428	- 11.55	431	- 4.62
3. Mining	30	30	-	30	-	30	-
4. Food and beverages	12,410	12,409	- 0.08	12,375	- 2.82	12,401	- 0.73
5. Tobacco	1,188	1,160	- 6.85	1,155	- 11.13	1,161	- 5.99
6. Textiles	937	936	- 1.07	932	- 5.34	935	- 2.13
7. Clothing and apparel, soft furnishings	3,199	3,193	- 1.88	3,180	- 5.94	3,192	- 2.19
8. Leather, hides and footwear	957	954	- 3.13	952	- 5.22	955	- 2.09
9. Woodworking industries	770	767	- 3.90	766	- 5.19	769	- 1.30
10. Metal industries	1,149	1,147	-	1,144	-	1,146	-
11. Mechanical engineering (not including repair work)	1,577	1,572	- 1.75	1,566	- 4.35	1,572	- 2.61
12. Manufacture of transport vehicles	1,012	1,007	- 3.17	1,002	- 6.98	1,007	- 3.17
13. Car, motorcycle, cycle and sundry mechanical repair	136	139	- 4.94	139	- 9.88	137	- 4.94
14. Conversion of non-metallic ores	1,672	1,683	22.06	1,681	22.06	1,682	7.35
15. Chemical and related industries	2,348	2,374	6.58	2,381	5.38	2,371	5.98
16. Oil and coal products	252	252	11.07	251	14.05	252	9.80
17. Rubber	60	58	-33.33	58	- 3.97	59	-16.67
18. Paper and board	776	772	- 5.15	768	-33.33	772	- 5.15
19. Printing and publishing	287	287	-	287	-10.31	287	-
20. Other manufacturing industries	45	45	-	44	-	45	-
21. Construction	45	45	-	45	-22.22	45	-
22. Power generation and distribution	771	770	- 1.30	768	- 3.85	770	- 1.30
23. Gas production and distribution, methane distribution	202	201	- 4.95	200	- 9.90	201	- 4.95
24. Water supplies	86	83	-34.88	83	-34.88	84	-23.26
25. Distributive and related industries, hotels, shops, etc.	1,708	1,692	- 9.37	1,686	-12.88	1,682	-15.22
26. Transport, ancillary transport and communications activities	1,697	1,698	0.59	1,692	- 2.95	1,696	- 0.59
27. Credit institutions, insurance companies, finance management	806	797	-11.17	792	-17.37	798	- 9.93
28. Various services	4,452	4,442	- 2.25	4,424	- 6.29	4,440	- 2.70
29. Rental of housing	4,131	4,126	- 1.21	4,112	- 4.60	4,121	- 2.42
30. Government services	9,400	9,345	- 5.85	9,301	-10.53	9,345	- 5.85
TOTAL	59,776	59,664	- 1.87	59,465	- 5.20	59,632	- 2.41

N.B. The absolute values are given at 1970 prices, revalued to allow for the increase in prices in the three schemes A, B and C.

114

Table 9e. LEVELS OF CONSUMPTION, AND RELEVANT CHANGES, BY SECTOR OF PRODUCTION – FOURTH ALTERNATIVE

SECTOR OF PRODUCTION	ISPE ESTIMATES (NO POLLUTION CONTROL PROGRAMME) LIRE '000 MILLION, 1970	ESTIMATED FIGURES FOR SCHEME A		ESTIMATED FIGURES FOR SCHEME B		ESTIMATED FIGURES FOR SCHEME C	
		ABSOLUTE VALUE	PERCENTAGE CHANGE	ABSOLUTE VALUE	PERCENTAGE CHANGE	ABSOLUTE VALUE	PERCENTAGE CHANGE
1. Animal and crop farming, forestry, trapping	7,305	7,310	0.68	7,308	0.41	7,312	0.96
2. Fishing	433	432	- 2.31	431	- 4.62	433	-
3. Mining	30	30	-	30	-	30	-
4. Food and Beverages	12,410	12,436	2.10	12,442	2.58	12,436	2.10
5. Tobacco	1,168	1,163	- 4.28	1,161	- 5.99	1,164	- 3.42
6. Textiles	937	938	1.07	937	-	933	1.07
7. Clothing and apparel, soft furnishings	3,199	3,200	0.31	3,198	- 0.31	3,201	0.63
8. Leather, hides and footwear	957	956	- 1.04	957	-	958	1.04
9. Woodworking industries	770	769	- 1.30	770	-	771	1.30
10. Metal industries	-	-	-	-	-	-	-
11. Mechanical engineering (not including repair work)	1,149	1,150	0.87	1,150	0.87	1,150	0.87
12. Manufacture of transport vehicles	1,577	1,575	- 1.27	1,574	- 1.90	1,576	- 0.63
13. Car, motorcycle, cycle and sundry mechanical repairs	1,012	1,009	- 2.96	1,008	- 3.95	1,010	- 1.98
14. Conversion of non-metallic ores	136	139	22.06	139	22.06	138	14.71
15. Chemical and related industries	1,672	1,687	8.97	1,690	10.77	1,687	8.97
16. Oil and coal products	2,348	2,379	13.20	2,394	19.59	2,378	12.78
17. Rubber	252	252	-	253	3.97	252	-
18. Paper and board	60	59	-16.67	59	-16.67	59	-16.67
19. Printing and publishing	776	773	- 3.87	772	- 5.15	775	- 1.29
20. Other manufacturing industries	287	288	3.48	288	3.48	288	3.48
21. Construction	45	45	-	45	-	45	-
22. Power generation and distribution	771	772	1.30	773	2.59	773	2.59
23. Gas production and distribution, methane distribution	202	201	- 4.95	201	- 4.95	201	- 4.95
24. Water supplies	86	84	-23.26	84	-23.26	84	-23.26
25. Distributive and related industries, hotels, shops, etc.	1,708	1,696	- 7.03	1,695	- 7.61	1,687	-12.30
26. Transport, ancilliary transport and communications activities	1,697	1,702	2.95	1,701	2.36	1,701	2.36
27. Credit institutions, insurance companies, finance management	806	799	- 8.68	796	-12.41	800	- 7.44
28. Various services	4,452	4,452	-	4,448	- 0.90	4,453	0.22
29. Rental of housing	4,131	4,135	0.97	4,135	0.97	4,133	0.48
30. Government services	9,400	9,635	- 3.73	9,352	5.11	9,371	- 3.09
TOTAL	59,776	59,796	3.35	59,791	2.51	59,804	4.68

N.B.   The absolute values are given at 1970 prices, revalued to allow for the increase in prices in the three schemes, A, B and C.

Table 10a. LEVELS OF IMPORTS, AND RELEVANT CHANGES, BY SECTOR OF PRODUCTION IN 1975

SECTOR OF PRODUCTION	ISPE ESTIMATES (NO POLLUTION CONTROL PROGRAMME) LIRE '000 MILLION, 1970	ESTIMATED FIGURES FOR SCHEME A		ESTIMATED FIGURES FOR SCHEME B		ESTIMATED FIGURES FOR SCHEME C	
		ABSOLUTE VALUE	PERCENTAGE CHANGE	ABSOLUTE VALUE	PERCENTAGE CHANGE	ABSOLUTE VALUE	PERCENTAGE CHANGE
1. Animal and crop farming, forestry, trapping	3,611	3,611	–	3,611	–	3,611	–
2. Fishing	111	111	–	111	–	111	–
3. Mining	3,268	3,279	3.37	3,281	3.98	3,277	2.75
4. Food and Beverages	1,060	1,069	8.49	1,072	11.32	1,068	7.55
5. Tobacco	215	215	–	215	–	215	–
6. Textiles	487	491	8.21	493	12.32	491	8.21
7. Clothing and apparel, soft furnishings	110	111	9.09	111	9.09	110	–
8. Leather, hides and footwear	116	117	8.62	117	8.62	117	8.62
9. Woodworking industries	356	357	2.81	357	2.81	357	2.81
10. Metal industries	2,039	2,059	9.81	2,068	14.22	2,058	9.32
11. Mechanical engineering (not including repair work)	2,241	2,245	1.78	2,246	2.23	2,245	1.78
12. Manufacture of transport vehicles	1,284	1,284	–	1,284	–	1,284	–
13. Car, motorcycle, cycle and sundry mechanical repairs	–	–	–	–	–	–	–
14. Conversion of non-metallic ores	267	274	26.22	274	26.22	272	18.73
15. Chemical and related industries	1,575	1,633	36.82	1,649	46.98	1,630	34.92
16. Oil and coal products	1,166	1,207	35.17	1,224	49.74	1,204	32.59
17. Rubber	104	105	9.62	105	9.62	105	9.62
18. Paper and board	375	375	–	375	–	375	–
19. Printing and publishing	57	57	–	57	–	57	–
20. Other manufacturing industries	338	339	2.96	340	5.92	339	2.96
21. Construction	–	–	–	–	–	–	–
22. Power generation and distribution	–						
23. Gas production and distribution, methane distribution	–						
24. Water supplies	–						
25. Distributive and related industries, hotels, shops, etc.	486	490	8.23	491	1.03	489	6.17
26. Transport, ancilliary transport and communications activities	656	658	3.05	659	4.57	658	3.05
27. Credit institutions, insurance companies, finance management	654	655	1.53	655	1.53	654	–
28. Various services	377	378	2.65	379	5.31	378	2.65
29. Rental of housing	–						
30. Government services	–						
TOTAL	20,953	21,120	7.97	21,174	10.55	21,105	7.25

N.B. Absolute values at 1970 prices, revalued to allow for the effects of pollution control measures on prices.

116

Table 10b. LEVELS OF EXPORTS, AND RELEVANT CHANGES, BY SECTOR OF PRODUCTION IN 1975

SECTOR OF PRODUCTION	ISPE ESTIMATES (NO POLLUTION CONTROL PROGRAMME) LIRE '000 MILLION, 1970	ESTIMATED FIGURES FOR SCHEME A		ESTIMATED FIGURES FOR SCHEME B		ESTIMATED FIGURES FOR SCHEME C	
		ABSOLUTE VALUE	PERCENTAGE CHANGE	ABSOLUTE VALUE	PERCENTAGE CHANGE	ABSOLUTE VALUE	PERCENTAGE CHANGE
1. Animal and crop farming, forestry, trapping	611	611	-	611	-	611	-
2. Fishing	14	14	-	14	-	14	-
3. Mining	77	77	-	77	-	77	-
4. Food and beverages	410	410	-	410	-	410	-
5. Tobacco	15	15	-	15	-	15	-
6. Textiles	1,551	1,551	-	1,551	-	1,551	-
7. Clothing and apparel, soft furnishings	280	279	- 3.57	279	- 3.57	279	- 3.57
8. Leather, hides and footwear	775	779	5.16	780	6.45	778	3.87
9. Woodworking industries	222	221	- 4.50	222	-	222	-
10. Metal industries	688	688	-	689	1.45	688	-
11. Mechanical engineering (not including repair work)	4,947	4,943	- 0.81	4,946	- 0.20	4,947	-
12. Manufacture of transport vehicles	1,887	1,887	-	1,887	-	1,887	-
13. Car, motocycle, cycle and sundry mechanical repairs	2	2	-	2	-	2	-
14. Conversion of non-metallic ores	461	459	- 4.34	459	- 4.34	460	- 2.17
15. Chemical and related industries	1,604	1,604	-	1,604	-	1,604	-
16. Oil and coal products	783	778	- 6.39	775	-10.22	778	- 6.39
17. Rubber	215	215	-	215	-	215	-
18. Paper and board	475	175	-	175	-	175	-
19. Printing and publishing	130	129	- 7.69	129	- 7.69	130	-
20. Other manufacturing industries	410	409	- 2.44	409	- 2.44	409	- 2.44
21. Construction	6	6	-	6	-	6	-
22. Power generation and distribution	3	3	-	3	-	3	-
23. Gas production and distribution, methane distribution	-	-	-	-	-	-	-
24. Water supplies	2	2	-	2	-	2	-
25. Distributive and related industries, hotels, shops, etc.	439	441	4.56	442	6.83	441	4.56
26. Transport, ancilliary transport and communications activities	1,729	1,732	1.74	1,733	2.31	1,732	1.74
27. Credit institutions, insurance companies, finance management	354	354	-	1,354	-	354	-
28. Various services	243	244	4.12	244	4.12	243	-
29. Rental of housing	-	-	-	-	-	-	-
30. Government services	9	9	-	9	-	9	-
TOTAL	18,042	18,037	- 0.28	18,042	-	18,042	-

N.B.   Absolute values at 1970 prices, revalued to allow for the effects of pollution control measures on prices.

117

Table 10c.   GROSS PRODUCT AT 1975 MARKET PRICES
ON THE BASIS OF THE THREE SCHEMES AND
IN RELATION TO THE VARIOUS
CYCLICAL EVENTUALITIES

	FIRST CYCLICAL EVENTUALITY	SECOND CYCLICAL EVENTUALITY	THIRD CYCLICAL EVENTUALITY	FOURTH CYCLICAL EVENTUALITY
Scheme A ...	75,847	75,718	75,495	75,626
Scheme B ...	76,103	75,780	75,474	75,798
Scheme C ...	75,879	75,709	75,526	75,698

N.B.   The gross product forecast by ISPE for 1975 is Lire 75,653,000 million.

Table 10d.   CONSUMPTION ON THE BASIS
OF THE THREE SCHEMES AND THE VARIOUS
CYCLICAL EVENTUALITIES

	FIRST CYCLICAL EVENTUALITY	SECOND CYCLICAL EVENTUALITY	THIRD CYCLICAL EVENTUALITY	FOURTH CYCLICAL EVENTUALITY
Scheme A ...	59,796	59,667	59,444	59,575
Scheme B ...	59,791	59,468	59,162	59,486
Scheme C ...	59,804	59,634	59,451	59,623

N.B.   The ISPE consumption forecast for 1975 is Lire 59,776 million.

Table 10e.   PERCENTAGE CHANGE IN ADDED VALUE
AT CONSTANT PRICES;
SCHEME A - CYCLICAL EVENTUALITIES 1 AND 3

SECTOR OF PRODUCTION	CYCLICAL EVEN-TUALITY 1	CYCLICAL EVEN-TUALITY 2
1. Animal and crop farming, forestry, trapping	4.93	- 4.49
2. Fishing	4.81	- 9.58
3. Mining	-41.11	-52.54
4. Food and beverages	4.82	- 4.11
5. Tobacco	5.39	- 3.83
6. Textiles	1.18	- 3.16
7. Clothing and apparel, soft furnishings	9.20	0.47
8. Leather, hides and footwear	9.77	1.80
9. Woodworking industries	5.95	- 2.04
10. Metal industries	-28.09	-35.19
11. Mechanical engineering (not including repair work)	-12.35	-37.49
12. Manufacture of transport vehicles	2.49	- 5.04
13. Car, motorcycle, cycle and sundry mechanical repair	8.54	0.20
14. Conversion of non-metallic ores	-12.84	-19.79
15. Chemical and related industries	- 0.66	- 9.08
16. Oil and coal products	23.00	14.40
17. Rubber	3.40	- 9.57
18. Paper and board	-59.30	-67.49
19. Printing and publishing	35.65	27.02
20. Other manufacturing industries	- 2.50	-10.31
21. Construction	- 1.27	- 8.01
22. Power generation and distribution	-32.01	-39.98
23. Gas production and distribution, methane distribution	0.66	- 7.76
24. Water supplies	2.55	-11.24
25. Distributive and related industries, hotels, shops, etc.	4.27	- 4.18
26. Transport, ancilliary transport and communications activities	9.52	1.46
27. Credit institutions, insurance companies, finance management	3.43	- 4.48
28. Various services	10.90	2.21
29. Rental of housing	16.37	7.44
30. Government services	-	-
TOTAL	2.56	- 2.10

Table 10f. PERCENTAGE CHANGE IN ADDED VALUE AT CONSTANT PRICES; SCHEME B - CYCLICAL EVENTUALITIES 1 AND 2

SECTOR OF PRODUCTION	CYCLICAL EVEN-TUALITY 1	CYCLICAL EVEN-TUALITY 2
1. Animal and crop farming, forestry, trapping	3.75	- 5.72
2. Fishing	- 0.96	-10.36
3. Mining	-30.86	-42.38
4. Food and beverages	2.26	- 6.71
5. Tobacco	3.64	- 5.63
6. Textiles	2.35	-10.47
7. Clothing and apparel, soft furnishings	8.22	- 0.56
8. Leather, hides and footwear	10.15	2.13
9. Woodworking industries	10.22	2.14
10. Metal industries	-28.44	-35.59
11. Mechanical engineering (not including repair work)	3.66	- 3.57
12. Manufacture of transport vehicles	- 0.82	- 8.39
13. Car, motorcycle, cycle and sundry mechanical repair	10.81	2.39
14. Conversion of non-metallic ores	- 7.65	-14.70
15. Chemical and related industries	- 0.29	- 8.78
16. Oil and coal products	- 1.53	25.37
17. Rubber	34.13	- 9.53
18. Paper and board	-79.11	-87.18
19. Printing and publishing	36.58	27.89
20. Other manufacturing industries	2.21	- 5.66
21. Construction	12.48	5.58
22. Power generation and distribution	-30.43	-38.46
23. Gas production and distribution, methane distribution	1.53	- 6.97
24. Water supplies	- 3.03	-11.77
25. Distributive and related industries, hotels, shops, etc.	8.68	0.16
26. Transport, ancilliary transport and communications activities	11.18	3.04
27. Credit institutions, insurance companies, finance management	8.65	0.69
28. Various services	12.14	3.38
29. Rental of housing	17.91	5.39
30. Government services	10.35	3.58
TOTAL	5.94	- 2.36

ECONOMIC CONSEQUENCES OF POLLUTION CONTROL*

Foreword

The economic aspects of the pollution problem and of the policy aimed at tackling that problem are at least as important as the technological aspects. Consequently, in May 1971 the then Minister of Economic Affairs requested information from the Central Planning Bureau on the economic consequences of anti-pollution measures.

A Steering Group on Macro-Economic Analysis of Environmental Control (MEAM) was established. ** This Steering Group assists the Central Planning Bureau with the relevant work, and specifically with the collection of the indispensable reference data about the environment and environmental pollution.

Preliminary information on this subject was contained in the Central Planning Bureau's study, which was undertaken as part of the work of the MEAM Steering Group and is entitled "Economic Consequences of Controlling Water Pollution from Biodegradable Organic Substances". This study was published as an appendix to the explanatory memorandum on the 1973 budget of the Ministry of Economic Affairs***. The present study is a continuation and amplification of the first one. Apart from water pollution control, the present study also deals with the control of air pollution and with the disposal of solid waste. It also takes initial steps in the direction of a more detailed breakdown by sector and outlines the long-term consequences of our economic outlook.

The investigation and contents of the present study, including the assumptions made in it, are the responsibility of the Central Planning Bureau. The investigation was supervised by H. den Hartog. The study was undertaken by A. Houweling, H. D. Nagtegaal and T. F. L. de Waal with the assistance of H. S. Tjan and P. H. Gommers.

C. A. van den Beld
Director

---

* This is an abridged version of the complete study, Sections 2, 3, 4 and 5 of Chapter II, providing the basic data and Appendices I, II and III, given the description of the model have been excluded here.

** By order of the Minister of Economic Affairs, dated 13 May 1971.

*** Also published as CPB Monograph No. 16, The Hague, 1972.

I. INTRODUCTION

I. 1.   Definition of the problem

Because of his economic activities of production and consumption, man causes changes in his natural environment. These changes mainly result from
- the demand made on space
- the extraction of raw materials and
- the disposal of polluting substances in the environment. *

This level, pattern and growth rate of economic activities determine the extent to which the environment is affected. If these make a proportionately high demand on space, raw material resources and/or the assimilative capacity of the biosphere, they may be accompanied by severe failure of environmental performance which will also jeopardize the quality of life for future generations. Such changes compel countermeasures to be taken. The present study deals with the economic aspects of such measures.

In the first instance we shall restrict our considerations to measures aimed at controlling the (harmful) discharge of polluting subtances** into the environment, this being the last of the three causes of environmental change mentioned above. This is the first major restriction of the subject. The reasons for it are chiefly practical ones. The topical nature of the pollution problem is mainly determined by the direct threat that human activities constitute for the environment. This threat now seems to come a head in the form of the harmful effects resulting from the discharge of polluting substances. The present level of such discharge, particularly in highly industrialized and densely populated areas, is already imposing such a heavy burden on the environment both locally and regionally that counter-measures are imperative.

Consequently, one of the main objectives in the field of environmental control in the Netherlands is: to ensure the preservation or

---

* In the sense of material waste (solids, liquids and gases) or physical phenomena (sound, heat and radiation).

** This restriction means that the infrastructural facilities which are also being considered from the viewpoint of nature conservation - the East Scheldt river estuary (Oosterschelde), for instance - are not included in the problem. Other areas which are disregarded because of the definition of the subject include the withdrawal of ground water, over-fertilization and the additional costs of preparing drinking water (see also II. 1).

realization of an acceptable quality of the physical environment by
controlling or reducing the level of pollution. * In the light of this,
legislation has been passed relating specifically to the discharge of
waste substances. The Surface Waters Pollution Act, 1969 took effect
on 1st December 1970 and the Air Pollution Act, 1970 on 18 September
1972. The bills for the Chemical Waste Act and Sea-Water Pollution
Act are being discussed by the States General. In the meantime (March
1975) the Bill on Waste Removal has been submitted to the States General.
Acts relating to Noise Nuisance and Soil Conservation are being prepared.

Of the many economic problems raised by the disposal of Polluting
Substances and the relevant counter-measures, only one has been considered: What consequences does controlling the (harmful) disposal of
waste materials have for the economic policy objectives? This is a
second restriction of the subject. As the present study gives a detailed
elaboration of the problem within the Dutch situation, the principal
reason for this restriction is to provide information geared to the immediate requirements of economic and environmental policy-making
and policy implementation. Obviously, this information will make it
easier to choose between the instruments offered by environmental
legislation. This need for information does not of course relate solely
to the direct instruments for pollution abatement, such as emission
standards, product standards or pollution levies. An evaluation must
also be made of the consequences of other policy instruments for the
environment, especially now that ensuring a better quality of the natural
environment has been accepted as a major element of the government's
tasks.

Restricting the subject to the economic consequences of anti-
pollution measures also means - and this point must be emphasized -
that no attention is devoted to questions involving the evaluation of the
failure of environmental performance. Nor to questions of measuring
the standards of prosperity and welfare. ** Similarly, no consideration
has been given to the direct effects of the quality of the environment on
such economic variables as labour productivity, the stock of capital
goods (including houses) and the level of medical and recreational

---

* Another main objective it to promote the adaptability in ecosystems of human
activities. Cf. the Explanatory Memorandum to the 1975 Budget of the Ministry of Public
Health and Environmental Control, Appendix 2, p. 170.

** For the problems involved in evaluation and measurement see: E.F. Denison,
"Welfare Measurement and the GNP", Survey of Current Business, Vol. 51, pp. 1-8;
R. Hueting, "Nieuwe Schaarste en Economische Groei" (New Scarcity and Economic Growth),
Agon Elsevier, Amsterdam/Brussels, 1974; J.B. Opschoor, "Economische Waardering van
Milieuverontreiniging" (Economic Evaluation of Environmental Pollution), Van Gorcum,
Assen/Amsterdam, 1974; H.J. Peskin, "National Accounting and the Environment", Article
No. 50, Central Bureau of Statistics, Oslo, 1972.

facilities.* This is not an attempt to deny the importance of these
particular aspects. On the contrary: the basic premise of this study
is that high priority should be accorded to a concrete approach to
pollution pending the facts that may be brought to light by evaluation,
measurement and the actual effects.

While this may imply a fairly stringent limitation on the scope of
the economic problem being dealt with, the actual elaboration is ultimately restricted by the shortage of statistical data. In particular, it
was not possible to review counter-measures against all types of pollution. This can be interpreted in two senses. Firstly, only the control
of present-day waste disposal and emissions can be included in the
scope of this study. Whether the cumulative effects of pollution on the
environment must also be tackled (known as "restoring" the environment) has been disregarded.** Secondly, the list of waste material
types used in the calculations cannot be regarded as complete.

The last point calls for further explanation. In selecting the set of
anti-pollution measures whose economic impact is to be studied, only
the most widespread effects on the environmental components of water,
air and soil were included. Where it was possible to collect statistical
material, the selection was mainly based on the anti-pollution activities
within the Netherlands*** which, on the basis of the purification costs,
could be regarded as the most important ones.

In view of this selection criterion, which is determined by the
nature of the study (viz. economic consequences of pollution control),
the findings may be assumed to cover most of the environmental control
measures in force at the present time.

As already mentioned above, the subject matter of this study is
restricted to one of the aspects of the impact on the environment viz.
the disposal of waste substances. Other aspects, such as the demand
made on space and the extraction of raw materials, are not discussed.
The "pollution interchange" between various "anti-pollution activities"
dealt with later on in this study is in turn a source of pollution, which

---

* An estimate of the damage caused, for example, by air pollution to health,
materials, crops and houses can be found in: H. M. A. Jansen, G. J. van der Meer, J. B.
Opschoor and J. H. A. Stapel, "Een Raming van de Schade door Luchtverontreiniging in
Nederland, 1970" (An Estimate of the Damage caused by Air Pollution in the Netherlands,
1970), Surveys by the Institute for Environmental Studies of the Free University, Series A,
No. 8, Amsterdam, 1974.

** For a differentiation between current waste disposal levels and the harmful
accumulation of waste material in the environment see: H. Den Hartog, A. Houweling and
H. S. Tjan, "Economische Gevolgen van Anti-Vervuilingsactiviteiten" (Economic Consequences
of Anti-Pollution Activities), in "Milieu en Economie" (ed. P. Nijkamp), Universitaire
Pers Rotterdam, 1974.

*** What is known as "transfrontier pollution" (incl. water pollution caused by
salinization) is not discussed in the present study. In any case, such pollution can, apart
from a few exceptions, only be effectively combated at the source - which means abroad.

means that such activities must be <u>synchronized</u>. This aspect is still within the scope of this study. Despite this, the control of pollution makes demands on space (especially for water purification plants, refuse tips and cooling towers) and on raw materials (energy in particular). Basically, this in turn prejudices the sought-after favourable effect of anti-pollution activities. That is the reason why some attention is also devoted to the demand on space and the energy consumption resulting from measures aimed at controlling waste disposal.

I. 2.   Summary of the contents

The wide-ranging nature of the economic consequences of an environmental policy necessitated the development of a separate model specifically attuned to the environmental problems involved. The structure and functioning of this extensive economic model are discussed in detail in the Central Planning Bureau's Monograph No. 16. * The use of the model in that publication was limited to measures against the pollution of water by biodegradable organic substances. Applying the model method to air pollution and waste disposal called for an increase in the number of interdependent relationships, including the synchronization of individual "anti-pollution activities". Thus, for instance, the available possibilities for disposing of sludge from purification plants may constitute a bottleneck in waste water treatment. If such a processing possibility does exist, for example in the form of "dry incineration" together with household refuse, this may in turn impose a heavier burden on the air as an environmental component. Countering this drawback by means of, say, gas scrubbing will in principle again result in water pollution. Needless to say, the model to which these interdependent factors have now been added is otherwise completely unchanged as far as its structure and functioning are concerned, which means that the above-mentioned publication can be consulted for the <u>characteristics</u> of the model, for the way in which the "anti-pollution activities" (also called the environmental sector) are integrated in the model and for a <u>description of the mechanism.</u>

Despite the severely restricted definition of the subject of this study and the simplification of the problems because of the model-based approach, a large number of basic data are still required to answer the question outlined in the previous section. Most of these basic data relate to the various types of pollution and the relevant control measures. These data will be presented and accounted for in Chapter II.

First of all, Chapter II gives a summary of the state of affairs as regards the <u>effects</u> and <u>extent</u> of the various forms of waste disposal,

---

    * Central Planning Bureau, "Economische Gevolgen van de Bestrijding van Waterverontreiniging met Afbreekbaar Organisch Materiaal" (Economic Consequences of Controlling Water Pollution from Biodegradable Organic Substances), Government Publishing Office, The Hague, 1972.

broken down according to sources (industry and households) in 1973. This summary serves as a basis for the calculations. After illustrating the extent of the environmental problem by contrasting the level of waste disposal in the basic situation with the current level of purification, the chapter goes on to deal with information on the purification measures geared to the remaining level of pollution. A differentiation is made between "anti-pollution activities" covering the following areas:

- water purification in publicly-run biological waste water treatment plants ;
- reduction of water pollution in privately-run waste water treatment plants and by sanitation ;
- reduction of air pollution by the modification of the powered internal combustion engine in motor vehicles ;
- reduction of air pollution by the desulphurization of gas oil and heavy fuel oils ;
- the disposal of non-chemical waste.

On the whole, the criteria used to determine the extent of the purification link up fairly well with the practical policy objectives. They imply an effective approach to the problem, though it should be noted here in passing that the efficiency of the control techniques available at the moment, especially those in the field of air pollution, is not much higher than 70-90%.

For various types of pollution there are as yet no techniques available for achieving a major reduction. In the case of air pollution, for instance, this applies to nitrogen oxides.

The purification measures, the relevant policy instruments and the implementation of "the polluter-pays principle", are described in broad outline in Chapter II, after which more detailed attention is devoted to the key economic data (per unit of pollution eliminated), such as the annual costs, the investments and the labour requirements.

The results of the model calculations are presented in Chapter III. At this juncture it is necessary to give some indication of the terms used. The expressions "clearing up the backlog" or "making up for areas" are used to indicate that purification facilities must in any event be created for the pollution existing in the basic situation. Such pollution is already so extensive that this will require a number of years. The situation that will then arise is that during the "catching-up period" additional pollution will be created as a result of new investments and this pollution will also have to be prevented or reduced. If mention is made of completing "the major cleaning operation" within a "programme period" of, say, 10 years, then this must obviously relate to both the "arrears" and the "dirty growth". Once the "cleaning operation" has been completed it is a question of maintaining the clean situation. "Maintaining order" must, however, also be undertaken during the "cleaning period", since the degree of purification attained in the basic situation will, of course, continue to exist.

The results of the model calculations relate in the first instance to the macro-economic consequences. What is chiefly involved here is the consequences that can be expected for production as a whole. Production in the environmental sector is also counted as part of this. In the event of adverse consequences for production as a whole, the production decrease (or reduced growth rate) in the (traditional) industrial sector will be higher still, because the environmental sector makes a positive contribution equal to its own production level.

The results of the model calculations are presented in the form of a number of variants. These review the effect of the length of time taken to complete the cleaning operation and what can be expected if foreign price trends of relevance to the Netherlands are influenced by a corresponding environmental policy abroad. Not only are the macro-results (production, consumption, employment, etc.) stated for each variant, but also the "sector results". The sectoral breakdown has not, however, been highly elaborated: apart from five environmental sectors, the model distinguishes between the four "big" (traditional) sectors - agriculture, industry, the building trade and services. The model therefore merely provides fairly approximate information which is not geared to specific branches of industry.

A concession is made towards the need for such information by ascertaining the maximum anticipated price increases for 23 separate branches of industry* after completion of the "cleaning programme". The method used to compute this is explained in the General Planning Bureau's "Occasional Paper" 1974 No. 1 and does not differ in its main outlines - by which is meant the interdependence of branches of industry within the assumptions of the traditional input-output system - from the mechanism also used to compute the price increases for four main sectors in the environmental model.

As has already been said, Chapter III concentrates on the "major cleaning operation" which, solely by way of hypothesis, should be completed in 1985. The size of the environmental sector by that time and the consequences of this for pollution, energy consumption and the demand on space are discussed in Chapter IV. The same chapter then goes on to make a very tentative exploration of developments in pollution and in the environmental sector after the "cleaning period" up to the year 2000. This principally involves the question of how the environmental sectors claim on national resources will develop in the light of long-term growth.

---

* Based on the Union Nations "International Standard Industrial Classification of All Economic Activities".

II. BASIC DATA

<u>II. 1. General</u>

As stated in the Introduction, the set of anti-pollution activities whose economic consequences are reviewed cannot be regarded as complete. Firstly, because insufficient statistical material is available and, secondly, because the investigation was concentrated on those purification activities which could be considered as amongst the most important in terms of cost. Both these reasons result in an under-estimation of the economic consequences. This calls for further explanation.

In the first place, the following factors have provisionally been disregarded in collecting the basic data:
- the thermal pollutional load,
- the radiation hazards of radioactive material or waste and
- pollution caused by production of synthetic gas.

Even apart from the question of whether agreement currently exists on the standards to be set or whether adequate anti-pollution technology is already available, it is not expected that there will be any costs of macro-economic significance in these areas <u>within the time-span of the</u> "major cleaning operation". Over the much longer term this will very probably be the case, particularly if a decision is taken to generate nuclear energy on a large scale and if fuel gasification becomes more popular. The fact that the areas mentioned here and later on in this section are disregarded does not mean, however, that there is no present need for urgent environmental measures in these fields.

Secondly, the lack of statistical information meant that in collecting the basic data we were compelled to disregard the following areas:
- air pollution caused by diesel-powered motor vehicles
- air pollution caused by industrial process emissions
- the disposal of chemical waste (e. g. heavy metals, insecticides, etc.)
- noise pollution, and
- air pollution through emission of nitrogen oxides, hydrocarbons and carbon monoxide from combustion furnaces.

Data are available on the amount of pollution caused by diesel engines, but the relevant anti-pollution technology is not yet sufficiently advanced whilst the need to deal with total emissions is in fact not quite as urgent as in the case of petrol engine emissions. As regards process emissions (also including nitrogen oxides and particles) and as regards the almost endless series of suspect (chemical) waste substances, the big problem is, rather, to take stock of the physical data. There is growing understanding of means of tackling noise pollution. The problems involved in this are complex, firstly because of the great diversity of noise sources and, secondly, because of the consequences for town and country planning. The draft "Noise Nuisance Act" has meanwhile been prepared (June 1975). In the case of nitrogen oxides, hydrocarbons and carbon monoxide, data are available on pollution levels but the anti-pollution technology aimed at dealing with pollution from existing sources has not been developed far enough to enable any major reduction in the emission level.

Lastly, the following areas were also disregarded in the model because of their comparatively low expected cost levels, even over the longer term:
- disposal and processing of car wrecks and car tyres
- desulphurisation of diesel oil (gas-oil) for the transport sector
- control of air pollution caused by aerosols (aerosol particles) from combustion furnaces.

As has been said, the incompleteness of the set of anti-pollution activities under review here will result in an underestimation of the economic consequences. This is offset by the fact that in those cases where uncertainty exists as to the level of pollution or the cost of combating it, maximum hypotheses have been used. What is even more important is that no allowance could be made for a future improvement in anti-pollution technology. This tends to give rise to some degree of overestimation against the background of the assumed effective limits and targets.

Before dealing in the next section with those areas of the "cleaning programme" to be reviewed, first some information about the sources of the basic data. Two agencies were responsible for collecting and processing the data which originated from many other, scattered sources. These agencies were the Central Bureau of Statistics and the Central Planning Bureau. The fact-finding activities initiated by the Central Planning Bureau and undertaken in conjunction with the Central Bureau of Statistics as part of the work of the MEAM Steering Group were mainly centred around the specific objectives of analysis and forecasting of the CPB. Most of the data contained in the present chapter are taken from two publications by the Central Bureau of Statistics, * whilst the remainder are derived from reports by the

---

* Central Bureau of Statistics, "Waterverontreiniging met afbreekbaar organisch en eutrofiërend materiaal" (Water Pollution from Biodegradable Organic and eutroficating substances), Government Publishing Office, The Hague, 1972 ; and Central Bureau of Statistics, "Luchtverontreiniging door verbranding van fossiele brandstoffen, 1960-1972" (Air pollution from combustion of fossil fuels, 1960-1972), The Hague, Government Publishing Office, 1975.

the MEAM Steering Group.* These data are in fact still subject
to changes.

* The reports of the MEAM Steering Group have not been published but can be obtained from the Central Planning Bureau. The reports - issued during the 1971-1974 period
- reflect the intermediate position of the fact-finding activities. In a number of cases
more recent data have become available; these have been incorporated in the present
study.

III. THE ECONOMIC CONSEQUENCES

III. 1. Introduction

The abatement of the major proportion - in terms of costs - of the pollution existing in the basic situation (1973) will require an investment of almost Fl. 12,000 million in 1973 prices, whilst this will be accompanied by annual (or current) costs of almost Fl. 2,500 million - likewise in 1973 prices.

Those amounts only apply in the first instance.

Upon completion of the programme, changes will occur in two respects. Firstly, investments and annual costs will result from the synchronization of the various anti-pollution activities to comply with the own pollution of these activities. Secondly, the growth of anti-pollution activities* will affect the traditional activities (as will be reflected, for instance, by a drop in production), and thus will in turn influence the level of pollution and the costs of combating it.

Obviously, these changes can only be determined with the aid of a fairly comprehensive economic model. The structure and functioning of such a model were previously discussed in the Central Planning Bureau's Monograph No. 16. **

This model method has also been applied here to environmental components other than water (i.e. air and soil). However, the model which has now been expanded by adding the necessary equations still has the same structure and functioning, which means that the publication referred to previously should be consulted for a characterization of the model and for a description of the mechanism.

Lastly, a few comments on the contents of the present chapter. Sections III.2. and III.5. deal with the macro-economic consequences. In the first of these two sections, a short discussion of the instruments

---

* The size of the environmental sector is determined partly exogenously and partly endogenously. The environmental protection standards for the quality of the relevant environmental component are exogenous. These standards define, as it were, the relative level of "anti-pollution activities" in relation to the (potential) actual pollution. This pollution may be high or not so high - depending on activities in the remainder of the economy. The absolute level of the "anti-pollution activities" is therefore determined endogenously.

** Central Planning Bureau, "Economic Consequences of Controlling Water Pollution from Biodegradable Organic Substance, Government Publishing Office, The Hague, 1972.

used is followed by a presentation of the findings which reflect the resultant consequences for the existing level of production and consumption in the basic situation (1973), and for other factors. This therefore relates to the consequences of "clearing up the backlog of pollution" with regard to the pollution at the level existing in the basic situation. The latter-mentioned section also deals with the consequences of new activities or of the expansion of existing activities. The creation of anti-pollution facilities for new activities thus results in "clean growth".

Lastly, sections III.3. and III.4. deal respectively with the consequences for big sectors* and for the prices of separate industrial sectors. **

III.2.   Clearing up the backlog of pollution

The environmental problem has currently become acute for the specific reason that the existing environmental facilities are inadequate in many areas. This is one of the reasons why growth measures in traditional terms has become debatable.

As far as the pollution of water with biodegradable organic substances is concerned, this backlog in treatment facilities was pinpointed in the foregoing. Without any increase in purification facilities and sanitation measures, waste water with an estimated oxygen-consuming capacity of approx. 41 million p.e. was discharged*** in 1973. And this makes no allowance for pollution caused by oxygen consuming substances entering via trans-frontier rivers. The discharged pollution is many times higher than the natural self-purification capacity of the available surface water.

It is true that in the case of air pollution caused by sulphur dioxide the emission level has decreased in recent years because of the penetration of natural gas consumption, which has resulted in most places in what may be regarded as acceptable limits. However, the anticipated growth of mineral oil consumption particularly during the programme period combined with the efficiency of purification techniques which on average is currently still on the low side make it necessary for existing emissions also to be reduced (proportionately) by means of more far-reaching elimination measures.

The large quantities of motor vehicles exhaust gases (particularly from those fitted with petrol engines) emitted in areas with a high traffic density have for a number of years been adversely affecting the

---

    *   Agriculture, industry, building industry, services and environmental sector.

    **   Classification of industries (23 industrial sectors) based on the United Nations "International Standard Industrial Classification of all Economic Activities" and 5 anti-pollution sectors.

    ***   See Table 1: 40,110 p.e. plus 839,000 p.e. effluent from purification plants.

environment of the quality of life, especially in cities. In view of the concentrations currently being measured, some components of the exhaust gases have already reached a fairly harmful level. *

Their harmfulness is also indirectly reflected in the substantial contribution they make to the formation of (photochemical) smog. In view of the anticipated growth in the number of motor vehicles on the road, this situation might deteriorate considerably during the programme period.

A large proportion of household refuse, industrial waste and other refuse - estimated at about three-quarters - was tipped on over 550 refuse tips in 1973 in a manner which is unacceptable from a viewpoint of public health and environmental control and also from a viewpoint of its effects on the countryside. To ensure that ultimately a greatly improved situation will be achieved, the most important point is that an effective disposal of waste can only be realized by implementing economies of scale in its collection and treatment. Regional cooperation between municipalities based on provincial plans (possibly with a certain degree of government influence as regards nationally operating waste treatment plant) would seem the most suitable method of achieving this.

Instruments

The above situation as outlined for the environmental components of water, air and soil, together with a further increase in the pollution load as a result of a growth in production and consumption, must be described as absolutely untenable. The model calculations are therefore geared in the first instance to the economic consequences of a policy programme aimed at putting matters in order.

The initiation of such a programme by the government therefore calls for specific tailor-made instruments. These have been or will be provided for in the environmental legislation which is now being developed.

The most important part of this set of policy instruments is formed by the physical regulations and levies. In this context reference should be made to the "Paper on Instruments for the Environmental Control Policy - Levies and Physical Regulations". **

In the case of levies a differentiation can be made between pure redistribution levies, incentive levies and damage related.

In the said Paper an investigation is made of the possibilities of using regulating or inhibiting levies - in contrast to physical regulation -

---

* Because it combines with the haemoglobin, carbon monoxide reduces the oxygen-carrying capacity of the blood. This is reflected, amongst other things, in a reduction of the ability of sensory perception and in an increased risk of heart ailments. Nitrogen oxides are a potential health hazard; lengthy exposure to them is harmful to the lungs in particular.

** Appendix 1 to the Explanatory Memorandum on the 1975 Budget of the Ministry of Public Health and Environmental Hygiene.

as instruments for reducing pollution or polluting activities and for encouraging the use of less-polluting technology. The Paper's conclusion is that "physical regulation will, in the future as well, continue to be the predominant instrument of environmental policy in the majority of cases in view of the nature of many types of pollution and in view of the fact that they are often concentrated locally. On this basis, the greater certainty which is inherent in this instrument will prevail over any advantages that levies may have as regards their effectiveness. This does not preclude the fact that a more comprehensive application of levies may provide a useful supplement to the set of instruments."

The effectiveness of the policy can be backed by encouraging the development of a clean technology and also - especially over the longer term - by influencing and promoting "environment-consciousness.

As regards the set of policy instruments which are being or will be used for controlling the types of pollution distinguished in the present study, the instrument of physical regulation has - in accordance with what was stated above - been considered to be applicable in most cases.

In controlling the pollution of water by degradable organic substances and in the disposal of waste materials, a major role is played by organisational aspects.

Licences for the disposal of waste water or waste are issued by the local authorities which cooperate on a regional or provincial level. However, the licensing policy for the discharge of waste water into the main "national" waters is still the responsibility of the government. The preparation of the Indicative Multi-Year Programme (IMP) - which officially does not in fact have any binding authority - for the implementation of water purification measures proposed throughout the entire country and for the issuing of any "declaration of inadequacy" on the basis of the targets set in the IMP creates the framework within which the effective implementation of proposed measures is made possible.

The pollution of air by sulphur dioxide from the combustion of gas-oil and fuel oil is caused by the wholesale and widespread use of a polluted product (sulphurous oil). In this case the instruments are aimed both at eliminating the pollution prior to combustion (fuel desulphurization "at the source" by oil refineries) by setting "product requirements"* and at purification after combustion (flue gas desulphurization by big consumers) by imposing emission control standards. The possibilities also include indirect instruments aimed at promoting a clean technology - in this case, two-stage combustion.

A phased reduction in air pollution caused by petrol-engine motor vehicles, achieved at the same rate as the vehicle population is renewed

---

* In October 1974 the "Decree on the Sulphur Content of Fuels" became effective in the form of a General Administrative Order. This decree specifies maximum sulphur contents for current consumption. The decree also specifies the subsequent stages in a phased reduction and enables a continuing abatement of sulphur dioxide emissions.

can be realized by setting emission control standards* for exhaust gases of new annual models (new model inspections). ** A suitable means of ensuring that the standards are always met is the periodical inspection. ***

Directives relating to the maximum content of pollutants in exhaust gases are drawn up following consultation with the European Community countries and with the European Commission.

In such consultation priority has hitherto been accorded to the reduction of carbon monoxide and hydrocarbons. It may be assumed that the example of the United States will be followed and that requirements will also be made relating to the emission of nitrogen oxides.

As has been said, physical regulation is the main instrument of environmental policy in the cases outlined above. Where levies are applied, they are usually utilization levies. In the case of the pollution of water by degradable organic substances and the case of the disposal of waste, the levies are used to defray the operating costs of purification plants run by the local authorities. The draft Waste Removal Act also provides for a regulating levy.

To finance the investments to be made by the local authorities, use is normally made of the capital market. A differing arrangement is in force as regards the financing of investments in water purification plants used to ensure clean "national waters". Since the government does not itself undertake the construction and running of water purification plants used to ensure clean national waters, but leaves this to the local authorities and (in the case of a limited number of plants) to enterprises, the revenue from the (utilization) levies on unpurified discharges into national waters (National Levies Fund) can be used almost entirely as a means of financing the construction of water purification plants used to ensure clean national waters.

The existing system of redistribution levies has also been proved in practice to have a clearly inhibitive effect on the pollution level. This even holds true at the present time - when the levies have still not reached their ultimate level (i.e. after the regional purification programme has been executed in full).

Municipalities will still have to invest considerable sums in sewerage systems and pumping stations. To finance such work, use will be made in the first instance of the possibilities offered by the existing arrangements for municipal finances and municipal sewerage taxes.

In the model calculations "the polluter-pays principle" was consistently applied. The water pollution and waste disposal levies described above will not reach their ultimate levels until the various

---

* In addition measures for limiting the lead content of petrol are being considered in the Netherlands.

** Decree relating to new model inspection for motor vehicles (air pollution), State Gazette 1973, 356.

*** A bill relating to the periodical inspection of motor vehicles may possibly come into effect in 1976.

reorganisation programmes have been completed and the levies will then be equal to the costs of running the collective facilities.

The operating costs of privately-run facilities (purification or sanitation) will, of course, be charged directly to the polluters.

The desulphurization of gas-oil, domestic heating oil and fuel oil and of the flue gases from fuel oil will give rise to higher prices for the (potential) polluters, in this instance the consumers of the fuel.

The users of petrol-engine motor vehicles will likewise be confronted with higher prices as a result of the necessary measures for reducing pollution caused by exhaust gases. Converted to an annual basis, these increases will involve the capital costs of the higher retail price of the motor vehicle together with the costs of the (anticipated) higher petrol consumption.

Just as is the case with water pollution control, levies are also imposed to combat air pollution (in this case they are imposed on fossil fuels). These are redistribution levies, though because of their relatively low level they do not have any direct inhibitive effect on the use of "dirty" fuels. The levies are used to defray the costs of implementing the Air Pollution Act* as well as - specifically - the expenditure on measures for preventing or limiting air pollution.

Since there are no publicly run purification facilities, the air pollution levies should not be regarded as user-charges, as is the case with the water pollution and waste disposal levies. For this reason and also because of their low level, the air pollution levies have been disregarded in the model calculations.

Variants

As regards the use of the instruments described above, the following concrete assumptions were made in the model calculations.

The required investments will be financed in the usual way. For the local authorities this will be the capital market, though in the case of water purification it will be supplemented further by payments from the National Levies Fund. Payments from this Fund are only of importance for a few companies;** as regards the remaining industrial investments (in desulphurization plant, cleaner means of transport), it has been assumed that there will be no deviation from the customary financing pattern (capital market, self-financing).

In the case of the current costs the principle of "the polluter pays" has been applied in the sense that the operating costs (including the capital costs) of purification facilities will be borne entirely by the polluters. In the case of polluters in the industrial sector the costs are usually passed on via the price mechanism. This is, however,

---

* Costs of issuing licences, inspecting, measuring, etc.

** Viz. those enterprises with their own water purification facilities for cleaning waste water discharged into national waters.

subject to limits as a results of (international) market relations. In the calculations it has been assumed that all costs will be passed on. In the case of polluters in the other sectors, particularly households, the disposable income is reduced proportionately.

In the model calculations three variants are examined in more detail.

Firstly, a differentiation is made between two alternatives as regards the time-span of the programme period. A study has been made of what consequences will result if matters are put in order in the 1973-1980 and 1973-1985 periods respectively.

Secondly, an examination has been made of what consequences would result if allowance is made for price increases occurring abroad as a result of a corresponding environmental policy. This has been worked out for a period of 12 years, as it is not likely that all countries which compete with or export to the Netherlands will initiate an environmental policy over the shorter term to the same extent as in this country.

The standards set for the quality of the environment are identical in all variants and simply in practical terms the almost complete control of the relevant types of pollution. Only in the case of dephosphatization and disinfection has less widespread application been assumed, in accordance with what was stated in section II.2.2. above.

The pollution still remaining after implementation of all measures will then be determined solely by the purification efficiency of the various control techniques* which are expected to be used.

Results

The macro-results of the variants outlined above are shown in Table 1.

Since the model-based approach was discussed in detail in Monograph No. 16 of the Central Planning Bureau** it should be sufficient here to give a brief explanation of the main assumptions underlying the model equations which have resulted in the economic consequences presented here.

In the first place, the introduction of "anti-pollution activities" creates an additional demand on the scarce production resources. Firstly, because substantial investments will have to be made in new environmental facilities and, secondly, because the operation of these facilities will entail current costs.

---

* This efficiency averages 85-95% for oxidative-biological purification, 70-90% for desulphurization and 65-90% for the "clean" petrol engine working according to the stratified charge principle.

** Central Planning Bureau, "Economic Consequences of Controlling Water Pollution from Biodegradable Organic Substances, Government Publishing Office, The Hague, 1972.

Table 1. Consequences of three variants for a policy programme aimed at controlling the pollution of water by biodegradable organic substances, the disposal of waste materials and the control of air pollution by sulphur dioxide caused by the burning of oil products in stationary combustion sources and from exhaust gases of petrol-engine motor vehicles ("putting matters in order"); macro-results [a]

	DURATION OF PROGRAMME PERIOD		
	7 YEARS	12 YEARS	12 YEARS INCLUDING CORRESPONDING POLICY ABROAD
	CHANGES FOR THE ENTIRE PROGRAMME PERIOD IN %		
Volume of personal consumption	-6.2	-6.4	-5.2
Volume of investments by industry (excluding houses) [b]	-7.1	-4.2	-3.3
Volume of investments in dwelling	-2.7	-1.8	-1.2
Volume of exports of goods	-4.0	-3.5	-2.9
Volume of imports of goods and services [b]	-2.3	-2.4	-1.7
Production volume in enterprises [b]	-5.1	-5.1	-4.2
Production volume in enterprises [c]	-3.6	-3.5	-2.6
Employment level in enterprises [b]	-1.5	-1.4	-1.0
Employment level in enterprises [c]	-1.3	-1.2	-0.8
Wages bill per employee in enterprises	-4.4	-5.0	-2.1
Other income [b]	0.5	0.3	1.4
Price level personal consumption	1.2	1.0	2.4
Price level investments by enterprises	0.8	0.6	2.4
Price level goods exports	2.0	1.7	3.4
	CHANGES FOR THE ENTIRE PROGRAMME PERIOD		
Balance of payments, current account (Fl. mln.)	435	530	295
Unemployment ('000s)	16.5	10.9	7.4
Investment ratio (%) [c]	0.9	0.9	0.9

a) The results are valid provided the investments in the "environmental sector" are spread evenly over the relevant programme period.
b) Excluding the "environmental sector".
c) Including the "environmental sector".

138

There are very limited possibilities of supplying additional resources for the environmental sector or for other countries out of un-
exploited production factors. The scope needed for the environmental
sector will therefore be created almost entirely at the expense of
(further) growth in traditional sectors.

It is assumed in the model equations that the prices and incomes
determination will be the main means of deciding how much of the
scarce resources can be allocated to the environmental sector.

The price effects result from the fact that the current costs of the
"anti-pollution activities" are "charged" to the polluting activities
themselves. The increasing pressure resulting from the higher investment requirement also has the effect of raising prices, because
it has been assumed that real savings will not increase proportionately
in the first instance. The cost increases are passed on in the ultimate
prices and will, in view of the assumed negative price elasticities for
domestic and foreign demand, cause a reduction in sales volume
(initially for consumption and export).

A further downward adjustment of the sales of (traditional) industries is effectuated by means of a drop in disposable income.

A real decrease in disposable income occurs because it has been
assumed that price increases which are directly related to "anti-
pollution activities" do not fall within the wage indexation system. A
further decrease in disposable income occurs because the costs of
combating pollution caused directly by consumers are charges to that
group. In addition, the (disposable) earned income is further affected
by the (adverse) consequences of a change in labour productivity* and
of a lessening of over-employment.

The downward adjustment of the production volume caused by
price and income effects also changes the outlook for future production
growth, thus reducing the investments (project-wise) that have been
assumed for that. Against these lower investments in the traditional
sectors are, however, investments undertaken in the environmental
sectors. As the results show, the higher capital intensities of anti-
pollution activities will lead to a net increase in the total investment
volume, but will not provide enough additional jobs to compensate for
the declining employment level in other sectors. The change in unemployment is fairly limited, especially in the light of the extent of
the facilities created in the environmental sector. It should be emphasized in this context that quite considerable shifts have been assumed
in international migration and in the numbers of registered unemployed.
The drop in employment, which will not have reached its ultimate level
until the end of the programme period, is considerably higher.

As regards the eventual effect that a more stringent environmental
policy will have on the balance-of-payments position, a number of

---

* Production includes that of the environmental sector.

mutually compensating trends are of importance. It is true that the volume of both imports and exports will drop, but on the one hand the decline in imports will, by comparison, be less sharp because of price effects, whilst on the other hand a slight price increase may have a compensating effect as regards exports. As the results show, the model tends to indicate favourable effects for the net balance of payments.

The overall tendency in these and other macro-results is approximately the same for each of the variants and corresponds to what could initially have been expected on the basis of the assumptions made. For comparison purposes, however, some further explanation seems appropriate.

The results are comparatively sensitive to the time-span during which matters would have to be put in order. Shortening the programme period from 12 to 7 years in fact leads to substantially greater pressure. This results firstly from the fact that annual investments in the environmental sector will be almost doubled. In particular, the greater pressure causes a bigger price increase. The decrease in the wage ratio is therefore slightly less for a 7-year programme period than for a 12-year one. Apart from the index-linking of wages, (partial) compensation for the higher price increase is also provided by an increased pressure on the labour market during the entire period. The fact that unemployment is still higher at the end of the shorter period is due to the downward production adjustments which in that case are on average slightly bigger.

Lastly, a variant is presented in which it has been assumed that foreign prices of relevance to the Netherlands have been influenced by a corresponding environmental policy. In the model calculations this hypothesis was put into concrete terms simply by causing the foreign prices (competing export prices and all import prices) to increase at the same rate as the price rise occurring in the Netherlands as a result of the environmental policy being implemented here.

This hypothesis has been worked out for the 12-year programme period, as it is unlikely that all countries which compete with or export to the Netherlands will initiate an environmental policy to the same extent over the shorter term.

The resultant volume and price effects move in the same direction as in the other variants. Compared with the other variant for a 12-year programme period, the (negative) effects on volume are, in general, smaller, though the (positive) price effects are in fact somewhat higher. The volume of exports is stimulated by the higher prices of competing exports, and the volume of personal consumption by a higher disposable income. The improved income position results from less unemployment and the higher price compensation given via index-linked wages to cover the increased (import) prices.

The higher import prices will also bring upward pressure to bear on domestic prices and will thus partially cancel out the initial competitive advantage as soon as they are passed on in export prices.

Lastly, it should be noted that the economic consequences will be more favourable if a corresponding environmental policy is pursued abroad as well.

III.3. Sector results for clearing up the backlog of pollution

The preceding sections show the salient macro-economic consequences of an environmental policy. Such an environmental policy may have divergent consequences for different sectors, one of the reasons being that major differences exist between the degree to which the individual sectors pollute the environment. The present section reviews a number of the characteristic consequences that "clearing up the backlog of pollution" will have for the various sectors. It should be noted that the model calculations for the sector results as presented in Table 2 were based on the same set of "anti-pollution activities" as used for the macro-results.

The classification according to sectors has not been highly elaborated. Besides the environmental sector, a differentiation is made between the four "big" sectors: agriculture, industry, the building industry and services. This classification makes allowance for the (very) big differences that exist between these sectors as regards their impact on the environment.

Because of the lack of statistical data it was not possible for a more far-reaching classification, specially within the industrial and services sector, to be applied within the framework of the model. Consequently, the sector results only provide fairly approximate information not geared to specific industrial sectors. *

In the model-based approach all new "anti-pollution activities" are grouped within a separate sector called the "environmental sector". Within this environmental sector a further distinction is made between five sub-sectors, ** each with its own cost structure and its own sources for the required investments. All anti-pollution activities have been combined together within the environmental sector irrespective of whether or not the activities are initiated by enterprises themselves or whether they are undertaken by one central, publicly run facility which the polluters can make use of. The advantage of this approach is that the initial impulse caused by an intensification of "anti-pollution activities" can be completely categorized.

The cost structure and the investment requirement of the separate sub-sectors thus determine the extent to which an intensification of such activities will have a further effect on the other (traditional) sectors.

---

* One aspect of the possible consequences, viz. the effect on prices, is in fact discussed for 23 industrial sectors in section III.5.

** Viz. two for water, two for air and one for soil. See also Chapter II.

Table 2. Consequences of three variants for a policy programme
aimed at controlling the pollution of water by decomposable organic substances,
the disposal of waste materials and the control of air pollution by sulphur
dioxide caused by the burning of oil products in stationary combustion sources
and from exhaust gases of petrol-engine motor vehicles
("putting matters in order"); sector results[a]

| | DURATION OF PROGRAMME PERIOD | | |
	7 YEARS	12 YEARS	12 YEARS INCLUDING CORRESPONDING POLICY ABROAD
	CHANGES FOR THE ENTIRE PROGRAMME PERIOD IN %		
Volume of investments according to destination			
Agriculture	-3.1	-1.8	-1.4
Industry	-6.5	-3.7	-2.9
Building industry	-2.4	-2.8	-1.1
Services	-8.4	-5.1	-4.0
Production volume			
Agriculture	-5.0	-4.7	-3.9
Industry	-6.5	-6.2	-5.3
Building industry	-0.1	-0.7	-0.1
Services	-5.0	-5.1	-4.1
Prices			
Agriculture	1.6	1.4	2.6
Industry	2.3	2.0	3.7
Building industry	0.7	0.4	2.3
Services	0.9	0.5	2.1
Environmental sector	5.1	5.2	6.4
Employment			
Agriculture	-3.2	-2.8	-2.2
Industry	-1.6	-1.2	-1.0
Building industry	1.6	1.2	1.4
Services	-2.0	-1.9	-1.5
	LEVELS		
Environmental sector			
Investments (Fl. mln per annum)	1,735	1,010	1,020
Added value upon completion of programme (Fl. mln.)	1,760	1,760	1,770
Employment upon completion of programme ('000 man-years)	8.0	8.0	8.0

a) The results are valid if the investments in the "environmental sector" are spread evenly over the relevant programme period.

The resultant consequences can be broken down in the first instance into effects on prices and spending. Since the principle of "the polluter pays" is applied, cost increases arise which are passed on in the end-prices charged by the sectors. This causes changes in the prices structure, because the cost increases vary according to sector. These differences are principally related to the level of pollution caused by each sector.

It is striking that the price increase is still highest of all in the environmental sector. The reason is that not only do the costs of goods and services supplied by traditional sectors increase, but also the costs of those supplied by the environmental sector itself. This latter is due to the fact that the various environmental (sub-) sectors are attuned to the processing of one anothers' waste.

The sectoral pattern of the results for the variants is likewise striking as regards its effects on production and employment. In all variants there is considerable pressure on the production level of the traditional sectors - except for the building industry, where the decline in production is extremely limited owing to investment in "building-intensive" projects for water purification facilities. The drop in employment is substantially lower than the decrease in production, whilst in the building industry employment even increases. This is caused by two factors which compensate to a certain extent for the negative consequences of the production drop. Firstly, a substitution of labour for capital takes place because of a change in the factor-price ratio. Secondly, the fact that the drop in employment tends as a rule to lag somewhat behind the drop in production has a compensatory effect.

There is a variation in the spending effects on sales broken down by sector. This is illustrated by the shifts which occur in the various final sales categories owing to the intensification of the environmental policy. The effects shown in Table 3 occur over a programme period of 12 years, excluding an environmental policy abroad.

The shifts are brought about by several factors. Firstly, the prices structure changes and, secondly, price and spending elasticities vary according to sector. In the case of consumer sales it is not only the change in price (also vis-à-vis competing imports) but also the change in real income which influence sales; in the case of exports the changed competitive position is responsible for this. In the case of investment shifts according to sector of origin, a decisive role is played by the sources of the investments in the environmental sector.

The most striking features are the divergent price increases per sector; these are mainly linked to the level of pollution in each sector. Apart from income shifts, it is these price changes which cause a reallocation of activities, and hence of investments and labour, between sectors. A reallocation which ultimately brings the economy "into line" with the more stringent environmental quality requirements.

Table 3. Consequences for the volume of exports of goods, personal consumption and investments, broken down by sector of origin ("putting matters in order" in 12 years; excluding environmental policy abroad

	EXPORTS OF GOODS	PERSONAL CONSUMPTION	INVESTMENTS BY ENTERPRISES[a]
	CHANGES DURING THE ENTIRE 12-YEAR PROGRAMME PERIOD IN %		
Agriculture	-1.4	-3.7	-
Industry	-3.8	-6.8	-0.5
Building trade	-0.4	-3.5	4.1
Services	-3.5	-6.9	1.1
Import	0.0	-5.0	-1.8
Total	-3.5	-6.4	0.5

a) Excluding houses, including environmental sector.

III. 4. Price effects for the industrial sector

As outlined above, income and price changes play an important role in the execution of the environmental policy. The present section goes into the price effects in more detail by breaking down the sectoral pattern of the industrial sector. This is done for 23 separate branches of the industrial sector within the four "big" sectors. The industry classification used here is derived from the International Standard Industrial Classification of all Economic Activities (ISIC) of the United Nations Statistical Office. *

In determining the price effects shown in Table 17 the same set of anti-pollution activities was used as for the macro-results and sector results.

The price changes were computed with the aid of the "traditional" input-output analysis method. "Anti-pollution activities" are specified according to the branches of industry for which these activities are actually undertaken. The cost structures of the "anti-pollution activities" are also included in the input-output model. ** Together with the

---

* Statistical Office of the United Nations, "International Standard Classification of all Economic Activities", Statistical Papers, Series M, No 4, 1st rev. N.Y.

** See also H. den Hartog and A. Houweling, "Pollution, Pollution Abatement and the Economic Structure: Empirical Results of Input-Output Computations for the Netherlands", Occasional Papers No. 1/1974, Central Planning Bureau.

specifications of the turnover and cost structure of the anti-pollution activities, this determines the mechanism used for passing on the costs. Imports of raw materials, semi-manufactures and services have been broken down according to competing (domestic) branches of industry. This establishes the extent to which the environmental policy abroad will affect the domestic price level via import prices.

The foregoing describes that part of the mechanism which causes price differentiation according to branch of industry. The previously described pressure involving the financing of additional investments and the changes in the costs of the primary inputs (wage costs per product unit, depreciation) have been disregarded within the framework of the input-output analysis, as they are more remote interdependencies. Above all, this appears to have consequences for the level of the figures. It is also of importance here that the upward pressure on prices is to a certain extent compensated for by the declining wage costs per product unit. Hence, the detailed price effects presented here are indicative of the changes in the prices structures which will result from a more stringent environmental policy.

Table 4 makes a detailed review of two situations from the time angle. Firstly, calculations were made of the price effects which will result from the level* of "anti-pollution activities" already existing in the basic situation of this study - in the year 1973. Information of this is given in Chapter II.

Secondly, a closer review is made of the price level increase upon completion of the programme. This increase also includes the above-mentioned price increase which had already occurred. Both cases not only give the part of the price increase that results from the fact that the costs of domestic "anti-pollution activities" are passed on, but also state the price increase which allows for the effects of a hypothetical environment policy abroad - via the impact of import prices on the domestic price level.

Exact information about the environmental policy abroad is extremely scarce, at least in such a form as would enable it to be used in the model method of the present study. But the impression cannot be avoided that the Netherlands, which was already a densely populated country prior to the basic situation (1973), ought to take more far-reaching measures than most of its supplying countries.

Over the longer term this differential might become very much smaller or might even disappear entirely.

Lastly, it has been assumed in the calculations that the import price trend will to a certain extent be in line with that for domestic prices. In order to limit the number of possibilities it has been assumed that as regards the price increase realized in the basic situation the increase in import prices will amount to half the domestic price increase, whilst upon completion of the programme it will be equal to the then current rate of the domestic price increase.

---

* No really substantial start was made with control activities until the late 'sixties.

Table 4.   Consequences for the price level of the gross production of 23 branches of industry if "the polluter pays principle" is consistently applied. Percentage changes realized in 1973 and after completion of programme, excluding and including effects of environmental policy abroad on domestic price level via import prices

	% CHANGES REALIZED IN 1973		% CHANGES AFTER COMPLETION OF PROGRAMME	
	EXCLUDING POLICY ABROAD	INCLUDING POLICY ABROAD	EXCLUDING POLICY ABROAD	INCLUDING POLICY ABROAD
Agriculture	0.20	0.23	1.33	1.74
Industry .... of which:	0.29	0.34	1.46	2.11
Coal-mining	0.05	0.07	0.42	0.70
Other mining	0.13	0.14	0.66	0.88
Food stuffs animal	0.58	0.62	2.72	3.21
Foods stuffs other	0.44	0.53	2.17	3.23
Beverages and tobacco	0.50	0.53	1.98	2.40
Textile	0.86	1.04	3.30	5.16
Clothing and footwear	0.19	0.32	0.94	2.36
Paper	0.81	0.93	3.34	4.63
Chemical industry	0.43	0.50	1.93	2.70
Oil refineries	0.08	0.12	1.27	1.85
Metal industry	0.10	0.13	0.87	1.41
Construction	0.08	0.10	0.51	0.91
Electrical engineering	0.06	0.08	0.34	0.72
Transport vehicles	0.15	0.18	0.76	1.18
Other industries	0.19	0.23	1.00	1.49
Public utilities	0.05	0.06	1.09	1.27
Building industry	0.14	0.17	0.83	1.21
Services .... of which:	0.12	0.13	0.66	0.83
Trade	0.07	0.09	0.55	0.72
Housing	0.03	0.03	0.16	0.23
Sea and air transport	0.04	0.08	0.26	0.77
Other transport and Post Office ..	0.04	0.06	0.45	0.64
Other services	0.23	0.24	1.03	1.17
Not specified separately	0.04	0.14	0.19	1.20
Enterprises	0.21	0.25	1.12	1.57
Environmental sector	1.59	1.59	6.56	6.69

Theoretically, the input-output analysis enables a fairly accurate assessment to be made of the price effects created owing to implementation of the principle of "the polluter pays". In fact, however, the accuracy of the results also depends on the (presupposed) homogeneity of the industrial sector and on the degree of aggregation that has been applied. In consequence, the price changes now calculated may turn out to be considerably higher or lower if certain industrial classes are broken down in more detail.

Deviations from the calculated percentages may still occur, of course, because a number of enterprises will not be able to pass on their higher costs in full as a result of international market relations. This problem will gradually lose its significance according as the environmental policy is intensified in other countries.

III.5.   "Clean" growth and "dirty" growth

As has been shown in the previous sections, "clearing up the backlog of pollution" will adversely affect growth during the programm period. The question now arises as to which consequences for growth may be anticipated if all new activities must also comply with the more stringent standards.

To answer this question the most important factor is the change occurring in the (macro-economic) composition of investments, at least in so far as such a change is linked to the higher standards for environmental quality. It can be ascertained how many extra investments in the environmental sector will be needed to cope with an annual "dirty" growth rate of approx. 3.5% provided the required investments for this growth were to meet with the standards. "Dirty" growth is then taken to mean the growth that would otherwise have been possible had the assumed intensification of the environmental policy not taken place. In this instance, production (value added) is measured on the basis of the existing range and therefore excludes activities in the environmental sector, or their added value.

The amount of additional investments thus established as being necessary for "clean" growth during any specific period is relatively low. In the case of a shift of this size in investments, the macro-effects on an annual basis are very small. Over a 12-year period in particular (concluding year 1985), the "clean" growth of industrial production (excluding the environmental sector) is found to be about 2.7% less than in the case of "dirty" growth. In all cases, "clean" and "dirty" are taken to mean controlling and not controlling pollution respectively. The reduction in the growth rate is of course slightly lower if the production of the environmental sector is included in the production of the total industrial sector. The decrease in growth over 12 years then works out at a mere 2%.

Compared to the assumed annual "dirty" growth rate of 3.5%, the reduction of 2% over a period of 12 years implies a "clean" growth of almost 3.4% per annum. This reduction arises in the following way.

147

Additional investments in an improved quality of the environment also mean fewer investments in traditional activities. In turn, this implies less growth in these latter activities and hence, on balance, a smaller increase in potential or latent pollution. In the long run, this has the effect of pushing down the required additional investments for maintaining the quality of the environment. The ultimate extra investments for "clean" growth therefore work out slightly lower than initially forecast. The reduced growth is thus the result of two changes.

First, passing on the real costs of environmental facilities lays claim to part of the added value of traditional activities. Interpreted in economic terms, this in fact means that the capital ratios of these traditional activities become higher if new investments have to comply with more stringent environmental requirements. In other words, there is a drop in the yield of investments in terms of the value they add to the traditional range of activities. There is some compensation for this, however, by the production or added value of the environmental sector.

Second, most of the loss of growth is caused by those investments of "clean" growth which replace investments in traditional activities. This replacement is mainly made at the expense of investments in the industrial and services sectors. Only a small proportion of the environmental facilities can be financed from additional savings.

IV.   THE ENVIRONMENTAL SECTOR

IV. 1.   Clearing up the backlog of pollution

As has been said before, the size of the environmental sector is
determined partly exogenously and partly endogenously.   The quality
standards set for the relevant environmental components are exogenous.
These standards define the level of the "anti-pollution activities" in
relation to the (potential) pollution level.   This pollution level may be
high or not so high - depending on activities in the rest of the economy.
In this latter respect, therefore, "anti-pollution activities" are determined endogenously.

The (exogenous) setting of standards is by far the most important
determining factor for the actual size of the environmental sector.   As
the results of Table 2 show, the endogenously determined size of the
environmental sector is only a few per cent lower than would have been
initially required.   This is a result of a slightly lower production level
in the remaining sectors of the economy following the process of "putting
matters in order".

These negligible endogenous effects on the size of the environmental
sector are further disregarded here.   Table 5 gives a summary of the
key figures for the "anti-pollution activities" differentiated in the model
at the level that would initially have been required (df. Chapter II).

These figures are self-explanatory.   Later on in the present section, however, attention is paid to three other important aspects of the
environmental sector.   These are: waste disposal by the environmental
sector itself, its energy consumption and its demand on space.

In the case of waste discharge by an "anti-pollution activity", a
distinction can be made between waste of the same type that the activity
is directed against, and other types of waste whose control lies in the
sphere of other anti-pollution activities.

As a rule the purification efficiency of the various techniques is
expressed as a percentage of the activity's "own" waste.   The efficiency
of the biological waste water treatment of decomposable organic substances amounts, for example, to an average of 90%.   This is therefore
the percentage of the pollution that is converted into (harmless) carbon
dioxide, water vapour and purified sludge.   The average efficiency of
the desulphurization of oil products is 84%* and that of the CVCC engine

---

*   The efficiency amounts to 80% if allowance is made for the sulphur dioxide
emitted by the oil burned during the desulphurization process.

Table 5. KEY FIGURES FOR THE ENVIRONMENTAL SECTOR (1973)[a]

ANTI-POLLUTION ACTIVITIES	RESIDUAL POLLUTION			ANNUAL COSTS		INVESTMENTS		ADDED VALUE, TOTAL	EMPLOY-MENT, TOTAL IN MAN-YEARS
	SIZE	UNIT	AS % OF TOTAL POLLUTION	PER UNIT	TOTAL	PER UNIT	TOTAL		
			%	Fl.	Fl. mln.	Fl.	Fl. mln.		('000s)
Public waste water treatment	17.1	mln.p.e.[b]	69	69	1,180	431	7,370	1,050	3.51
Private waste water treatment and sanitation	20.0	mln.p.e.	81	9	180	64	1,275	158	0.52
Stratified charge-engines instead of conventional engines	3.4	mln. vehicles[c]	100	173	588	366	1,244	276	0
Desulphurization of oil	10.4	mln.tons of oil	86	25.1	261	75.8	788	148	0.97
Disposal of solid waste	10.0	mln.tons[d]	75	20	200	105	1,050	161	2.22
Environmental sector .					2,409		11,727	1,793	7.22

a) Figures relate to residual pollution (that part of the 1973 pollution level for which no environmental facilities were available in that year).

b) Population equivalents (COD).

c) Passenger cars and delivery vans fitted with petrol engines.

d) Gas-oil, domestic heating oil and fuel oil.

is 70% as compared to emissions from a conventional petrol fuelled internal combustion engine (1971 type).

The model calculations are based on the cost levels in line with these efficiencies. In addition, the model equations also allow for a number of interdependencies linked to the waste eliminated by the other environmental sectors within the range being studied.

It is likely, for example, that in the case of water purification bottle-necks will arise as regards the destination of a large proportion of the purified sludge. In view of the already extensive manure surplus from the livestock herd, it is thought that no further expansion will occur in the (traditional) sales of sludge for fertilizing purposes, whilst it is anticipated that restrictions will be made on (uncontrolled) tipping on nearby sites. The purified sludge surplus has been regarded as solid waste and has been removed at the costs applicable to such waste. In the case of water purification allowance has also been made, for completeness' sake, for the relatively minor costs of adapting the vehicles in use in that sector to bring them into line with the more stringent emission control standards.

The incineration of waste materials imposes a higher pollutional load on the environmental component air. Countering this drawback by, say, gas washing gives rise to water pollution. This latter can in turn be controlled by purifying the process water. In the case of the controlled tipping of waste it has been assumed that pollution of surface water and ground water can be completely eliminated by purifying the percolation water.

Table 6 gives an indication of the (initial) cost increases which will result from controlling waste discharges which originate from "anti-pollution activities" and which have been allowed for in the model equations.

The figures in Table 6 show that the initial cost increase for the smaller sub-sectors will be quite substantial. For the environmental sector as a whole the cost increase of 5.5% is fairly modest. The ultimate price increase computed using the model appears to be between 6% and 7%.

To sum up, it may be concluded that the available figures give no reason for fearing that attuning the separate "anti-pollution activities" to one another's waste discharges might result in a substantial accumulation of waste and/or costs.

One major aspect of the consequences of the environmental policy is the effect of the introduction of "anti-pollution activities" on energy consumption. A very cautious estimate is given below of the energy that would be required annually for operating the environmental facilities outlined in previous sections. The energy consumption has been estimated for the pollution still remaining in the reference year (1973) and is expressed as a percentage of the (national) energy consumption in that year.

If the pollution still to be eliminated in 1973 is indeed tackled in accordance with the standards assumed in the preceding sections and on the basis of the average assumed contributions made by the various techniques to the elimination, then the environmental sector's energy consumption will reveal the following pattern.

Table 6. Effect of controlling pollution caused by "anti-pollution activities" on the cost of such activities (1973 prices)

ANTI POLLUTION ACTIVITIES	ANNUAL COSTS		
	PRICE [b]	UNIT	CHANGE [a] IN %
	Fl.		%
Public waste water treatment	69	p. e. [c]	3. 0
Private waste water treatment and sanitation	9	p. e. [c]	14. 5
Modification of petrol engines	173	vehicle	–
Desulphurization of oil	27	ton	6. 0 [d]
Disposal of solid waste	20	ton	24. 5
Environmental sector			5. 4

a) In the sense of the initial cost increase.
b) Price level for efficiency levels mentioned in text.
c) Population equivalent on COD basis.
d) Costs resulting from desulphurization of oil burned in this sub-sector.

For waste water treatment in publicly run plants the aeration of the waste water requires the most energy. In addition, some energy is needed for supply and discharge of the water and for sludge off take and dephosphatization. After consulting information from various sources,* a quantity of 23 Tcal (tera-calories) per mln. population equivalents on a COD basis has been assumed.

This figure was likewise used as a basis for private biological waste water treatment by enterprises. Sanitations achieved via process changes usually requires less than half the energy (per population equivalent).

* a) Stichting Toekomstbeeld der Techniek: Energy Conservation: Ways and Means, The Hague, 1974, p. 132.
b) E. Hirst, Energy Implications of Several Environmental Quality Strategies, Oak Ridge National Laboratory, USA, 1973.
c) J. Zeper, Kostenaspecten van behandeling van afvalwater (Cost Aspects of Wastewater Treatment), Intermediair, 7th year, No. 29, 23 July 1971.

It is roughly estimated that an average of 12 Tcal per mln. population equivalents is required for all privately run waste water treatment facilities taken together.

Consequently, the energy required for purifying water polluted with decomposable organic substances amounts to less than 1,500 Tcal, which is less than 0.25% of the national (primary) energy consumption in 1973. *

The measures to restrict the emission of pollutants in the exhaust cases of petrol-engine vehicles would give rise to an extra petrol consumption of about 10%. This figure is mainly based on the additional consumption of engines operating according to the stratified charge principle (see section II.4.2.). The 10% figure is not absolutely certain, since the various sources differ in this respect. For the total vehicle population (petrol-engines) of approx. 3.5 mln. passenger cars and delivery vans, almost 3,000 Tcal more energy would be required, or almost 0.5% of the total national consumption.

The desulphurization of gas-oil (incl. domestic heating oil) and of fuel oil requires a considerable amount of energy. On the basis of figures from various sources, ** the following percentages have been assumed for the fuel loss: flue gas desulphurization 1%, gas-oil desulphurization 5% and fuel oil desulphurization 10%. If allowance is made for the participation percentages of the various techniques given in Table 6 (section II.3.2.), the average fuel loss works out at almost 6% of the 10.4 mln. tons of oil to be desulphurized. This is equal to about 1% of the total national energy consumption.

The energy required for the disposal of waste treatment comprises energy for collection transport, for further transport and for treatment (tipping, composting and incineration). Figures have been derived from a report by the Waste Disposal Association (SVA) *** as regards transport (excl. collection transport) **** and treatment. In total, the energy requirement for the disposal of waste amounts to over 500 Tcal for approx. 10.5 mln. tons of waste. This is not much, and is in fact less than 0.1% of the total national energy consumption in 1973.

The resultant energy consumption for the separate "anti-pollution activities" on the basis of the figures given above is summarized in Table 7. The table shows that the energy consumption for running the environmental facilities to be created after 1973 for the pollution level

---

* Incl. 64.6 mln. tons oil equivalent (TOE) not used for energy purposes.
** a) See footnote * a); p. 152 ; and b) below.
   b) Study of the costs of residue and gasoil desulphurization for the Commission of the European Communities, Report No. 13/72, Concawe, The Hague, December 1972.
*** "Benodigde hoeveelheid energie t.b.v. de afvalverwijdering" (Amount of energy required for waste disposal), SVA Report 569, Amersfoort, 1973.
**** The ernegy consumption of the (satisfactorily operating) collection activities has not been taken into consideration; see also section II.5.2.

Table 7. Energy consumption of "anti-pollution activities" during implementation of a hypothetical policy programme for the residual pollution in 1973, related to total national energy consumption in 1973, broken down according to types of energy

ANTI-POLLUTION ACTIVITIES	TOTAL DIRECT CONSUMPTION	OF WHICH:			PRIMARY ENERGY a)	
		PETROLEUM PRODUCTS	GAS	ELECTRICITY	TOTAL	PROPORTION OF TOTAL WITHIN NATIONAL CONSUMPTION
	x 100 TOE b)	%			x 100 TOE b)	%
Public waste water treatment	393	9	-	91	1,109	0.17
Private waste water treatment and sanitation	240	42	50	8	278	0.05
Modification of petrol engines	2,958	100	-	-	2,958	0.46
Desulphurization of oil	6,053	94	-	6	6,739	1.04
Disposal of solid waste	484	98	-	2	505	0.08
Environment sector	10,128	91.3	1.3	7.4	11,589	1.80

a) Fuel input has been valued at 3 times the production of electricity.

b) TOE = tons oil equivalent.

154

occurring in that year would amount to about 1.8% of the total national energy consumption in 1973.

This figure calls for a few extra comments. In the first place, as the foregoing shows, a substantial proportion of the extra fuel will be used in the desulphurization sector. Since it is expected that the proportion of oil fired in combustion furnaces will start to increase again after 1980, energy consumption by the desulphurization sector will also increase accordingly.

Secondly, as has been mentioned earlier, no allowance has been made in the estimate for a number of possibilities for achieving savings in the energy consumption of anti-pollution activities over the somewhat longer term.

Such possibilities include coupling electricity generation with waste incineration on a larger scale than is undertaken at present. In the case of biological waste water treatment, energy consumption can be reduced even further by making use of the exploitable methane gas produced during (controlled) sludge fermentation. It might also be possible to achieve further energy savings (and reductions in waste) via the increased recycling of suitable materials. Besides the already considerable amounts of the traditional raw materials steel and paper which are recycled, aluminium would be another suitable product.

It may be concluded therefore that the total energy consumption of "anti-pollution activities" of almost 1.2 mln. tons oil equivalent is about the same size as that of a big branch of industry such as the building industry. Moreover, compared with other activities, the relative energy requirement is fairly high, even higher than in energy-intensive sectors such as the paper industry and metal industry. This comparison is merely meant to be illustrative. It is not valid as a favourable or unfavourable qualification of anti-pollution activities for the very reason that such activities are by necessity linked to the existence of other branches of industry such as paper-making and metal industry. If, for instance, these latter branches of industry were no longer to occur in our country because of their relatively high energy requirements, this would mean the discontinuation of the "anti-pollution activity" geared to them.

Lastly, it should be mentioned that the additional energy consumption in the environmental sector would be more than offset by a reduced consumption of energy as a result of the downward production adjustments in the traditional sectors.

This latter would then be a result of the production loss which, as has been shown above, * will occur in the traditional sectors because of the environmental policy. A reallocation of energy uses would therefore likewise occur.

---

*   The reduced consumption in the traditional sectors amounts to approx. 1.8 mln. TOE for a 12-year programme period and if it is assumed that no corresponding environmental policy is pursued abroad. The variant with a 12-year programme period incl. environmental policy abroad results in a reduced energy consumption of approx. 1.3 mln. TOE in the traditional sectors.

The introduction of "anti-pollution activities" makes a demand on space. As is shown below, this is mainly a demand for storage space in the countryside for waste water treatment plants and waste disposal tips. Just as above, the estimate of the demand on space relates to that part of the pollution still not eliminated in 1973.

For biological waste water treatment the demand on space is very much dependent on the depth of the aeration tanks and the method of sludge treatment.* The bigger the plant capacity the faster the reduction in the required site area per population equivalent, since use can then be made of deeper aeration tanks and mechanical methods of sludge dewatering. On the basis of a number of data** it has been assumed that the average demand on space will be $0.55m^2$ per population equivalent (COD) for publicly run plants and $0.3\,m^2$ per p.e. for the private waste water treatment plants within industry (since these are on average somewhat bigger).

The reduction of water pollution by means of sanitation measures requires much less space. Sanitation in the form of process adaptations does not normally make any additional demand on space at all. But sanitation in the form of controlling the discharge of slimes does require some space. For all reorganisation measures together a surface area of $0.03\,m^2$ per population equivalent has been assumed.

On the basis of the above figures, controlling the pollution of water by decomposable organic substances would require a total area of approx. 1,135 hectares.

Air pollution control requires much less space. Modification of the petrol powered traction engines so that they emit cleaner exhaust gases can be completely disregarded here. As regards desulphurization activities, the demand on space made by the oil-refineries may be considered as representative. An approximate calculation puts this at around 0.1 hectare per mln. guilders sales.*** If this figure is applied to the desulphurization sector, the resultant site area requirement is 28 hectares.

Of all the various "anti-pollution activities" the disposal of waste requires most space. Even when waste is incinerated, storage capacity in the countryside is still needed for the quarter part that is left over. In the case of composting as undertaken at present (1974–75), seventy to to eighty per cent of the waste supplied is tipped (both straight away and in the form of the residue left after composting). The total amount of waste after incineration and after composting, plus the waste that is tipped directly, accounts for approx. 7 mln. tons.

* Sludge dewatering on drying beds, or mechanical drying (possibly combined with thermal drying).

** a) Prof. A.C.J. Koot, De oxydatiesloot (The oxidation ditch), in H2O, periodical for drinking water supply and waste water treatment, 4th year 1971, p.457.

   b) National Institute for Waste water Purification (Rijksinstitut voor de Zuivering van Afvalwater - RIZA) supplied data on plants already built.

*** See also the (slightly outdated) figures given in: Dr. L. Bax, Het industriële terreingebruik in Nederland (Industrial Land-Use in the Netherlands), 1961.

If the average tipping height is above five metres after the waste has first been compressed, this means that a site area of 0.30 m^2 per ton of waste is required. * For a waste quantity of 7 mln. tons, therefore, the annual growth-rate of tipping sites will be approx. 210 hectares.

The permanent demand on space made by an annual quantity of 7 mln. tons is a few times higher still. If waste burial sites are included in regional development plans and if, after a certain period, ** they ca be put to some other use, *** then the permanently required site area can be estimated at almost 1,600 hectares.

Table 8.   Demand on space made by anti-pollution activities
during implementation of a hypothetical policy programme
for the proportion of pollution not yet eliminated in 1973.

ANTI-POLLUTION ACTIVITIES	DEMAND ON SPACE (x 1 HECTARE)
Public waste water treatment	940
Private waste water treatment and sanitation	195
Modification of petrol engines	0
Desulphurization of oil	28
Disposal of solid waste	1,575
Environmental sector	2,738

Supplementary aspects of the demand for space by tipping sites, such as access roads and aesthetic requirements, are also of importance in deciding which tipping sites will be permanently in use. It should be noted that the proposed decentralization, to be achieved via

---

* a) Information from the Waste Disposal Association (SVA) shows that 1.1 cubic metres of tipping space is required per ton of highly comminuted waste. With a tipping height of over 5 metres this works out at an area of 0.22 m^2 per ton of waste.

b) Th. A.M. van Keulen in "Plan" (Monthly for Design and Environment) No.2, 1973, p. 49. For a height of over 5 metres this source gives a required site area of 0.45 to 0.65 m^2 per ton of waste.

** Fifteen years has been assumed. On average, the waste's demand on space will then last for 7 1/2 years.

*** Agriculture, horticulture and forestry. There are also possible recreational uses.

regional cooperation between municipalities on the basis of provincial plans, will bring a considerable improvement compared to the 1973 situation when more than 550 refuse tips were still in existence.

The space required by the environmental sector amounts to about 2,700 hectares (see Table 8). This is quite considerable and is of the same magnitude as the surface area in use for cemeteries or for one-third of the parks and gardens within built-up areas. *

In the present section the "anti-pollution activities" have been discussed as regards their waste production, their energy consumption and the demand they make on space. The purification activities which have been disregarded (cf. section II. 1) imply an under-estimation, albeit a limited one, of the economic consequences. As a result, the consequences for energy consumption and the demand on space have also been underestimated. Part of this underestimation relates to the energy consumed in controlling air pollution caused by industrial process emissions, whilst the other part is the energy used in preventing thermal pollution of surface water which the aid of cooling towers, a technique which requires a great deal of energy and space.

As a conclusion to this section, the foregoing has shown that the environmental sector is an activity which is certainly not spotlessly clean, is energy-intensive and requires a great deal of space.

It should be emphasized once more that this is merely meant as a pure statement of fact. Upon closer examination, the characteristics of the environmental sector are found to be supplementary to the corresponding characteristics of the "traditional" sectors. For the fact is that where these latter sectors (have to) make use of "anti-pollution activities", the pollution, energy consumption and space requirements of the environmental sector can in fact be allocated to the traditional activities themselves.

IV.2. The growth of the environmental sector

As can be seen from the previous sub-section, "putting matters in order" in the basic situation (1973) will require almost Fl. 12,000 mln. (in 1973 prices), whilst this will be accompanied by an annual amount of almost Fl. 2,500 mln. for current current costs (also in 1973 prices). These sums therefore relate only to the arrears, i.e. the purification measures geared to the residual pollution existing in 1973. If allowance is made for the level of purification already existing in that year, the current costs of the environmental sector will total almost Fl. 3,000 mln. ** after "putting matters in order".

---

* Central Bureau of Statistics, Algemene Milieustatistiek (General Environmental Statistics), 1973, Table 1.1., page 16.

** Investments in the environmental sector prior to 1973 likewise amounted to almost Fl. 3,000 mln. (in 1973 prices).

The total current costs, or the gross production of the environmental sector, are used here as a yardstick for the demand made on resources by anti-pollution activities. The above-mentioned Fl. 3,000 mln. corresponds to approximately 1.8% of the Gross National Product. *

The present sub-section deals firstly with whether any changes (possibly major ones) may occur in the claim made by the environmental sector on the GNP if factors such as the long-term growth in production, population, the number of vehicles on the roads and energy consumption are taken into consideration. Secondly, an estimate is made of the growth of the stock of capital goods** in the environmental sector.

The above changes are related to the period up to 1985 - the year in which it has been assumed that most of the "major cleaning operation" will have been completed. Then, developments are briefly reviewed for the period up to the year 2000.

In view of the many uncertain factors, the estimates are of course merely intended to be purely indicative - and this applies in particular to the latter-mentioned period. Besides this uncertainty, the 1985-2000 period also differs from the period up to 1985 in that production after 1985 will no longer be held back by the pollution backlog which will have been cleared off by that time.

In estimating the development of the various types of pollution prior to elimination and the relevant level of "anti-pollution activities", very approximate assumptions were used as a basic. The most important of these assumptions are given below in brief.

In most instances it was assumed that the pollution prior to elimination will increase at the same rate as such factors as industrial production, the population level, the number of vehicles on the roads and the consumption of energy in combustion furnaces. In a number of cases, however, and specifically in the case of energy consumption, allowance was also made for shifts in distribution - in this case changes in the shares of the primary energy suppliers. A non-proportional development has also been assumed in estimating the manure surplus of the intensive livestock breeding industry and the quantity of household refuse. In the first instance the deviation is due to the fact that possible uses for natural fertilizers will remain practically at the same level as against an expanding production originating from a growing livestock herd, whilst in the second instance allowance has been made not only for the population growth but also for an "affluence effect" amounting to 2% per year.

As regards the population level, the "B alternative" of the Central Bureau of Statistics estimate has been used. This works out at 14.4 and 15.4 mln. people for the years 1985 and 2000 respectively. The

---

* Approx. Fl. 166,000 mln at market prices in 1973.

** This can in turn be used as a basis for estimates of environment investments.

estimate of the pollution caused by enterprises is based on a production growth of 3.5% p.a., with the exception of a number of cases where, owing to limitations in supply factors, * production is expected to grow at a slower rate. The personal car population, which was approx. 3.2 mln. in 1973, is expected to undergo a fairly big increase and reach 5.2 mln. cars in 1985.** It is expected that the increase will be considerably lower after 1985, but that it will still rise to approx. 6.5 mln. cars in the year 2000.

The estimates of energy consumption, which is specifically decisive for the growth of air pollution, obviously reveal a great many uncertainties, especially as regards the role that the various primary energy supplies will play within future supplies. But it is clear that the share of the low-polluting natural gas will decline over the long run and be replaced by more polluting fossil fuels (oils, coal) and by nuclear power. The estimate of air pollution up to the year 1985 caused by combustion of fossil fuels is based on the potential development trends in the energy situation up to that year as outlined in the "Energienota" ("Energy Paper"). ***

For the average growth of national energy consumption a variant**** on the estimate based on "unchanged policy" has been used. This shows increases of 5% and 3.7% during the 1973-80 and 1980-85 periods respectively.

For the 1985-2000 period***** an increase of 3.2% has been assumed. The politically controversial issue of nuclear power supplies will not play a predominant role until 2000, with a share of 2.5% in the total supplies. Of importance is the continuingly high dependence on imports of crude oil and coal, which will account respectively for 53% and 22% of total national consumption by the end of the century. This dominant position of oil and coal has major consequences for the growth of (potential) air pollution.

Table 9 summarizes the pollution prior to elimination which will exist in 1985 and 2000 for the various environmental components on the basis of the growth scenario outlined above.

Apart from a few exceptions, the previously mentioned effective standards (see Chapters II and III) were used for attuning the size of the environmental sector to the various types of pollution. Strictly speaking, in view of the fact that assimilative capacity of the natural environment is constant in absolute terms, even more stringent standards

---

* For instance, the food stuff industry based on processing potatoes and sugar beets. The cultivation areas available for these crops in the Netherlands are not expected to show any major increase.

** Based on car-density estimates in the Integral Traffic and Transportation Study of the Netherlands Institute of Economics (1972).

*** Lower House, 1974-75 session, 13122 Nos. 1-2.

**** For a description of the variants see the "Energienota" (Energy Paper), p. 65 ff.

***** CPB extrapolation.

Table 9. Pollutional load of waste discharge prior to elimination in 1973, 1985 and 2000

TYPE OF POLLUTION	POLLUTIONAL LOAD IN 1973 [a]		POLLUTION INDEX (1973 = 100)	
	LEVEL	UNIT	1985	2000
Biodegradable organic substances, purification in publicly operated sewage purification plants	24.8[b] mln s (COD)	p.e.	128	180
Biodegradable organic substances, private purification and sanitation within industry	24.7[c] mln (COD)	p.e.	152	236
Air pollution by road traffic caused by exhaust gases from petrol engines .	1,690 mln 60 mln 100 mln	kg carbon monoxides kg nitrogen oxides kg hydro- carbons	149	179
Sulphur dioxide due to the combustion of fossil fuels in stationary combustion sources	500 mln	kg sulphur oxides	308	433
Waste	15.4[e] mln	ton	148	243
Noise pollution	.[f]		.	.
Pollution not previously specified during generation of electricity [g] ..	.[f]		.[h]	.[h]

a) See Chapter II.

b Of which 7.7 mln. p.e. (COD) is purified.

c) Of this amount, 4.7 mln. p.e. (COD) has already been eliminated via sanitation or purification.

d) If, solely in order to gain an approximate overall impression, all pollutants (from stationary combustion sources, mobile sources and industrial process emissions) are weighted together with the weighting factors proposed by L.R. Babcock and N.L. Nagda, the resultant quantity for 1973 amounts to 1,473 mln. kg sulphur dioxide equivalents.

The indices for 1985 and 2000 are 217 and 403 respectively. The weighting factors used were as follows: carbon monoxide 0.03; nitrogen oxides 0.9; sulphur dioxides 1.0; lead-containing aerosols 13.0; other aerosols 1.6; hydrocarbons 0.3. For emissions at ground level (mobile combustion sources) the above factors have been doubled.

e) Approx. 3.5 mln. tons would have been processed according to the more stringent standards. The esti- mate of 15.4 mln. tons includes 2 mln. tons industrial waste (mainly chemical waste) which is difficult to process. The latter quantity is based on a provisional estimate taken from a survey conducted by the Waste Disposal Association (SVA).

f) . = insufficient data.

g) Thermal pollution; radioactive waste from nuclear power stations.

h) The indices of the estimated electricity consumption supplied by public power stations (3.4 mln. tons TOE in 1973) are 232 and 456 for 1985 and 2000 respectively.

(and correspondingly higher costs) should be used as a basis in a growth situation. It is quite possible, however, that the cost-raising effect which results in principle from an increase in purification efficiency will be compensated for by cost reductions resulting from improvements in anti-pollution technology.

In calculating the current costs and the capital goods stock of the environmental sector in 1985 and 2000, therefore, the figures given in Chapter II have been used. In presenting these and subsequently applying them to the model methods in Chapter III, a number of "anti-pollution activities" were disregarded (see section II. 1) for various reasons - either because the more substantial costs do not arise until after 1985, or because the detailed statistics needed for the model were not available. Nevertheless, in order to give an approximate impression, an indication of the environmental measures that were disregarded is given in Tables 9 and 11, and where any approximate cost estimates on these were available, such costs have been included and are reflected in the total figure. The fact that this part of the estimate is based on figures which is most instances have not yet been confirmed by several sources should, of course, be taken into account when interpreting the results.

Table 10 shows what the annual costs of the environmental sector will be on the basis of the assumed growth and standards and in accordance with the relevant cost assumptions. As can be seen from the table, the annual costs of the environmental sector in 1985 correspond to about 2% of the Gross National Product in 1985 market prices. The corresponding figure for annual environmental expenditure in the year 2000 is practically the same despite quite considerable shifts in the range of activities.

The findings relating to the growth of the capital goods stock up to 1985 and from 1985 to 2000 are summarized in Table 11. The total growth over the 1973-1985 period amounts to almost Fl. 21,000 mln, * or nearly 5% of the total (estimated) gross investments by enterprises** and by the government in that period.

The total growth during the (longer) period from 1985 to 2000 is considerably lower than in the preceding "cleaning-up" period since it will then no longer be necessary for any investments to be made on clearing away the pollution backlog. But in the 1985-2000 period a gradual start will be made on replacement investments in the environmental sector.

To sum up, the findings of the present section seem to indicate that the cost of the anticipated growth will not cause any major changes

---

* Of which an estimated 5% as government investments, 37% as industrial investments and 6% as non-recurrent expenditure by households (on anti-pollution devices in motor vehicles).

** Excl. investments in dwelling and stocks.

Table 10. Current costs (gross production) of environmental sectors 1973-2000, in mln. guilders, 1973 prices

	1973	1985	2000
	Fl. mln.		
Public waste water treatment	320	1,990	2,790
Private waste water treatment and sanitation	40	330	510
Stratified charged-engines instead of conventional petrol engines	–	930	1,160
Desulphurization of gas-oil, fuel oil and coal a)	20	1,050	1,985
Disposal of solid waste	65	410	660
Disposal of chemical waste b)	20	300	510
Air pollution by emission from diesel powered motor vehicles c)	–	. d)	.
Air pollution by industrial process emissions e)	–	50	80
Measures against noise pollution	.	.	
Mesures against thermal pollution ..	–	–	325 f)
Measures relating to radioactive waste g)	.	.	.
Total, memorandum item + ...	465	5,060	8,020
As percentage of GNP at market prices h)	0.3	2.0	1.9

a) Additional costs of generating electricity using partial combustion (2-stage combustion), compared to costs in conventional power stations, have been considered to represent costs of desulphurization.

b) Some sources give costs varying from Fl. 50 to Fl. 500 per ton, depending on type of waste. An average of Fl. 100 per ton has been assumed for a waste quantity of 2 mln. tons (cf. footnote e) in Table 9).

c) Technology not sufficiently advanced. Level of relevant air pollution in 1973 lower than that caused by petrol-engine vehicles.

d) . = insufficient data.

e) The estimate only includes the (large-scale) emissions of: sulphur dioxides from sulphuric acid plants (desulphurization techniques), aerosols from industry (dust separation) and emissions from oil tanks (those with floating roofs). Since details on certain emissions are unavailable, the figures should be regarded as a minimum estimate.

f) It has been assumed that in the year 2000 half of the electricity production will be achieved using an improved closed circuit cooling system, whilst (wet) cooling towers will still be in use for the other half.

g) As an indication: an increase of one percent in the cost of electricity generated in nuclear power stations (4 mln. TOE in 2000) to pay for environmental control facilities will involve a sum of approx. Fl. 20 mln. in 1985 and approx. 40 mln in 2000.

h) At 3.5% growth per annum this works out at Fl. 116, 250 and 420 billion in 1973, 1985 and 2000 respectively.

in the relative size of the environmental sector* which accounts for about 2% of the Gross National Product at market prices. The uncertainties in the estimate as regards growth, control standards and elimination costs are of course much greater for the 1985–2000 period than for the preceding period. The purely indicative nature of the extrapolation up to the year 2000 should therefore be emphasized once again.

---

* In terms of the pollution in the reference year 1973: approx. 1.8% of the GNP. Cf. p. 159, note *.

Table 11. Growth of capital goods stock in environmental sectors 1973-2000, Fl. mln. in 1973 prices

	1973-1985		1985-2000	
	TOTAL GROWTH	AVERAGE ANNUAL GROWTH	TOTAL GROWTH	AVERAGE ANNUAL GROWTH
	Fl. mln.			
Public waste water treatment	9,860	822	4,120	275
Private waste water treatment and sanitation	2,100	175	1,320	88
Stratified charge-engines instead of conventional petrol engines	1,980 a)	165	490 b)	33
Desulphurization of gas-oil, fuel oil and coal	3,420	285	3,970	265
Disposal of solid waste	1,780	148	1,350	90
Disposal of chemical waste ..	1,400	117	1,050	70
Air pollution by emission from diesel powered motor vehicles	. c)	.	.	.
Air pollution by industrial process emissions d)	200	17	100	7
Measures against noise pollution e)	.	.	.	.
Measures against thermal pollution	–	–	1,950	130
Measures relating to radioactive waste	.	.	.	.
Total, memorandum item + ..	20,740	1,730 f)	14,350	960

a) Of this, sums amounting to Fl. 1,240 mln. and Fl. 310 mln. in 1973-1985 and in 1985-2000 respectively do not fall within the statistical by households on more expensive cars).

b) See footnote a) in Table 10. If the gasification of fuel (especially coal) destined for use in power stations were not carried out in power stations but in the vicinity of the extraction sites, the investments would work out much lower, particularly during the 1985-2000 period. But in that case the imported, ready-made gas would be more expensive so that the buyers would still be affected by a price-increasing effect caused by environmental measures (abroad).

c) . = insufficient data.

d) Minimum estimate; see Table 10, footnote e).

e) Facilities in (certain) dwelling houses, roads and noise sources (traffic industry, equipment). If standards are made more stringent the control of noise pollution can be expected to involve substantial costs.

f) The gross investments of the industrial sector (excl. houses and stocks) and of the government together amount to almost Fl. 29,000 mln. in 1973.

V.   SUMMING-UP

Reducing the most important part (in terms of costs) of the environmental pollution occurring in the reference year 1973 will require almost Fl. 12,000 mln. in investments in 1973 prices, whilst this will be accompanied by almost Fl. 2,500 mln. in annual (or current) costs - likewise in 1973 prices. When these "arrears" have been made up for, the annual costs, including those of the existing level of elimination, will work out at almost Fl. 3,000 mln. and the capital goods stock installed in the environmental sector will be worth as much as Fl. 15,000 mln. (both amounts in 1973 prices).

Making up for arrears, or "putting matters in order", will take time. In the meantime the (potential) environmental pollution would be increasing further. If measures are taken to counter this increase, the annual costs are likely to climb to approx. Fl. 5,000 mln. (1973 prices) in 1985 and approx. Fl. 8,000 mln. (1973 prices) in the year 2000. Both these amounts represent an estimated 2 % of the gross national product. The stock of capital goods for use in implementation of the control measures would then be valued at as much as Fl. 24,000 mln. in 1985 and about Fl. 38,000 mln. in 2000, both amounts in 1973 prices.

In the case of "programmes" or claims of this size, and particularly as regards assessing their feasibility, the implications of the basic assumptions should be emphasized once more.

Firstly, this involves the degree of overestimation of investments and annual costs which is inherent in certain assumptions. It is important in this context that no allowance has been made for improvements in anti-pollution technology. In fact, the basis used was the currently available control techniques most suited to the task in hand. A forecast of, or even an approximate hypothesis about, the amount of technological progress to be attained in the future cannot at present be reasonably substantiated. At least not for the entire environmental sector as considered in the foregoing. To judge by specific examples in this field, however, further technological improvement does seem likely. But it is impossible to derive from this an overall impression as to the probable rate of progress. The most that can be assumed, for instance, is that for each percent of annual technological progress about 6% fewer investments (in volume) would be needed for making up for the arrears over a 12-year period. Provided, at least, that this progress is capital-saving. However, the shorter the period of making up for arrears the less it is possible to benefit from this saving. If this period is 10 years, for example, the saving for each percent of annual progress would be over 5% of the investments required otherwise.

Secondly, a possible element of overestimation may be inherent in the assumption that the same environmental measures must be taken for existing and for new activities. Obviously, there will be a difference, apart from the odd exception. In particular the difference will be that facilities for new activities are cheaper to realize than those for existing activities. In view of the fact that the present chapter deals mainly - if not exclusively - with measures for existing traditional activities, this aspect is of especial importance for the possible overestimation of the environmental facilities which are geared to growth (Cf. section IV. 2). It may also be possible, though, that this aspect involves some overestimation of the investments and current costs needed for putting matters in order. This applies in cases where putting matters in order can also be realized via the replacement or accelerated replacement of capital goods which have become economically or technically obsolete. The longer the period needed for making up for arrears the greater the possible impact of this element of overestimation. Nevertheless, this aspect may also be of significance over the shorter term if accelerated replacement were to be enforced as a result of more stringent environmental requirements, at least if the resultant capital loss were disregarded. Lastly, some overestimation - but probably not to a very great extent - is inherent in a number of maximum hypotheses relating to cost trends. This involves in particular to removal of phosphates from waste water and the treatment of purified sludge and manure surpluses. The cost of facilities in these areas may turn out lower than expected.

Besides overestimation there is also some underestimation. In this context it must be emphasized - perhaps unnecessarily - that the "set" of anti-pollution activities dealt with in the present study is not complete (cf. the list in section 1.2.). A quite considerable number of conceivable anti-pollution measures were not considered (cf. the lists in section II. 1.).

Where this relates to the flow of pollution to be controlled, the existing accumulation of waste in the environment was also disregarded in some cases. Relevant measures aimed at the "restoration" of the environment may require large investments. Measures of this type are not considered in the foregoing.

Where measures are reviewed it should be noted that these solely involve facilities which result from the tighter control standards for the quality of the environment. Anti-pollution facilities already in existence in 1973 are not included in the "environmental sector" as defined in this study (see the key data in Table 4).

Underestimation of the costs of environmental measures seems possible if the 1973 pollution backlog is in fact cleared away during subsequent years within what in all probability will be a further expanding economy. An expansion which must also be "clean". And yet the assimilative capacity of the natural environment is constant in absolute terms. In practice this means that the purification efficiency of planned facilities will be subject to higher requirements than would have been the case without expansion. In its turn this means higher investments and higher current costs per unit of waste eliminated.

Apart from the implications of the assumptions as regards overestimation and underestimation, reference should be made lastly to the uncertainties which may affect the outlined development of the economic consequences of pollution control measures. In this context it should be pointed out that direct - and hence also indirect - effects of the environmental quality on economic variables such as labour productivity, the capital goods stock and the standard of medical and recreational facilities were disregarded in the calculations. Nor was any allowance made for a possible adverse effect in the event of the environmental quality standards being made more stringent than assumed in the relationships used in the model. It is conceivable - by way of example - that the factors in choice of location for foreign enterprises in (some regions of) the Netherlands may change in such a way that new activities and perhaps activities already established in our country will be directed abroad.

This latter is of course also dependent on the environmental policy abroad. More generally speaking, this is a second important element of uncertainty in the results discussed above. As already shown in the foregoing, an assumed intensification of the environmental policy abroad would have quite a considerable favourable effect on the economic consequences of such a policy in our country. More specific information is still unavailable.

Finally, the nature of the actual economic situation within which a more stringent environmental policy will be developed is likewise uncertain. Where such a situation deviates from the one assumed in the calculations, it would seem that, generally speaking, some gradation of interpretation would be appropriate. In particular, the question arises as to how the economic consequences of an environmental policy would have to be viewed in the light of the present-day situation (1974-75) which is characterized in particular by a high level of unemployment. Unemployment which for the main part is structural and for the rest has cyclical causes.

In answering this question it should be stated first and foremost that the present study reviews the economic consequences of an environmental policy over the long term. Emphasis is therefore placed on the reallocation of investments and manpower ultimately needed to create the pollution-control facilities. The hurdle that has to be overcome here is formed by the available investment funds and not by the manpower situation. The reallocation required for environmental purposes even implies fewer jobs and hence more unemployment. In view of the long-term nature of these changes, such higher unemployment should be classed as structural. In this context the economic consequences of an environmental policy do not need to be substantially amended on the basis of the divergent situation in 1974–75. Even now the latitude for new claims on the national income is extremely limited or even non-existent, whilst unemployment is relatively high. In accordance with the calculations in Chapter III, an environmental policy would contribute in this situation, too, towards more pressures as regards the allocation of the national income between consumption and investments (either private or public) and would ultimately bring little or no relief in the employment situation.

As regards the latter, the reservation should be made that the consequences of the more stringent environmental policy may differ initially from the situation ultimately being aimed at. It is in fact conceivable that the positive employment effects or more investments in the environmental sector will predominate at first and will subsequently be ousted by the negatice effects on employment arising from the "revision" of the production structure.

This revision will certainly create problems for individual enterprises. For instance, the anticipated costs of environmental facilities may, if broken down in a different way, have substantial repercussions for specific enterprises or even whole industrial sectors. This may be reflected in the disappearance not only of high-pollution sectors but also of enterprises which are unable to pass on the costs and which are also faced with a poor yields position. In principle, acceptance of these consequences will necessitate measures aimed at dealing as effectively as possible with the resultant problems in the social and regional spheres.

Annex V

INTRODUCTION

This study represents an updating and continuation of the work
done in previous years by Chase Econometrics for the Council on
Environmental Quality (CEQ) and the Environmental Protection Agency
(EPA) in assessing the macroeconomic impact of Federal environmental
programs.*   The analysis uses abatement cost estimates for the period
1970-1983 supplied by CEQ for air and water pollution abatement; these
figures are given in Table 1.   The estimates include capital investment,
annualized capital costs, and operating and maintenance costs for each
of the years in the period of analysis, and are disaggregated by two-
digit industry.   The cost estimates are consistent with the "incremental
abatement costs" estimates published in the CEQ 1975 annual report.

The analysis was performed using the Chase Econometrics macro-
economic and input/output models, which are linked together to allow
analysis of both the impacts that different industries have on one another
and on the interaction between pollution control expenditures and
general economic factors such as the rate of growth, inflation, unemployment, and financial markets.

Most of the analysis is based upon the CEQ estimated level and
timing of costs superimposed on a general cyclical economic scenario
taken from a recent Chase Econometrics ten-year forecast.   The
impacts of the pollution control expenditures are estimated by comparing
the economic forecasts including these expenditures (the "with" scenario)
with a forecast which is similar in every respect except that it excludes
such additional environmental expenditures (the "without" scenario). It
should be noted, however, that the inclusion of these expenditures involves several sets of adjustments to the model, which are discussed
in greater detail in the Methodology and Assumptions section.   Two
additional simulations were calculated, one using 125 % of CEQ's best
estimate of pollution control expenditures, and the other using CEQ's
estimate superimposed on a full-employment economic scenario.   These
alternative scenarios are also discussed later in this report.

---

*   The Economic Impacts of Meeting Exhaust Emission Standards, 1971-1980,
October 1971; The Economic Impact of Pollution Control Upon the General Economy,
October, 1972; The Economic Impact of Pollution Control: Macroeconomic and Industry
Reports, July, 1973; The Economic Impact of Pollution Control: Macroeconomic and
Industry Reports, March, 1975.

Two separate sets of simulations were performed in calculating the economic impact of pollution control expenditures for the period 1970-1983. We first determined what effect pollution control has already had over the period 1970-1975. This was done by comparing the actual values of economic variables with those that would have occurred in the absence of incremental pollution control expenditures. Thus these expenditures were subtracted from the historical data. For the period 1976-1983 estimated pollution control expenditures are added to the baseline forecasts. The results which are reported here are thus the sum of the effects which have already occurred from 1970 to 1975 plus those which are expected to occur from 1976 to 1983.

PRINCIPAL CONCLUSIONS

Impact on Inflation

Over the period 1970-1983, the wholesale price index will have risen 5.8 % more, the consumer price index will have risen 4.7% more, the consumer price index will have risen 4.7% more, and the implicit GNP deflator will have risen 3.6% more than would have been the case in the absence of pollution control expenditures. These correspond to an average annual rate of increase of 0.5% for the WPI, 0.4% for the CPI and 0.3% for the GNP deflator over this period.

The largest single-year increments occur in 1977, when the WPI rises 0.7% more, the CPI rises 0.7% more, and the GNP deflator 0.5% more because of pollution control expenditures. The increases are almost this large in 1975 and 1976; thus during the three-year peak period the WPI rises 1.9% more, the CPI rises 1.4% more, and the GNP deflator 0.8% more.

Impact on Economic Growth

The stimulus of increased expenditures on pollution control growth offsets the negative effects of higher inflation and lower productivity growth in the early years of the period, and is projected to raise the rate of economic growth above what it would have otherwise been through 1976. The maximum differential constant-dollar GNP is 0.2% higher with pollution control expenditures. In the latter half of the period, however, lower levels of pollution control investment combined with a higher rate of inflation lead to a slower rate of economic growth. By 1983 real GNP is projected to be 2.2% below the baseline forecast.

Impact on Unemployment

In keeping with the pattern of overall economic growth, the unemployment rate is estimated to be 0.4 % lower in 1976 and 0.5%

lower in 1977 than it otherwise would have been. However, it gradually rises to a level of 0.2% above the baseline forecast by 1983. The increase in unemployment is somewhat less than might be expected for the decline in real GNP because of the lower level of labor productivity.

Impact on Investment

The CEQ cost estimates indicate that incremental pollution control investment will reach a peak of approximately 3-1/2 percent of total private plant and equipment expenditures in 1977. Depending on such general economic factors as the rate of unemployment and interest rates, this investment is expected to result in somewhat lower levels of other types of plant and equipment expenditures. In general, the closer the economy is to operating at full employment, the greater the degree of substitution.

However, the rate of substitution is usually less than a dollar of other investment for every dollar of pollution control investment.* Most of this substitution does not occur from other business investment, but rather from residential construction, which is particularly sensitive to high interest rates and the availability of loanable funds. Even this impact depends upon the policies being pursued by government, and the simulations reported here included no adjustment in such policies to compensate for any adverse impacts on interest rates.

The simulations show the Aa corporate bond yield rising almost 12% (1.1 percentage points above the base line) in 1977, and, in response, housing starts dropping by over 20% the following year. By 1983 the with and without projections begin to converge so that interest rates are 1.0 percentage points higher, housing starts 13.5% lower and plant and equipment investment 0.8% higher under the projection including pollution control expenditures.

The analysis in this study is carried only through 1983, and the results provide little indication of what can be expected after that date. For instance, the difference between real GNP with and without environmental expenditures is widening during the latter years of these projections. However, if pollution abatement expenditures were to drop rapidly after 1984, we would also expect the "with" and "without" projections to begin to come together again. Under these conditions we would also expect little difference in unemployment, and the difference in the price indices to stabilize (but not diminish).

---

* The average rate of substitution, based on a number of simulations performed with the Chase Econometrics macro model under different assumptions about underlying economic conditions, is $0.40 reduction in all other private investment for every $1.00 in pollution control investment.

POLLUTION ABATEMENT COSTS

The cost estimates used in this analysis are consistent with the most recent CEQ estimates of "incremental abatement costs" published in its 1975 annual report. The CEQ defines "incremental" abatement costs as expenditures made to satisfy the requirements of Federal environmental legislation beyond what would have been spent for pollution control in the absense of this legislation.

The cost estimates, which are predominantly based upon cost estimates provided by EPA, the National Commission on Water Quality, and private sources, are summarized in Table 1.* Those figures were made available to Chase Econometrics for 16 industrial classifications, most of them at the two-digit level. These figures were given on an annual basis for the years 1970 to 1983 and were separated into expenditures for air pollution and water pollution abatement. The estimates included investment cost, annual operation and maintenance costs, and depreciation and interest charges. All figures were given in 1974 dollars. In addition, figures were supplied for the cost of meeting mobile source emission standards for automobiles, and municipal water pollution abatement.

In addition to the basic analysis using the cost estimates summarized in Table 1, two other sensitivity analyses were run. The first alternative scenario assumed that all costs were increased by 25% in order to estimate the likely macroeconomic impact if the CEQ estimates were significantly understated. The second alternative scenario used the unadjusted CEQ estimates for pollution control expenditures but these were superimposed on an economic setting with very rapid growth and a return to full employment by 1980.

METHODOLOGY AND ASSUMPTIONS

The baseline values for the overall economic scenario are taken from the Chase Econometrics long-term macroeconomic outlook. In this forecast we predict a continuation of the boom throughout mid-1977, and a decline in the rate of unemployment to 6 1/2 %. After that, the economy is plummeted into another recession in 1978 with the unemployment rate reaching a peak of 10 %. The economy begins a prolonged recovery in 1980 but the unemployment rate remains above 6% until 1983. The indicated growth rate for real GNP for the period 1976-1979 averages only 2.1% but rebounds to 5.3% for the period 1980-1983. The rate of inflation as measured by the consumer price index averages 6.2% from 1976 to 1979 and then declines to 5.2% from 1980 to 1983.

---

* See the appendix to Chapter 4 of CEQ's 1975 annual report for a further description of sources for cost estimates.

Table 1. ESTIMATED INCREMENTAL POLLUTION CONTROL EXPENDITURES, 1970-1983

	AIR POLLUTION ABATEMENT COSTS 1970-75		WATER POLLUTION ABATEMENT COSTS 1970-75		AIR POLLUTION ABATEMENT COSTS 1976-83		WATER POLLUTION ABATEMENT COSTS 1976-83	
	INVESTMENT	ANNUAL	INVESTMENT	ANNUAL	INVESTMENT	ANNUAL	INVESTMENT	ANNUAL
Food and Bevarages a)	0.19	0.15	0.54	0.55	0.33	0.89	0.54	1.77
Textiles	0	0	0.08	0.10	0	0	0.23	0.38
Pulp and Paper Products	0.87	0.45	0.59	0.46	1.11	4.25	4.10	3.48
Chemicals...........................	0.84	0.79	0.84	0.85	1.27	3.54	7.61	10.74
Petroleum b)	1.43	0.86	1.21	1.77	0.57	3.29	2.36	4.51
Rubber and Miscenalleous Plastic Products ...	0.10	0.09	0	0	0.25	0.64	0	0
Other nondurables	0.09	0.04	0.11	0.09	0.24	0.55	0.54	0.73
Stone, Clay and Glass	0.65	0.62	0.06	0.21	1.37	3.32	0.03	0.53
Iron and Steel	1.19	1.25	0.35	0.32	1.88	6.17	1.81	1.80
Primary Nonferrous Metals	1.83	1.42	0.17	0.12	1.25	6.67	-0.02	0.39
Machinery	0.42	0.53	0.69	0.21	0.69	2.20	8.19	4.59
Motor Vehicles	0.08	0.08	0	0	0.01	0.29	0	0
Other Transportation Equipment	0.06	0.09	0.31	0.25	0.06	0.28	0.80	1.57
Other Durables	0.72	0.81	0.35	0.28	1.08	3.27	1.20	1.97
Total Industrial	8.50	7.17	5.29	5.21	10.11	35.34	27.40	32.46
Electricity	4.75	3.35	2.20	1.00	11.03	28.95	2.53	7.49
Utilities	0.10	0.07	0	0	0.26	0.61	0	0
Other manufacturing	0.18	0.20	0.41	0.13	0.17	1.73	0.75	1.63
Total Fixed Source	13.53	10.79	7.91	6.35	21.56	66.63	30.69	41.58
Mobile Source emission controls	5.59	22.93	0	0	32.02	56.81	0	0

a. Include feedlots.

b. Includes mining.

All figures are in billions of 1974 dollars.

The definitions of investment and annual costs are given on page 3.

174

Other major factors of the baseline forecast include the assumption that the Federal government budgets will remain at pproximately the $ 70 billion deficit expected this year. The personal savings rate will average 7.7 % for the period, indicating it will remain near its present level. However, this does represent an increase from the postwar average of 6 1/2 %, due primarily to a higher average rate of inflation. New car sales are projected to be 10.6 million units in 1976, declining to 9.4 million in 1978, and then rising from that point to 12.7 million units in 1983. Housing starts will decline from their level of 1.5 million units this year to 1.0 million units in 1978 but will rebound to an average of 2 million units for the 1980-1983 period.

The alternative economic scenario is the so-called "Path A" taken from the Five Year Budget Projections prepared by the Congressional Budget Office. Under these assumptions, real GNP will grow 7.5% in 1976, 7 % in 1977 and 1978, and then a gradual decline to 3.8% in 1981 and later years. The unemployment rate is assumed to decline from 7.4 % in 1976 to 4.5 % in 1980 and later years. The rate of inflation, as measured by the implicit GNP deflator, remains at 6.6% over the forecast period, while the annual rate of increase in the CPI declines gradually from 7.2% in 1976 to 6.6% in 1980 and later years.

We now consider the major steps which were taken to enter the EPA pollution cost figures into the Chase Econometrics industry and macro models. It should be noted that the procedure described below is used for the 1976-1983 period. For the 1970-1975 period, the procedure was followed in reverse; i.e., "add" become "subtract" in the following summary.

1. Enter the estimated investment costs for each industry into the model as an addition to the year-by-year demand for plant and equipment investment. These adjustments have two effects: a) they are added directly to the investment functions in the model (see |7| below), and (b) they increase the asset base on which firms must earn the normal rate of return, hence resulting in higher prices.

2. Enter the annual operation and maintenance costs and interest costs on pollution control investments into the model as an increase in each industry's production costs.

3. Apply "markup" factors to the increase in production costs, including capital depreciation, interest charges, and operation and maintenance, to determine the increase in prices. The markup factors, which represent the proportion of increased costs passed along as higher prices, have already been calculated on an industry-by-industry basis in the Chase Econometrics industrial models. The markups in general range from 0.8 to 1.0. A markup factor of 1.0 indicates that the average firm in the industry will raise its prices by the same proportion as the increase in costs.

175

4. Calculate the effect which these price increases will have on all industries. The previous step calculates only the direct effect of pollution controls on prices; that is, the amount that the price of steel (e.g.) rises because the steel industry invests in pollution control plant and equipment. However, we must also consider the effects which an increase in steel will have on machinery, autos, and other steel-using industries. In other words, we must measure the indirect as well as the direct effects of the price increases in each industry.

5. Convert the price increases by final demand categories to price increases by aggregate demand categories. We use a reverse bridge matrix to go from the 40 categories of final demand to the aggregate demand components contained in the Chase Econometrics macro model.

6. Translate the price increases which come from the input-output table and the bridge matrix - as given in (5) above - into actual ex post price changes by using the markup factors at the macro level. Until this has been accomplished we do not yet know what changes in final product prices will be, since the cost increases may not be fully passed along. Thus we use the markup factors at the final demand level (consumption, investment, and exports) to determine what the price rise will be before taking into account interactive and dynamic factors. These markup factors range from 0.8 to 1.1.

7. Adjust for changes in fixed business investment due to, pollution control expenditures. Since more investment will be needed, the constant terms in the investment functions should be raised accordingly. However, we adjust rental cost of capital upward by the percentage of investment for pollution control because it will now take more investment to produce a given amount of output. Hence the required rate of return on investment for capacity expansion will have to increase to offset the zero financial return on the pollution control investments.

8. Labor productivity was adjusted downward through the exogenous variable in the model which measures the rate of technological progress. This downward adjustment offsets the increase in productivity which otherwise would occur from an increase in the capital stock.

9. The index of industrial production was increased to represent the manufacture of auto emission control devices.

10. The consumption of transportation services was increased because of higher operating and maintenance costs due to the catalytic converters and other pollution control devices.

11. Corporate profits were adjusted downward to take into account the added costs of pollution control. The existing profit functions would show an increase in profits if prices rose and unit labor costs, raw material prices, interest rates, output and capacity utilization all stayed at the same level.

A final round of price and output changes were then obtained by solving the complete Chase macroeconomic model, taking into account the interactive and dynamic factors.

OPERATION OF MODEL

We now consider the interactive and dynamic features of the macroeconomic model. The additional plant and equipment expenditures for pollution control will reduce the amount of investment in the private sector undertaken for other purposes. Part of this effect has already been included by raising the value of the rental cost of capital term.* However, several other factors need to be taken into account. First, an increase in nominal investment will place greater pressure on the capital markets, thus increasing interest rates and lowering other investment. Second, the increased investment demand will cause an increase in the costs of construction materials, labor, and equipment which results in some decline in constant dollar investment for a given level of output and financial variables. Third, a significant substitution exists between residential and nonresidential construction. This substitution works through changes in three variables: credit availability, the cost of construction, and the availability of labor. Since housing is more sensitive than other construction to all three of these variables, it suffers the greatest decline when other sectors of investment increase. The average elasticity of substitution between pollution control expenditures and other fixed investment is approximately 0.4 as has been mentioned. This value can reach even larger values during periods of overfull employment and stringent monetary policy, although it does not in these simulations.

It should be mentioned that a higher rate of inflation leads to a slower rate of growth in the economy for a number of other reasons.

---

* The rental cost of capital is defined as $\dfrac{P_K \ (r + \delta) \ (1 - uz - k)}{P_W \ (1 - u)}$ where

P_K	=	supply price of capital goods	z	=	depreciation factor
r	=	cost of borrowed funds	k	=	investment tax credit rate
δ	=	depreciation rate	P_W	=	wholesale price index
u	=	marginal statuatory tax rate			

The most important link: a rise in the rate of inflation increases the savings rate and hence reduces consumption. According to the permanent income hypothesis, the marginal propensity to consume is lower for variable incomes than it is for fixed incomes. Yet clearly inflation penalizes those on fixed incomes at the expense of those on variable incomes. During inflation the decline in consumption by those on fixed incomes is not nearly matched by the increase in consumption by those on variable incomes - even if we assume that income changes are the same - and thus the savings rate rises. This is one of the important endogenous relationships in the macro model, and works through the income distribution and relative price terms in the consumption function. In addition there is a relative decline in durable purchases which is not balanced by the slightly higher spending on services.

The other channels by which a rise in prices lower real output are more straight forward and require only brief commentary. First, for a given nominal money supply, higher prices must lead to a lower real money supply and hence an increase in interest rates unless there has been a specific offsetting shift in the liquidity preference function; this leads to the effects on investment which have already been discussed. Second, an increase in domestic prices for a given level of foreign prices leads to a deterioration in the net foreign balance in constant prices, although if the sum of the price elasticities of exports and imports is less than unity, the balance in nominal terms may increase. Third, a government budget which is fixed in current dollars buys fewer goods and services and generates less employment if prices increase. If the government attempts to retain its real purchasing power, it can do so only by creating additional money, which will in turn raise prices, or by borrowing additional funds, which will raise interest rates. We have chosen to assume that this latter route is operative, as indicated in our earlier discussion of constant adjustments.

All of these linkages reinforce the result that a rise in costs and prices will reduce aggregate demand and raise unemployment. As soon as this happens, however, secondary effects which act in the opposite direction begin to surface. A rise in unemployment will result in a lower level of wags increases in following years. Thus unit labor costs and prices will not rise as much for a given increase in productivity. In addition, the lower level of capacity utilization leads to lower markup factors. When these events begin to increase in importance, the rate of price increase starts to diminish. The decline in real GNP and employment, which was originally caused by higher prices, also begins to slacken. As this continues, prices and real GNP tend to return toward the level which would have occurred if the additional costs had not been added. Under a fairly wide variety of assumptions it is likely that the economy will eventually return to the level of output and employment which would have occurred in the absence of expenditures for pollution control, although prices will remain somewhat higher because of a lower level of productivity.

RESULTS OF ANALYSIS

Impact on Prices

The economic effects of pollution control expenditures are found
to be rather modest. By 1983 the implicit GNP deflator is only 3.6%,
the wholesale price index 5.8%, and the consumer price index 4.7%
above their respective baseline values. The biggest price effect occurs
in 1977, when the GNP deflator with pollution control costs rises 0.5%
more than in the baseline scenario. The difference in all other years
is much less. The wholesale price index rises an additional 0.9%
in 1976 and 0.7% in 1977 because of pollution control expenditures,
while the consumer price index rises an additional 0.7% in 1977.

The fact that some price increase does occur is no surprise, since
it is assumed that pollution control expenditures do not increase output
per unit of labor or capital. The increased aggregate demand caused
by the pollution control expenditures with no compensating increase in
aggregate production inevitably results in higher prices. The amount
of inflation will depend upon how much "slack" there is in the economy.
At "full employment," the price increases caused by the additional
demand would be greater than during a period of sluggish economic
growth or actual decline. Even with a sluggish economy, however,
there will be some price increase as firms pass on higher production
costs in the form of higher prices, and as resources are competed
away from other sectors to the production and installation of pollution
control equipment.

Impact on Economic Growth

There has been a considerable amount of disagreement about
whether pollution control expenditures on balance increase or diminish
the rate of real growth and employment. Some economists have argued
that the additional expenditures associated with pollution control investment will result in a higher growth rate and hence a higher level of
employment. Our results support this analysis for the most of the
period before 1977, although the pattern is mixed for the 1973-1976
period beacuse of the countervailing forces of greater investment and
higher inflation. However, the negative effect of inflation clearly
outweighs the positive effect of higher investment on real growth in 1977
and later years. This latter effect works through several different
channels, which have already been described in the previous section.

As a result, we have a somewhat variegated picture of an incremental pattern of real growth over the forecast period. During the
early years - 1970 though 1973 - real GNP is higher than the baseline
solution and hence unemployment is lower. The pattern is mixed in
1974, 1975, and 1976, but by 1978 and succeeding years the picture is

Table 2. ESTIMATED IMPACT OF POLLUTION CONTROL EXPENDITURES ON THE ECONOMY (1970-1983)

	1970	1971	1972	1973	1974	1975	1976	1977	1978	1979	1980	1981	1982	1983
Gross National Product, Current Dollars														
Without pollution control costs	979.4	1,060.2	1,168.4	1,304.8	1,405.1	1,495.2	1,683.5	1,875.7	2,002.0	2,118.4	2,346.6	2,629.2	2,904.3	3,186.1
With pollution control costs	981.4	1,063.2	1,173.8	1,312.1	1,413.9	1,505.8	1,703.7	1,897.7	2,022.0	2,142.7	2,373.8	2,660.4	2,939.2	3,226.6
% Difference	.20	.28	.46	.56	.63	.71	1.20	1.17	.99	1.15	1.16	1.19	1.20	1.27
Gross National Product, 1974 Dollars														
Without pollution control costs	1,254.1	1,292.0	1,367.7	1,442.2	1,416.3	1,387.4	1,479.3	1,550.3	1,559.1	1,573.9	1,660.4	1,766.8	1,855.6	1,934.3
With pollution control costs	1,256.0	1,293.4	1,369.9	1,443.1	1,414.8	1,384.4	1,480.6	1,543.0	1,543.1	1,555.7	1,636.9	1,736.9	1,819.0	1,892.4
% Difference	.15	.11	.16	.06	-.11	-.22	.09	.48	-1.03	-1.16	-1.42	-1.70	-1.97	-2.17
Implicit GNP Deflator, 1974 = 100														
Without pollution control costs	78.0	82.1	85.6	90.4	99.2	107.8	113.7	120.9	128.4	134.6	141.3	148.8	156.5	170.6
With pollution control costs	78.1	82.2	85.7	90.9	100.0	108.7	115.0	122.9	131.0	137.7	145.0	153.2	161.6	
% Difference	.13	.12	.12	.55	.81	.83	1.14	1.65	2.02	2.30	2.62	2.96	3.26	3.58
Consumer Price Index, 1974 = 100														
Without pollution control costs	78.6	81.8	84.4	89.5	99.2	108.0	115.6	123.9	132.4	138.6	145.7	153.2	161.1	169.9
With pollution control costs	78.6	82.0	84.7	90.0	100.0	109.3	117.4	126.7	136.0	143.0	151.0	159.4	168.3	177.9
% Difference	.00	.24	.36	.56	.81	1.20	1.56	2.26	2.72	3.17	3.64	4.05	4.47	4.71
Wholesale Price Index, 1974 = 100														
Without pollution control costs	71.3	63.8	76.2	81.2	99.0	109.9	118.8	129.4	141.3	149.6	160.9	170.9	180.9	191.5
With pollution control costs	71.4	74.1	76.6	81.8	100.0	111.5	121.5	133.2	146.1	155.5	168.1	179.3	190.6	202.6
% Difference	.14	.41	.52	.74	1.01	1.46	2.27	2.94	3.40	3.94	4.47	4.92	5.36	5.80
Unemployment Rate, Percent														
Without pollution control costs	5.2	6.2	5.8	4.9	5.7	8.5	7.2	6.8	8.3	9.9	8.7	7.0	6.1	5.5
With pollution control costs	5.1	6.1	5.6	4.7	5.5	8.4	6.8	6.3	8.1	9.7	8.6	7.0	6.2	5.7
% Difference	-1.92	-1.61	-3.45	-4.08	-3.51	-1.18	-7.35	-7.35	-2.41	-2.02	-1.15	.00	1.64	3.64
Fixed Investment in Producers Durable Equipment, 1974 Dollars														
Without pollution control costs	73.3	71.7	79.6	92.2	91.1	79.4	91.1	104.8	102.3	96.3	102.3	117.4	130.6	141.8
With pollution control costs	74.3	72.9	81.7	94.6	93.2	82.0	96.6	110.0	106.0	100.2	106.6	119.6	131.7	142.3
% Difference	1.36	1.67	2.64	2.60	2.31	3.27	6.04	4.96	3.62	4.05	3.19	1.87	.84	.35
Fixed Investment in Nonresidential Structures 1974 Dollars														
Without pollution control costs	53.6	51.5	52.3	56.0	52.8	45.8	49.9	54.2	57.2	55.8	55.3	64.6	73.6	79.1
With pollution control costs	54.4	52.7	53.7	57.5	53.9	46.8	52.4	57.1	60.8	57.5	56.8	66.0	74.8	80.4
% Difference	1.49	2.33	2.68	2.68	2.08	2.18	5.01	5.35	6.29	3.05	2.71	2.17	1.63	1.64
Housing Starts, Millions of Units:														
Without pollution control costs	1.44	2.07	2.39	2.06	1.34	1.17	1.51	1.41	1.04	1.43	2.09	1.91	1.75	1.78
With pollution control costs	1.43	2.04	2.36	2.02	1.28	1.09	1.41	1.14	.82	1.24	1.88	1.67	1.52	1.54
% Difference	-.69	-1.45	-1.26	-1.94	-4.48	-6.84	-6.62	-19.15	-21.15	-13.29	-10.05	-12.57	-13.14	-13.48
Percentage Growth Rate of GNP, 1974 dollars														
Without pollution control	-.7	3.0	5.9	5.5	-1.8	-2.0	6.5	4.8	.6	1.0	5.5	6.4	5.0	4.2
With pollution control costs	-.6	3.0	5.9	5.3	-2.0	-2.2	6.6	4.0	-.2	.6	5.0	5.9	4.5	3.8
% Difference	.1	.0	.0	-.2	-.2	-.2	.1	-.8	-.8	-.4	-.5	-.5	-.5	-.4
Percentage Growth Rate of CPI														
Without pollution control costs	5.9	4.1	3.1	6.0	10.8	8.9	6.1	7.2	6.8	4.7	5.1	5.1	5.2	5.4
With pollution control costs	6.0	4.3	3.3	6.3	11.1	9.2	6.8	8.3	7.8	5.5	5.9	5.9	5.9	6.1
% Difference	.1	.2	.2	.3	.3	.3	.7	1.1	1.0	.8	.8	.8	.7	.7

Table 2 (Cont'd)

	1970	1971	1972	1973	1974	1975	1976	1977	1978	1979	1980	1981	1982	1983
Trade Balance, 1974 Dollars														
Without pollution control costs	-11.1	-14.1	-19.6	-4.9	8.5	21.7	7.9	4.4	8.5	11.6	8.3	7.3	12.8	18.1
With pollution control costs	-11.4	-14.4	-20.0	-5.4	8.5	21.5	7.3	3.9	9.3	11.8	8.2	8.3	14.0	19.5
% Difference	-2.70	-2.13	-2.04	-10.20	.00	-.92	-7.59	-11.36	9.41	1.72	4.82	13.70	9.38	7.73
Consumption of Autos and Parts, 1974 Dollars														
Without pollution control costs	91.8	101.8	116.6	127.3	118.7	114.2	131.1	142.4	142.1	140.2	152.9	167.8	177.3	185.8
With pollution control costs	91.9	101.9	116.6	126.9	118.1	113.4	130.3	140.3	138.4	136.0	148.0	161.6	169.9	177.4
% Difference	.11	.10	.00	-.31	-.51	-.70	-.61	-1.47	-2.60	-3.00	-3.20	-3.69	-4.17	-4.52
Consumption of Other Durables, 1974 Dollars														
Without pollution control costs	59.7	61.9	69.2	75.8	75.5	73.8	78.7	85.3	87.0	86.7	92.1	99.7	105.7	111.3
With pollution control costs	59.7	61.9	69.2	75.6	74.1	73.3	77.1	84.0	85.0	84.2	89.1	96.1	101.4	106.4
% Difference	.00	.00	.00	-.26	-1.85	-.68	-2.03	-1.52	-2.30	-2.88	-3.26	-3.61	-4.07	-4.40
Consumption of Nondurables, 1974 Dollars														
Without pollution control costs	353.5	358.1	372.2	384.5	376.0	379.8	404.0	421.2	430.7	432.8	443.4	460.8	477.7	492.1
With pollution control costs	353.8	358.2	372.5	384.7	375.9	379.4	403.7	420.3	428.1	429.2	438.6	454.7	469.7	482.6
% Difference	.08	.06	.08	.05	-.03	-.11	-.07	-.21	-.60	-.83	-1.08	-1.32	-1.67	-1.93
Consumption of Services, 1974 Dollars														
Without pollution control costs	335.2	346.4	367.1	384.0	394.3	402.0	407.0	421.7	434.5	447.4	468.2	489.8	510.4	529.2
With pollution control costs	335.4	346.6	367.1	384.1	394.2	401.6	406.8	420.5	431.6	443.0	462.5	482.7	502.9	519.0
% Difference	.03	.06	.00	.03	-.03	-.10	-.05	-.28	-.67	-.98	-1.22	-1.45	-1.67	-1.93
Disposable Personal Income, Current Dollars														
Without pollution control costs	683.7	738.6	796.0	896.9	976.2	1,066.6	1,187.5	1,329.5	1,432.4	1,511.6	1,665.2	1,835.0	2,004.3	2,181.7
With pollution control costs	684.6	740.6	799.4	902.0	982.0	1,075.9	1,201.1	1,349.1	1,453.1	1,535.2	1,691.9	1,864.8	2,036.9	2,217.8
% Difference	.13	.27	.43	.57	.72	.87	1.15	1.47	1.45	1.56	1.60	1.62	1.63	1.65
Corporate Profits Before Taxes, Current Dollars														
Without pollution control costs	72.2	83.1	97.9	118.9	133.5	118.3	151.1	175.4	161.9	170.8	198.7	217.0	240.8	266.4
With pollution control costs	72.0	82.7	97.3	118.1	132.5	117.1	148.4	172.4	158.6	167.2	194.8	212.3	236.3	261.6
% Difference	-.28	-.48	-.61	-.67	-.75	-1.01	-1.79	-1.71	-2.04	-2.11	-1.96	-1.94	-1.87	-1.80
Corporate Profits After Taxes, Current Dollars														
Without pollution control costs	37.3	44.9	55.5	69.8	80.2	71.8	91.9	108.4	102.9	109.2	127.2	141.4	157.2	173.4
With pollution control costs	37.2	44.7	55.2	69.4	79.7	71.3	90.7	107.2	101.5	107.8	125.8	139.8	155.0	171.7
% Difference	-.27	-.45	-.54	-.57	-.62	-.70	-1.31	-1.11	-1.36	-1.28	-1.10	-1.13	-1.40	-.98
Aa Corporate Bond Rate for New Issues														
Without pollution control costs	8.75	7.51	7.19	7.46	8.99	8.95	9.13	10.15	9.82	8.06	7.51	7.78	8.11	8.66
With pollution control costs	8.81	7.68	7.40	7.73	9.39	9.44	9.90	11.25	10.97	9.18	8.64	8.86	9.15	9.70
% Difference	.69	2.26	2.92	3.62	4.45	5.47	8.43	10.84	11.71	13.90	15.05	13.88	12.82	12.01
Index of Industrial Production, 1974 = 100														
Without pollution control costs	84.4	84.4	91.3	100.2	99.4	89.2	100.9	110.5	109.4	106.9	114.2	126.3	135.9	143.6
With pollution control costs	85.2	84.8	92.0	101.1	100.0	89.8	102.5	111.7	109.5	107.1	114.0	125.5	134.2	141.5
% Difference	.35	.47	.77	.90	.60	.67	1.59	1.09	.09	.19	-.18	-.63	-1.25	-1.46

definitely reversed. First, less new investment is being added in
1978 and subsequent years. Second, the additional price increases
resulting from the environmental expenditures set in motion forces
that lead to a slower rate of real growth causing real GNP to be lower
and unemployment higher in the "with" solution in the years 1977
though 1983. The greatest decrement in real growth is reached in
1983, when the perturbed real GNP is 2.2% below the baseline solution.

Impact of Investment

Turning to the major components of investment, we find that
constant dollar purchases of producers durable goods are up 6.0% in
1976, but most of this increase represents investment in pollution
control equipment. Thereafter, a relative reduction in pollution
control expenditures occurs, and the difference between the with and
without solutions declines steadily to almost zero by the end of 1983.
Nonresidential construction is 5% higher in 1976 and 1977 and 6% higher
in 1978, but only 1.6% higher in 1982 and 1983. The declines are due
entirely to higher costs and a lower level of economic activity, since
total incremental pollution control investment remains positive throughout the decade.

Housing starts are hard hit and decline by an average of 7% in 1975
and 1976 and 20% in 1977 and 1978 when monetary stringency is greatest.
After that the difference narows but new starts remain 13% below the
baseline solution by 1983. The impact on housing, of course, depends
very much on the particular monetary and fiscal policies being pursued
by the Federal government. The government, for instance, could
take steps directly to aid the housing market. To determine the impact
of such a policy on prices and GNP growth, we calculated additional
simulation exercises in which we returned housing to its baseline level.
We found that stimulating the housing industry simply resulted in
reducing the amount of funds available to the remaining borrowing
sectors, particularly fixed business investment, and hence had relatively little short-run effect on the overall macroeconomic picture.

Impact on Foreign Trade

The foreign trade balance in constant dollars declines slightly
through 1977 relative to the baseline projection. This decline is
caused by the combination of higher prices and a higher level of
economic activity. However, starting in 1978, the trade balance in
constant dollars improves marginally, as the lower level of income
depresses imports more than the higher level of domestic prices
depresses exports.

Other Economic Impacts

The major components of consumption follow the pattern which
might be expected. Beginning in 1973, auto sales are negatively

affected because of the mobile source emission controls, and decline by a peak amount of 4.5% in 1983; this corresponds to about 600,000 cars. The change in auto sales is due to a combination of factors which include changes in relative prices, disposable income, the rate of unemployment, and credit conditions. Gasoline prices are explicitly included in the new car equation, but other operations and maintenance costs are not considered as a separate variable.

Disposable personal income (DPI) in current dollars is slightly above the baseline solution in all years. In constant dollars, it follows the general pattern of other aggregate economic variables; it is higher through 1973, about the same for 1974 and then is lower for the remaining period. The actual changes in constant dollars can be calculated by substracting the percentage changes in the CPI from the percentage changes in DPI. Corporate profits remain below baseline levels in all years. This is partially caused by our assumption that only 90% of the increased costs of pollution controls are passed along in the form of higher prices. No measure for "constant dollar" corporate profits is given, since this term is not easily defined.

In the financial markets, the Aa corporate bond rate for new issues is higher than the baseline solution throughout the simulation period. It is greater by 0.8% (or an 8.4% increase) in 1976; the difference continues to widen to 1978, where the gap is a full 1.1% (or an 11.7% increase). After that it diminishes slightly but still remains 1.0% higher (or a 12% increase) by 1983. Finally, the index of industrial production follows much the same pattern as constant-dollar GNP, with the peak positive difference of 1.6% being recorded in 1976 and the peak negative difference of 1.5% occuring in 1983. The projected levels and differences in interest rates depend, of course, upon monetary policy.

Industry Effects

The effects of pollution control expenditures on 31 major industries are given in Table 2, which shows the percentage changes for prices, out-put, and employment between the baseline forecast and the simulation with pollution control expenditures. These differences are shown for both 1978 and 1983.

As would be expected, the largest increases in prices occur in those industries which are most directly affected by pollution controls - utilities, nonferrous metals, paper, autos, iron and steel, stone, clay and glass, chemicals, and petroleum. However, it is also interesting to note that all 31 industries show some increase in prices, even those which are not directly affected to any substantial degree by pollution control expenditures. The increases in 1983 are larger than those in 1978 for all industries. It should be noted that all of these figures are cumulative from 1970; in order to get the average annual rate of price increase, the figures in the 1978 column should be divided by 8 and those in the 1983 column by 13.

All industries show a decline in output in 1978 relative to the baseline forecast except for nonelectrical machinery, which represents the increase in purchases of pollution control equipment. By 1983 even this sector is below the "without" case because of the lower overall growth. The employment figures follow the same general pattern of fluctuation on an industry basis, but they do not decline as much because the slower growth in productive capital spending leads to a smaller increase in productivity.

The price increase for new cars includes the effect of mobile source emission standards as well as the stationary source standards considered elsewhere in this study. In 1976 the pollution control standards have raised the average price of a new car by $270. Of this amount, $190 represents mobile source emissions, $20 represents direct costs to the automobile industry for their own plant and equipment expenditures, and $60 represents the higher costs of purchased materials, mainly metals.

Sensitivity Analyses

We now consider the results of two alternative simulation analyses which tested changes in the underlying assumptions about the condition of the economy and the level of pollution abatement expenditures. First, we summarize the changes that occur when we superimpose the expected levels of pollution control costs on the "full employment" baseline. This scenario is the "Path A" baseline given in the Five-Year Budget Projections, Fiscal Years 1977-81 prepared by the Congressional Budget Office. The results are presented in Table 4. As would be expected under this scenario, the price increases are slightly larger although the differences are modest. For example, by 1983 we find that the wholesale price index has increased by an additional 7% (6.2% over the without projection), the implicit GNP deflator by another 11% (4.0% over the without projection), and the GPI by an extra 13% (5.3% over the without projection) over the Chase cyclical economic scenario used in the earlier analyses. The decline in real GNP in 1983 is only 5% larger (2.3% less than the without projection). The increase in producers durable equipment and non residential construction and the decline in housing starts all follow the same pattern which occured in the standard simulation.

The second sensitivity analysis, summarized in Table 5, involved increasing all costs by 25% in order to test the impacts which could be expected in case the EPA/CEQ estimates were seriously understated.* This analysis showed the WPI, the implicit GNP deflator, and the CPI all rising by approximately 25% more. The decline in real GNP by

---

* In this analysis the historic as well as the projected cost estimates were increased by 25% although the historic numbers are based primarily on actual surveys of expenditures undertaken by the Bureau of Economic Analysis.

Table 3. ESTIMATED IMPACTS ON INDIVIDUAL INDUSTRIES

INDUSTRY	BY 1978			BY 1983		
	Prices	Output	Employment	Prices	Output	Employment
Agriculture	0.3	-0.8	+0.6	0.6	-1.3	+1.3
Mining	0.4	-1.2	-0.1	0.7	-2.5	-0.4
Construction	0.1	-2.1	-0.4	0.2	-3.5	-0.2
Food	0.7	-0.5	+0.7	1.2	-1.5	+1.2
Tobacco	0.2	-1.0	+0.6	0.4	-2.7	+0.9
Textiles	0.5	-1.4	-0.1	0.9	-2.5	-0.2
Apparel	0.3	-1.2	-0.2	0.5	-2.2	-0.6
Lumber	0.6	-4.4	-1.3	1.5	-4.4	-0.6
Furniture	0.3	-1.5	-0.7	0.5	-3.1	-1.3
Paper	3.0	-1.3	-0.2	6.2	-2.9	-1.0
Printing	0.2	-1.2	-0.1	0.3	-3.1	-1.3
Chemicals	1.7	-1.2	-0.3	4.8	-2.8	-1.1
Petroleum	1.6	-1.0	+0.4	2.3	-2.0	+0.7
Rubber	0.6	-1.6	-0.5	1.0	-4.2	-1.4
Leather	0.4	-0.8	0.0	0.9	-1.4	-0.3
Stone, Clay and Glass	2.0	-2.0	-0.7	3.2	-3.4	-1.0
Iron and Steel	2.3	-1.4	-0.2	4.1	-2.9	-0.3
Nonferrous Metals	5.4	-0.7	+0.4	8.1	-2.4	+0.3
Fabricated Metals	0.4	-1.2	0.0	0.8	-3.1	-0.6
Nonelectrical Machinery	1.0	+0.2	+1.1	2.8	-1.6	+0.3
Electrical Machinery	0.5	-1.4	-0.3	1.2	-3.5	-1.0
Autos	2.5	-2.1	-0.5	5.5	-5.6	-2.4
Other Trans. Eqpt	0.3	-1.0	+0.2	0.6	-0.9	+0.8
Instruments	0.2	-0.7	+0.4	0.4	-2.7	-0.4
Miscellaneous Manufacturing	0.2	-0.9	+0.3	0.4	-1.7	-0.7
Transportation Services	0.3	-1.1	+0.4	0.5	-2.7	+0.5
Communications	0.2	-1.2	-0.1	0.4	-4.0	-1.5
Utilities	15.2	-0.7	+0.5	27.8	-1.8	+0.6
Trade	0.3	-1.0	+0.2	0.6	-2.7	-0.8
Finance, Insurance and Real Estate	0.5	-0.8	+0.1	0.8	-2.4	-1.0
Other Services	0.4	-1.1	+0.8	0.7	-2.6	+1.6

Table 4. SENSITIVITY ANALYSIS FOR FULL EMPLOYMENT ECONOMIC SCENARIO

	1976	1977	1978	1979	1980	1981	1982	1983
Gross National Product, Current Dollars								
Without pollution control costs	1,717.8	1,958.3	2,238.6	2,522.7	2,809.4	3,110.1	3,430.3	3,781.5
With pollution control costs	1,738.4	1,979.9	2,263.1	2,554.7	2,848.4	3,154.0	3,482.6	3,840.0
% Difference	1.20	1.10	1.09	1.27	1.39	1.41	1.52	1.55
Gross National Product, 1974 Dollars								
Without pollution control costs	1,492.3	1,595.1	1,708.6	1,805.6	1,892.5	1,970.4	2,045.0	2,121.1
With pollution control costs	1,493.9	1,586.7	1,692.7	1,784.6	1,865.8	1,936.1	2,005.1	2,072.9
% Difference	.11	-.53	-.93	-1.16	-1.41	-1.74	-1.95	-2.27
Implicit GNP Deflator, 1974 = 100								
Without pollution control costs	115.0	122.7	131.0	139.7	148.4	157.8	167.7	178.2
With pollution control costs	116.3	124.7	133.7	143.2	152.7	162.9	173.8	185.4
% Difference	1.13	1.63	2.06	2.51	2.90	3.23	3.64	4.04
Consumer Price Index, 1974 = 100								
Without pollution control costs	116.8	125.0	133.1	141.6	150.9	160.9	171.8	183.5
With pollution control costs	118.6	127.9	136.8	146.4	156.7	168.0	180.0	193.3
% Difference	1.54	2.32	2.78	3.39	3.84	4.41	4.77	5.34
Wholesale Price Index, 1974 = 100								
Without pollution control costs	119.6	131.0	143.0	150.8	159.4	169.1	179.3	190.2
With pollution control costs	122.4	134.9	148.1	157.1	166.8	178.0	189.6	202.0
% Difference	2.34	2.98	3.57	4.18	4.64	5.26	5.74	6.20
Unemployment Rate, Percent								
Without pollution control costs	7.3	6.3	5.5	4.7	4.4	4.2	4.5	4.4
With pollution control costs	6.9	5.8	5.3	4.6	4.3	4.2	4.4	4.6
% Difference	-5.48	-7.94	-3.64	-2.13	-2.27	.00	-2.22	-4.55
Fixed Investment in Producers Durable Equipment, 1974 Dollars								
Without pollution control costs	96.5	113.8	130.5	144.8	154.3	162.4	174.4	185.1
With pollution control costs	102.0	119.5	134.1	148.5	157.5	164.6	175.3	185.5
% Difference	5.70	5.01	2.76	2.56	2.07	1.35	.52	.22
Fixed Investment in Nonresidential Structures, 1974 Dollars								
Without pollution control costs	50.6	55.0	63.0	73.2	77.4	82.2	86.6	89.9
With pollution control costs	53.0	57.9	66.3	74.6	78.6	82.9	86.7	90.0
% Difference	4.74	5.27	5.24	1.91	1.55	.85	.12	.11
Housing Starts, Millions of Units								
Without pollution control costs	1.58	2.06	2.12	2.19	2.25	2.10	1.90	1.86
With pollution control costs	1.48	1.78	1.87	1.98	2.01	1.84	1.62	1.55
% Difference	-6.33	-13.59	-11.79	-9.59	-10.67	-12.38	-14.74	-16.65
Percentage Growth Rate of GNP, 1974 Dollars								
Without pollution control costs	7.4	6.9	7.1	5.7	4.8	4.1	3.8	3.7
With pollution control costs	7.6	6.0	6.5	5.2	4.3	3.6	3.4	3.2
% Difference	.2	-.9	-.6	-.5	-.5	-.5	-.4	-.5
Percentage Growth Rate of CPI								
Without pollution control costs	7.2	7.0	6.5	6.4	6.5	6.7	6.7	6.9
With pollution control costs	8.0	8.2	7.4	7.3	7.4	7.5	7.5	7.7
% Difference	.3	1.2	.9	.9	.9	.8	.8	.8

Table 4   (Cont'd)

	1976	1977	1978	1979	1980	1981	1982	1983
Trade Balance, 1974 Dollars								
Without pollution control costs	8.4	4.2	5.5	5.7	8.1	10.7	13.5	16.0
With pollution control costs	9.6	3.9	6.3	6.2	8.6	12.1	14.8	17.8
% Difference	14.29	-7.14	14.55	8.77	6.17	13.08	9.63	11.25
Consumption of Autos and Parts 1974 Dollars								
Without pollution control costs	130.0	144.8	162.9	173.2	185.6	196.4	205.3	215.4
With pollution control costs	129.4	142.7	159.0	168.6	180.1	189.9	197.8	206.1
% Difference	-.46	-1.45	-2.39	-2.66	-2.96	-3.31	-3.65	-4.32
Consumption of Other Durables, 1974 Dollars								
Without pollution control costs	77.5	84.5	92.7	100.6	110.1	118.5	125.5	132.5
With pollution control costs	76.9	83.3	90.6	97.8	106.8	114.5	120.8	127.1
% Difference	-.77	-1.42	-2.27	-2.78	-3.00	-3.38	-3.75	-4.08
Consumption of Nondurables, 1974 Dollars								
Without pollution control costs	401.0	420.7	442.0	462.5	486.4	502.8	515.6	528.5
With pollution control costs	400.6	419.4	439.2	458.6	481.3	495.8	506.9	518.2
% Difference	-.10	-.31	-.63	-.84	-1.05	-1.39	-1.69	-1.95
Consumption of Services, 1974 Dollars								
Without pollution control costs	413.2	439.3	465.0	494.3	523.4	552.6	578.6	601.6
With pollution control costs	413.0	438.1	462.1	490.0	517.6	545.3	569.7	590.1
% Difference	-.05	-.27	-.62	-.87	-1.11	-1.32	-1.54	-1.91
Disposable Personal Income, Current Dollars								
Without pollution control costs	1,196.0	1,346.2	1,500.9	1,667.8	1,866.8	2,058.1	2,257.0	2,484.9
With pollution control costs	1,209.9	1,365.8	1,523.4	1,695.5	1,900.1	2,096.1	2,300.9	2,537.2
% Difference	1.16	1.46	1.50	1.66	1.78	1.85	1.95	2.10
Corporate Profits Before Taxes, Current Dollars								
Without pollution control costs	161.8	200.6	229.1	263.0	288.0	309.5	332.9	359.1
With pollution control costs	159.5	197.4	226.4	259.3	284.1	306.9	330.7	356.4
% Difference	-1.42	-1.60	-1.18	-1.41	-1.35	-.84	-.66	-.75
Corporate Profits After Taxes, Current Dollars								
Without pollution control costs	98.2	123.2	142.5	165.7	183.6	199.9	215.8	232.6
With pollution control costs	97.4	121.9	142.0	164.3	182.4	199.7	215.8	232.6
% Difference	-.81	-1.06	-.35	-.84	-.65	-.10	.00	.00
Aa Corporate Bond Rate for New Issues								
Without pollution control costs	9.08	9.69	9.58	9.72	9.92	9.69	9.89	10.30
With pollution control costs	9.85	10.81	10.77	10.95	11.20	10.94	11.13	11.68
% Difference	8.48	11.56	12.42	12.65	12.90	12.90	12.54	13.40
Index of Industrial Production, 1974 = 100								
Without pollution control costs	102.5	114.8	126.3	136.6	144.8	151.7	159.1	166.2
With pollution control costs	104.2	116.0	126.5	136.7	144.4	150.4	157.4	163.8
% Difference	1.66	1.05	.24	.07	-.28	-.86	-1.07	-1.44

187

Table 5.   SENSITIVITY ANALYSIS FOR 25% INCREASE IN POLLUTION CONTROL COST ESTIMATES

	1970	1971	1972	1973	1974	1975	1976	1977	1978	1979	1980	1981	1982	1983
Gross National Product, Current Dollars														
Without pollution control costs	978.9	1,059.4	1,167.1	1,303.0	1,403.0	1,492.4	1,683.5	1,875.7	2,002.2	2,118.4	2,346.6	2,629.2	2,904.3	3,186.1
With pollution control costs	981.4	1,063.2	1,173.8	1,312.1	1,413.9	1,505.8	1,708.9	1,902.6	2,026.6	2,149.4	2,381.5	2,669.2	2,948.8	3,237.6
% Difference	.26	.36	.57	.70	.78	.90	1.51	1.43	1.22	1.46	1.49	1.52	1.53	1.62
Gross National Product, 1974 Dollars														
Without pollution control costs	1,253.7	1,291.5	1,367.1	1,442.0	1,416.6	1,387.8	1,479.3	1,550.5	1,559.1	1,573.9	1,660.4	1,766.8	1,855.6	1,934.3
With pollution control costs	1,256.0	1,293.4	1,369.9	1,443.1	1,414.8	1,384.4	1,481.3	1,541.4	1,539.2	1,551.8	1,631.7	1,729.9	1,810.4	1,882.4
% Difference	.18	.15	.20	.08	-.13	-.24	-.14	-.59	-1.28	-1.40	-1.73	-2.09	-2.44	-2.68
Implicit GNP Deflator, 1974 = 100														
Without pollution control costs	78.0	82.0	85.4	90.4	99.1	107.5	113.7	120.9	128.4	134.6	141.3	148.8	156.5	164.7
With pollution control costs	78.1	82.2	85.7	90.9	100.0	108.7	115.4	123.5	131.7	138.5	146.0	154.4	163.0	172.2
% Difference	.13	.24	.35	.55	.91	1.12	1.50	2.15	2.57	2.90	3.33	3.76	4.15	4.55
Consumer Price Index, 1974 = 100														
Without pollution control costs	78.6	81.8	84.3	89.4	99.0	107.7	115.6	123.9	132.4	138.6	145.7	153.2	161.1	169.9
With pollution control costs	78.6	82.0	84.7	90.0	100.0	109.3	117.7	127.3	136.9	144.0	152.3	160.9	170.1	180.0
% Difference	.00	.24	.47	.67	1.01	1.49	1.82	2.74	3.40	3.90	4.53	5.03	5.59	5.94
Wholesale Price Index, 1974 = 100														
Without pollution control costs	71.3	73.8	76.1	81.1	98.7	109.6	118.8	129.4	141.3	149.6	160.9	170.9	180.9	191.5
With pollution control costs	71.4	74.1	76.6	81.8	100.0	111.5	122.1	134.1	147.2	156.9	169.7	181.4	192.9	205.3
% Difference	.14	.41	.66	.86	1.32	1.73	2.78	3.63	4.18	4.88	5.47	6.14	6.63	7.21
Unemployment Rate, Percent														
Without pollution control costs	5.2	6.3	5.8	5.0	5.7	8.6	7.2	6.8	8.3	9.9	8.7	7.0	6.1	5.5
With pollution control costs	5.1	6.1	5.6	4.7	5.5	8.4	6.6	6.1	8.0	9.6	8.5	6.9	6.1	5.6
% Difference	-1.92	-3.17	-3.45	-6.00	-3.51	-2.33	-8.33	-10.29	-3.61	-3.03	-2.30	-1.43	.00	1.82
Fixed Investment in Producers Durable Equipment, 1974 Dollars														
Without pollution control costs	73.1	71.5	79.0	91.6	90.6	78.8	91.1	104.8	102.3	96.3	103.3	117.4	130.6	141.8
With pollution control costs	74.3	72.9	81.7	94.6	93.2	82.0	97.9	111.1	106.9	101.1	107.5	120.2	131.8	142.5
% Difference	1.64	1.96	3.42	3.28	2.87	4.06	7.46	6.01	4.50	4.98	4.07	2.39	.92	.49
Fixed Investment in Nonresidential Structures, 1974 Dollars														
Without pollution control costs	53.3	51.3	51.9	55.6	52.5	45.5	49.9	54.2	57.2	55.8	55.3	64.6	73.6	79.1
With pollution control costs	54.4	52.7	53.7	57.5	53.9	46.8	52.9	57.9	61.7	58.0	57.3	66.3	75.1	80.9
% Difference	2.06	2.73	3.47	3.42	2.67	2.86	6.01	6.83	7.87	3.94	3.62	2.63	2.04	2.28
Housing Starts, Millions of Units														
Without pollution control costs	1.44	2.08	2.39	2.07	1.35	1.18	1.51	1.41	1.04	1.43	2.09	1.91	1.75	1.78
With pollution control costs	1.43	2.04	2.36	2.02	1.28	1.09	1.39	1.08	.78	1.21	1.83	1.63	1.47	1.48
% Difference	-.69	-1.92	-1.26	-2.42	-5.19	-7.63	-7.95	-23.40	-25.00	-15.38	-12.44	-14.66	-16.00	-16.85
Growth Rate of GNP, 1974 Dollars Percentage														
Without pollution control costs	-.8	3.0	5.9	5.5	-1.8	-2.0	6.5	4.8	.6	1.0	5.5	6.4	5.0	4.2
With pollution control costs	-.6	3.0	5.9	5.3	-2.0	-2.2	6.7	3.8	-.3	.6	4.9	5.8	4.4	3.8
% Difference	.2	.0	.0	-.2	-.2	-.2	-.2	-1.0	-.9	-.4	-.6	-.6	-.6	-.4

Table 5 (Cont'd)

	1970	1971	1972	1973	1974	1975	1976	1977	1978	1979	1980	1981	1982	1983
Percentage Growth Rate of CPI														
Without pollution control costs	5.9	4.1	3.1	6.0	10.7	8.8	6.1	7.2	6.8	4.7	5.1	5.1	5.2	5.4
With pollution control costs	6.0	4.3	3.3	6.3	11.1	9.2	7.0	8.6	8.0	5.7	6.2	6.2	6.1	6.3
% Difference	.1	.2	.2	.3	.4	.4	.9	1.4	1.2	1.0	1.1	1.1	.9	.9
Trade Balance, 1974 Dollars														
Without pollution control costs	-11.1	-14.1	-19.6	-4.9	8.5	21.7	7.9	4.4	8.5	11.6	8.3	7.3	12.8	18.1
With pollution control costs	-11.4	-14.4	-20.0	-5.4	8.5	21.5	7.2	3.9	9.4	11.8	8.8	8.6	14.3	20.0
% Difference	-2.70	-2.13	-2.04	-10.20	.00	-.92	-8.86	-11.36	10.59	1.72	6.02	17.81	11.72	10.50
Consumption of Autos and Parts, 1974 Dollars														
Without pollution control costs	91.8	101.8	116.6	127.3	118.8	114.4	131.1	142.4	142.1	140.2	152.9	167.8	177.3	185.8
With pollution control costs	91.9	101.9	116.6	126.9	118.1	113.4	130.0	139.8	137.4	135.0	146.7	160.1	168.2	175.4
% Difference	.11	.10	.00	-.31	-.59	-.87	-.84	-1.83	-3.31	-3.71	-4.05	-4.59	-5.13	-5.60
Consumption of Other Durables, 1974 Dollars														
Without pollution control costs	59.7	61.9	69.3	75.9	75.6	73.8	78.7	85.3	87.0	86.7	92.1	99.7	105.7	111.3
With pollution control costs	59.7	61.9	69.2	75.6	74.1	73.3	78.0	83.7	84.6	83.7	88.6	95.3	100.6	105.4
% Difference	.00	.00	-.14	-.40	-1.98	-.68	-.89	-1.88	-2.76	-3.46	-3.80	-4.41	-4.82	-5.30
Consumption of Nondurables, 1974 Dollars														
Without pollution control costs	353.5	357.9	372.2	384.5	376.1	379.9	404.0	421.2	430.7	432.8	443.4	460.8	477.7	492.1
With pollution control costs	353.8	358.3	372.5	384.7	375.9	379.4	403.6	419.9	427.3	428.3	437.4	453.1	467.7	480.2
% Difference	.08	.11	.08	.05	-.05	-.13	-.10	-.31	-.79	-1.04	-1.35	-1.67	-2.09	-2.42
Consumption of Services, 1974 Dollars														
Without pollution control costs	335.3	346.4	367.0	384.0	394.3	402.1	407.0	421.7	434.5	447.4	468.2	489.8	510.4	529.2
With pollution control costs	335.4	346.6	367.1	384.1	394.2	401.6	406.7	420.3	430.9	441.8	461.1	481.2	500.0	516.6
% Difference	.03	.06	.03	.03	-.03	-.12	-.07	-.33	-.83	-1.25	-1.52	-1.76	-2.04	-2.38
Disposable Personal Income, Current Dollars														
Without pollution control costs	683.5	738.1	795.2	895.7	974.7	1,064.4	1,187.5	1,329.5	1,432.4	1,511.6	1,665.2	1,835.0	2,004.3	2,181.7
With pollution control costs	684.6	740.6	799.4	902.0	983.2	1,075.9	1,204.7	1,353.8	1,458.0	1,541.2	1,698.8	1,872.5	2,045.4	2,227.1
% Difference	.16	.34	.53	.70	.87	1.08	1.45	1.83	1.79	1.96	2.02	2.04	2.05	2.08
Corporate Profits Before Taxes, Current Dollars														
Without pollution control costs	72.2	83.2	98.0	119.1	133.7	118.5	151.1	175.4	161.9	170.8	198.7	217.0	240.8	266.4
With pollution control costs	72.0	82.7	97.3	118.1	132.5	117.1	147.8	171.6	157.9	166.7	194.1	212.0	235.3	260.6
% Difference	-.28	-.60	-.71	-.84	-.90	-1.18	-2.18	-2.17	-2.47	-2.40	-2.32	-2.30	-2.28	-2.18
Corporate Profits After Taxes, Current Dollars														
Without pollution control costs	37.3	44.9	55.5	69.8	80.2	71.8	91.9	108.4	102.9	109.2	127.2	141.4	157.2	173.4
With pollution control costs	37.2	44.7	55.2	69.4	79.7	71.3	90.5	107.1	101.2	107.7	125.6	139.7	155.2	171.5
% Difference	-.27	-.45	-.54	-.57	-.62	-.70	-1.52	-1.20	-1.65	-1.37	-1.26	-1.20	-1.27	-1.10
Aa Corporate Bond Rate for New Issues														
Without pollution control costs	8.74	7.47	7.14	7.40	8.91	8.83	9.13	10.15	9.82	8.06	7.51	7.78	8.11	8.66
With pollution control costs	8.81	7.68	7.40	7.73	9.39	9.44	10.09	11.52	11.25	9.48	8.93	9.14	9.41	9.96
% Difference	.80	2.81	3.64	4.46	5.39	6.91	10.51	13.50	14.56	17.62	18.91	17.48	16.03	15.01
Index of Industrial Production, 1974 = 100														
Without pollution control costs	84.8	84.3	91.1	100.0	99.4	89.0	100.9	110.5	109.4	106.9	114.2	126.3	135.9	143.6
With pollution control costs	85.2	84.8	92.0	101.1	100.0	89.8	103.1	112.1	109.6	107.2	114.1	125.3	133.9	141.0
% Difference	.47	.59	.99	1.10	.60	.90	2.18	1.45	.18	.28	-.09	-.79	-1.47	-1.81

REAL GROSS NATIONAL PRODUCT (CONSTANT $ 1974)

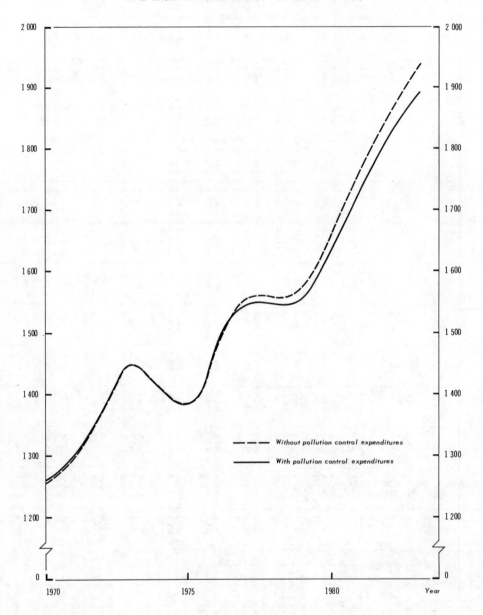

Without pollution control expenditures

With pollution control expenditures

Aa CORPORATE BOND RATE FOR NEW ISSUES

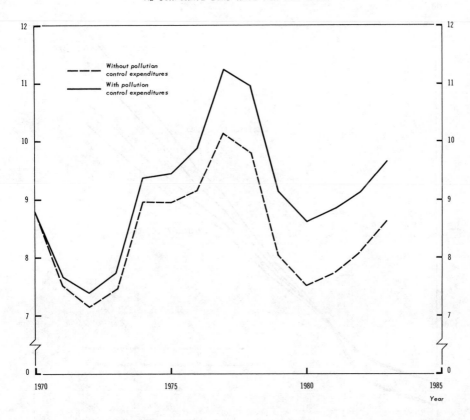

PRICE INDEX (1974 = 100)

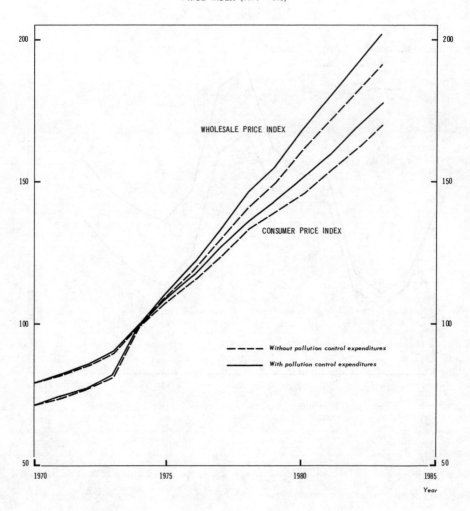

UNEMPLOYMENT RATE, %

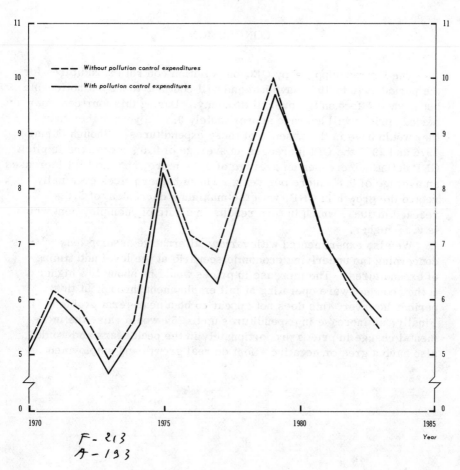

F- 213
A - 193

1983 is - 2.7%, compared to -2.3% in the standard simulation. In general the changes tend to be proportional; at the level of pollution control expenditures contained in this study, an additional 25% is not sufficient to produce additional nonlinearities.

CONCLUSION

The figures supplied by CEQ on pollution control expenditures for the period 1970 to 1983 have had and will continue to have a noticeable but modest effect on the overall economy. During this fourteen-year period, prices will average approximately 0.4% a year higher than they would have in the absence of these expenditures, although during 1976 and 1977 the CPI increases an average of 0.6% more, the implicit GNP deflator increases an average of 0.5% more, and the WPI increases an average of 0.8% more per year. These higher prices eventually retard the growth in GNP, with the maximum decrement of 2.2% reached in 1983, which in turn results in a rate of unemployment which is 0.2% higher.

We also experimented with various alternative assumptions concerning the underlying economic scenario at the level and timing of expenditures. The increase in prices would be about 10% higher if the economy were operating at full employment throughout this period; however, this does not appear to be a near-term problem. Finally, an increase in expenditures up to 25% would raise the incremental change in prices proportionately in the peak years and would also have a greater negative effect on real growth and employment.

OECD SALES AGENTS
DÉPOSITAIRES DES PUBLICATIONS DE L'OCDE

ARGENTINA – ARGENTINE
Carlos Hirsch S.R.L., Florida 165,
BUENOS-AIRES, ☎33-1787-2391 Y 30-7122

AUSTRALIA – AUSTRALIE
International B.C.N. Library Suppliers Pty Ltd.,
161 Sturt St., South MELBOURNE, Vic. 3205. ☎699-6388
658 Pittwater Road, BROOKVALE NSW 2100. ☎ 938 2267

AUSTRIA – AUTRICHE
Gerold and Co., Graben 31, WIEN 1. ☎52.22.35

BELGIUM – BELGIQUE
Librairie des Sciences,
Coudenberg 76-78, B 1000 BRUXELLES 1. ☎512-05-60

BRAZIL – BRÉSIL
Mestre Jou S.A., Rua Guaipá 518,
Caixa Postal 24090, 05089 SAO PAULO 10. ☎261-1920
Rua Senador Dantas 19 s/205-6, RIO DE JANEIRO GB.
☎232-07. 32

CANADA
Renouf Publishing Company Limited,
2182 St. Catherine Street West,
MONTREAL, Quebec H3H 1M7 ☎(514) 937-3519

DENMARK – DANEMARK
Munksgaards Boghandel,
Nørregade 6, 1165 KØBENHAVN K. ☎(01) 12 69 70

FINLAND – FINLANDE
Akateeminen Kirjakauppa
Keskuskatu 1, 00100 HELSINKI 10. ☎625.901

FRANCE
Bureau des Publications de l'OCDE,
2 rue André-Pascal, 75775 PARIS CEDEX 16.
☎524.81.67
Principal correspondant :
13602 AIX-EN-PROVENCE : Librairie de l'Université.
☎26.18.08

GERMANY – ALLEMAGNE
Verlag Weltarchiv G.m.b.H.
D 2000 HAMBURG 36, Neuer Jungfernstieg 21.
☎040-35-62-500

GREECE – GRÈCE
Librairie Kauffmann, 28 rue du Stade,
ATHÈNES 132. ☎322.21.60

HONG-KONG
Government Information Services,
Sales and Publications Office, Beaconsfield House, 1st floor,
Queen's Road, Central. ☎H-233191

ICELAND – ISLANDE
Snaebjörn Jónsson and Co., h.f.,
Hafnarstraeti 4 and 9, P.O.B. 1131, REYKJAVIC.
☎13133/14281/11936

INDIA – INDE
Oxford Book and Stationery Co.:
NEW DELHI, Scindia House. ☎45896
CALCUTTA, 17 Park Street. ☎240832

IRELAND - IRLANDE
Eason and Son, 40 Lower O'Connell Street,
P.O.B. 42, DUBLIN 1. ☎74 39 35

ISRAËL
Emanuel Brown: 35 Allenby Road, TEL AVIV. ☎51049/54082
also at:
9, Shlomzion Hamalka Street, JERUSALEM. ☎234807
48 Nahlath Benjamin Street, TEL AVIV. ☎53276

ITALY – ITALIE
Libreria Commissionaria Sansoni:
Via Lamarmora 45, 50121 FIRENZE. ☎579751
Via Bartolini 29, 20155 MILANO. ☎365083
Sous-dépositaires :
Editrice e Libreria Herder,
Piazza Montecitorio 120, 00 186 ROMA. ☎674628
Libreria Hoepli, Via Hoepli 5, 20121 MILANO. ☎865446
Libreria Lattes, Via Garibaldi 3, 10122 TORINO. ☎519274
La diffusione delle edizioni OCDE è inoltre assicurata dalle migliori

JAPAN – JAPON
OECD Publications Centre,
Akasaka Park Building, 2-3-4 Akasaka, Minato-ku,
TOKYO 107. ☎586-2016

KOREA - CORÉE
Pan Korea Book Corporation,
P.O.Box n°101 Kwangwhamun, SÉOUL. ☎72-7369

LEBANON – LIBAN
Documenta Scientifica/Redico,
Edison Building, Bliss Street, P.O.Box 5641, BEIRUT.
☎354429–344425

THE NETHERLANDS – PAYS-BAS
Staatsuitgeverij
Chr. Plantijnstraat
'S-GRAVENHAGE. ☎ 070-814511
Voor bestellingen: ☎ 070-624551

NEW ZEALAND - NOUVELLE-ZÉLANDE
The Publications Manager,
Government Printing Office,
WELLINGTON: Mulgrave Street (Private Bag),
World Trade Centre, Cubacade, Cuba Street,
Rutherford House, Lambton Quay, ☎737-320
AUCKLAND: Rutland Street (P.O.Box 5344), ☎32.919
CHRISTCHURCH: 130 Oxford Tce (Private Bag), ☎50.331
HAMILTON: Barton Street (P.O.Box 857), ☎80.103
DUNEDIN: T & G Building, Princes Street (P.O.Box 1104),
☎78.294

NORWAY – NORVÈGE
Johan Grundt Tanums Bokhandel,
Karl Johansgate 41/43, OSLO 1. ☎02-332980

PAKISTAN
Mirza Book Agency, 65 Shahrah Quaid-E-Azam, LAHORE 3.
☎66839

PHILIPPINES
R.M. Garcia Publishing House, 903 Quezon Blvd. Ext.,
QUEZON CITY, P.O.Box 1860 – MANILA. ☎99.98.47

PORTUGAL
Livraria Portugal, Rua do Carmo 70-74, LISBOA 2. ☎360582/3

SPAIN – ESPAGNE
Mundi-Prensa Libros, S.A.
Castelló 37, Apartado 1223, MADRID-1. ☎275.46.55
Libreria Bastinos, Pelayo, 52, BARCELONA 1. ☎222.06.00

SWEDEN – SUÈDE
AB CE FRITZES KUNGL HOVBOKHANDEL,
Box 16 356, S 103 27 STH, Regeringsgatan 12,
DS STOCKHOLM. ☎08/23 89 00

SWITZERLAND – SUISSE
Librairie Payot, 6 rue Grenus, 1211 GENÈVE 11. ☎022-31.89.50

TAIWAN – FORMOSE
National Book Company,
84-5 Sing Sung Rd., Sec. 3, TAIPEI 107. ☎321.0698

TURKEY – TURQUIE
Librairie Hachette,
469 Istiklal Caddesi, Beyoglu, ISTANBUL. ☎44.94.70
et 14 E Ziya Gökalp Caddesi, ANKARA. ☎12.10.80

UNITED KINGDOM – ROYAUME-UNI
H.M. Stationery Office, P.O.B. 569,
LONDON SEI 9 NH. ☎01-928-6977, Ext.410
or
49 High Holborn, LONDON WC1V 6 HB (personal callers)
Branches at: EDINBURGH, BIRMINGHAM, BRISTOL,
MANCHESTER, CARDIFF, BELFAST.

UNITED STATES OF AMERICA
OECD Publications Center, Suite 1207, 1750 Pennsylvania Ave.,
N.W. WASHINGTON, D.C.20006. ☎(202)298-8755

VENEZUELA
Libreria del Este, Avda. F. Miranda 52, Edificio Galipán,
CARACAS 106. ☎32 23 01/33 26 04/33 24 73

YUGOSLAVIA – YOUGOSLAVIE
Jugoslovenska Knjiga, Terazije 27, P.O.B. 36, BEOGRAD.
☎621-992

Les commandes provenant de pays où l'OCDE n'a pas encore désigné de dépositaire peuvent être adressées à :
OCDE, Bureau des Publications, 2 rue André-Pascal, 75775 PARIS CEDEX 16.
Orders and inquiries from countries where sales agents have not yet been appointed may be sent to:
OECD, Publications Office, 2 rue André-Pascal, 75775 PARIS CEDEX 16.

OECD PUBLICATIONS, 2, rue André-Pascal, 75775 Paris Cedex 16 - No. 39.797 1978

PRINTED IN FRANCE

SOCIAL SCIENCE LIBRARY

Manor Road Building
Manor Road
Oxford OX1 3UQ
Tel: (2)71093 (enquiries and renewals)
http://www.ssl.ox.ac.uk

This is a NORMAL LOAN item.

We will email you a reminder before this item is due.

Please see http://www.ssl.ox.ac.uk/lending.html
for details on:

- loan policies; these are also displayed on the
  notice boards and in our library guide.

- how to check when your books are due back.

- how to renew your books, including information
  on the maximum number of renewals.
  Items may be renewed if not reserved by
  another reader. Items must be renewed before
  the library closes on the due date.

- level of fines; fines are charged on overdue books.

Please note that this item may be recalled during Term.